THRIVE

EXPERIENCING MORE IN YOUR DAILY WALK WITH GOD

KENNETH KUYKENDALL

Thrive:
Experiencing More in Your Daily Walk with God
© 2017 by Kenneth Kuykendall
Cross Roads Publications
ISBN: 978-0-9978232-3-3

Cover design created and formatted by Daniel Ertley

Published and Printed by
Cross Roads Publications
1391 Braselton Hwy.
Lawrenceville, GA. 30043
www.crossroadspublications.org

All rights reserved. No part of this publication may be reproduced, stored in a retrieval system, or transmitted in any form- electronic, mechanical, recording, or any other - except for brief quotations embodied in critical articles or printed reviews, without prior permission in writing from publisher.

Printed and Published in the United States of America

To the individuals in my life who live passionately and courageously for Christ…your hunger for the holy creates a desire in my heart to thrive for God.

thrive

[thrīv] / verb

1. to grow vigorously;
2. to progress toward a realized goal despite or because of circumstances;
3. to prosper and to flourish.

When it comes to a relationship with God, there are three kinds of believers:
1. Those who are alive,
2. Those who survive,
3. Those who thrive.

If you are genuinely saved, you are alive in Christ and He is alive in you. Eternal, everlasting life is flowing through and beating in your heart. Positionally, you are secure in Christ Jesus forever. You are alive with resurrection power, even as Jesus is alive.

Then there are those who survive. I would venture to say this is where many believers find themselves in their daily walk with

God. They are saved, they are involved with religious activities and even embrace spiritual realities; but if the truth were known, they live in survival mode. They are alive, yet they merely maintain a spiritual status quo. It's not that they go backwards in their faith, but they never find themselves moving forward. They accept monotony, yield to apathy, and settle for the ordinary. Days, weeks, months, and sadly, even years pass without little-to-no spiritual growth.

Then there are those who thrive. As Webster declares, they "grow vigorously, they progress toward a realized goal, they prosper and flourish." Believers who thrive are not satisfied with yesterday's apex, they look for higher summits today. The water from last week's springs will not satisfy their present thirst, they need to taste the water again, and again, and again. Like the children of Israel, they need fresh manna for their souls. So, they advance, they push ahead, they pant for things divine. The goal for this kind of believer is not to survive only, but to thrive with passion and zeal.

Can this be said about your relationship with God? Jesus came, died on the cross, rose from the grave, ascended to His throne, and empowered us with the Holy Spirit, not so that you and I can experience life in survival mode. In John's gospel, Jesus said, "I am come that they might have life, and that they might have *life more abundantly*" (John 10:10). As the Chief Shepherd of our souls, Jesus came to impart abundant life to His sheep. The Greek word for "abundantly" in this passage is *perissos*; it means excessive, more than enough, exceedingly, to abound. Quite literally, it speaks of a life that operates "in the overflow." I believe it is safe to say that Jesus wants us to thrive. He died to give us this kind of life, and He victoriously lives so that we can experience this kind of life.

Do you want to thrive this year? Do you want your marriage to prosper like never before? Do you want your home to be zealous of spiritual things? Do you want to excel on your job or in your career? Do you long for a ministry that is so enamored with the glory of God that you find deep calling to deep in your heart? Do you want to develop, grow, and nurture your spiritual gifts? Are you tired of only surviving? Then I challenge you to make God's Word and this devotional part of your daily walk with Christ.

May God give you strength, hunger, and discipline to thrive!

Kenneth Kuykendall

JANUARY

JANUARY 1

STARTING THE NEW YEAR

"Resolution One- I will live for God. Resolution Two- If no one else does, I still will." –Jonathan Edwards

The start of a New Year affords many opportunities. It is not only a time to reflect and remember the past, but also a time to plan and prepare for the future. It reminds us of the importance of starting out right. The way you start something sets the pace and the potential for what you can achieve. Start the New Year with a few basic principles:

1. Start the New Year with God. Make it a priority to spend some time with God every day this year. Determine to read, pray, give, serve, and faithfully attend church with a renewed zeal and passion.

2. Start the New Year with Goals. George Lorimer said, "You've got to get up every morning with determination if you plan to go to bed with satisfaction." Limit your goals to an obtainable list and get to work!

3. Start the New Year with Grit. These next 365 days are sure to be filled with some adversities and hardships. Be ready and prepared for hard times and trust in God in advance to provide for your needs.

4. Start the New Year with Grace. Are there friendships that need restoring? Is there a person in your life that needs your forgiveness? Do you have grudges or feelings of ill will? Carry no resentment or bitterness into the New Year; extend God's grace in the same way you received it!

DAILY SCRIPTURE READING: Genesis 1-3

JANUARY 2

WHEN LIFE BEGINS

"The new birth is simply the impartation of a new nature- God's nature." –R.A. Torrey

Three preachers gathered at a coffee shop to discuss the theology of life. One preacher spoke up and said, "Life begins when a child takes its first breath in this world." The second preacher cleared his throat and adamantly said, "Sir, you are wrong. Life begins when a child is conceived in its mother's womb." The third preacher, who was a veteran pastor, spoke up and asserted, "Brethren, you are both wrong. Life begins when the last child leaves home and the dog finally dies."

I believe they are all wrong. True life begins when we place our faith in Jesus Christ and we become a new creature in Him. Jesus came to give us life and life more abundantly. Whosoever believeth in Him shall have everlasting life. Jesus is the Way, the Truth, and the Life. He is the Life, and the Resurrection; out of necessity therefore we must be born again –with His life.

The world constantly searches for meaning and purpose; but life has no real consolation without knowing Jesus Christ as Savior. Christ not only gives life, He gives significance to life. As someone anonymously said, "The life Christ lived qualified Him for the death He died, and the death He died qualifies us for the life we live." True life begins in Christ.

DAILY SCRIPTURE READING: Genesis 4-7

JANUARY 3
STAY ON YOUR OWN COURT

"Let every man abide in the same calling wherein he was called." –The Apostle Paul

On March 31, 1994 the sports world was surprised to learn that legendary basketball great Michael Jordan had reported to spring training in hopes of playing Minor-League baseball. Jordan, having won three basketball championships, now found himself in the Double-A division of the Chicago White Sox's minor league team the *Birmingham Barons*.

Although Jordan was a natural-born athlete he could not find his niche in the baseball world. With a terrible batting average and a multitude of errors it was obvious that he was struggling in his new field. For the first time in his professional career Jordan seemed like a fish out of water. After one year of being in the Minor Leagues, Jordan announced he would return to basketball. He went on to win three more championships with the Chicago Bulls, giving him a total of six titles. Arguably, he was the greatest player in the history of the game.

Jordan's failure as a baseball player proves one thing: we must abide in our calling. God gives each of us talents and abilities that are to be used in certain ways at certain times. When we try to do something we have not been created to do we will face frustration and failure. Stay on your own court and be the champion God designed you to be.

DAILY SCRIPTURE READING: Genesis 8-11

JANUARY 4

SATAN'S DESIRE FOR YOUR HOME

"Let the wife make the husband glad to come home, and let him make her sorry to see him leave." –Martin Luther

Have you ever noticed when Satan made his first appearance in Scripture? He came upon the scene immediately after God created and designed marriage. The serpent didn't seem to bother Adam until God gave him a wife. Soon after the marriage union was established the devilish assault against the home began. Consider what transpired once Adam and Eve were married:

- Satan attacked and beguiled Eve during a moment when she was separated from Adam (Separation)
- He promoted miscommunication among them and distorted what God had commanded (Miscommunication)
- He was able to make them turn their eyes upon the natural desires of the forbidden fruit (Worldliness)
- He destroyed their relationship with God (Disobedience)
- He got them kicked out of their home (Loss)

His intent for your home and marriage is still the same today. He wants to come between you and your spouse and cause division and dissension. His ultimate goal is to destroy your home and cause you to lose all God has given your family. Beware of his subtlety and guard your relationship against his devices.

DAILY SCRIPTURE READING: Genesis 12-15

JANUARY 5
REALITY IS A RARITY

"The most impressive part about you is simply you being you." –Kenneth Kuykendall

Our culture is inundated with a surplus of "reality shows." Whether it is catching alligators in the bayou or hanging out in a nightclub in New Jersey, these programs are suppose to document the "real life" of ordinary people. But in reality there is nothing real about these shows at all. They are produced by directors who place people in ridiculously scripted circumstances, and basically watch them react and respond to the programmed agenda.

However, in spite of their preposterous nature, I do believe "reality shows" operate as a commentary on society, perhaps even the church. In most of these shows you have ordinary people who are trying to become a "character" or "personality." They exaggerate and embellish who they are in pursuit of their fifteen-minutes of fame. They remind us that reality is a rarity these days.

Too often we simply play the part. We try to live up to other's expectations in hopes of their approval. We wear masks praying that no one will ever discover who we really are. But I have discovered that the most effective and influential people are those who are genuine and real. The most impressive part about you is simply you being you.

DAILY SCRIPTURE READING: Genesis 16-18

JANUARY 6

DON'T GAMBLE IT AWAY

"When I have any money, I get rid of it as soon as possible, lest it find a way into my heart." –John Wesley

There was a street-peddler in Las Vegas who approached a family for some financial help. He said to the father, "Sir, could you please give me some money? My wife is sick and in need of some medicine." Skeptically the father asked, "How do I know you won't take the money and go gambling with it?" The peddler responded, "Oh no, I wouldn't do that! I've already got gambling money."

The Bible has much to say about the stewardship of our finances. As a matter of fact, Jesus Himself spoke often of the subject teaching us to be good managers of His resources. Everything we have belongs to the Lord, including our life. Robert McCracken said, "Get to know two things about a man: how he earns his money and how he spends his money. You will them have a clue to his character."

Knowing that "my" possessions are borrowed from the Lord causes me to handle, with more sincerity, the resources He has provided. Your savings, your spending, and your investments are a testimony of your priorities. Keep track of your finances, and you might have a clearer understanding of your faith. "When you consider that we have the opportunity to successfully live with a divine mission and invest our lives in eternal purposes" said Paul Chappell, "anything less is a tragic waste."

DAILY SCRIPTURE READING: Genesis 19-21

JANUARY 7
BITTER ROOTS & BITTER FRUIT

"Bitterness hurts the vessel stored, more than the vessel poured." –Anonymous

We are instructed to live at peace with all men –those are not my words, those are the words of Scripture. The writer of Hebrews said, "Follow peace with all men, and holiness, without which no man shall see the Lord: Looking diligently lest any man fail of the grace of God; lest any *root of bitterness* springing up trouble you, and thereby many be defiled." Failure to live in peace with others often produces hostility and resentment in our lives. There are three primary truths when it comes to the subject of bitterness.

1. **Everyone has been hurt by someone.**
2. **If not guarded, that hurt turns into bitterness.**
3. **If not confronted, that bitterness hinders our relationship with God.**

Author John Courson said of bitterness, "It is like taking a bottle of poison, swallowing it, and waiting for the other person to die." Bitterness hurts me, not the person I am bitter with. As a root, bitterness gets covered up with smiles, laughs, and cordial exchanges; but the problem is that the root produces fruit, and the fruit of bitterness ultimately affects my relationship with the Lord. Remove bitterness at its source, and enjoy the liberty and freedom of not only being forgiven, but forgiving others.

DAILY SCRIPTURE READING: Genesis 22-24

JANUARY 8

BLESSINGS IN THE BRIAR PATCH

"A state of mind that sees God in everything is evidence of growth in grace and a thankful heart." –Charles Finney

On three separate occasions the apostle Paul asked the Lord to take away the thorn that was in his flesh. Instead of God taking it away, He sustained Paul with sufficient grace. Through the gift of grace Paul discovered three blessings while walking through the briar patch:

1. A Life of Peace. Strangely enough, Paul found peace in his problems, help in his hurting, and grace in his groaning. Speaking in the present-tense voice, the Lord said, "My grace is sufficient." What Paul did not realize was that God's grace had been sufficient the entire time; Paul didn't realize the grace of God until he needed it the most.

2. A Life of Praise. Once Paul understood the sufficiency of God, he began to praise the Lord for the thorn. Paul said he would "glory in infirmities." The very thing that made him cry was now making him rejoice. This thorn had brought him into the presence of God, and caused him to experience the Lord in ways like never before.

3. A Life of Power. Most interestingly, Paul said, "When I am weak then am I strong." It is only through our weaknesses do we discover the power and strength of Christ. Paul was a dynamic preacher, teacher and missionary not because of his abilities, but because of his thorn.

DAILY SCRIPTURE READING: Genesis 25-26

JANUARY 9

RUNNING WITH THE FATHER

"There is no such thing as a great man of God, only weak, pitiful, faithless men of a great and merciful God." –Paul Washer

During the 1992 Olympics in Barcelona, track star Derrick Redman pulled a hamstring while running the 400-meter. Falling to the ground he mustered up the strength to stand back up, and in heroic fashion began hobbling on one leg toward the finish line.

When Jim Redman, Derrick's father, saw the agony of his son he jumped the fence, ran to his side, and walked along Derrick until they both reached the finish line together. In one of the most iconic images in Olympic history, the crowd stood to their feet with roaring applause.

I am thankful to know that my heavenly Father does the same for me every single day. I stumble, I trip, and I fall, but never without the assistance of my great God and Savior. He is always there to help aid and assist me during those times when I run off course.

One day, together, we will cross the finish line for the final time. We will be met with a great cloud of witnesses who has cheered us on. I will be the one who wins, I will be the one who finished, but I would have never made it without Him helping me along the way. The true reward of the race will not be the prize you receive at the end, but finally meeting, face to face, the Person who walked with you long the way.

DAILY SCRIPTURE READING: Genesis 27-29

JANUARY 10
IT'S NEVER TOO LATE

"Gold medals aren't really made of gold. They're made of a hard to find alloy called guts." –Dan Gable

Fauja Singh holds just about every possible record in his age bracket for marathon running. At the age of 92 he set the world record as the oldest man to finish the 26.2 mile run in the fastest time –five hours and forty minutes.

At the strapping age of 100 he set five world records in various races at the Ontario Masters Association. And three days later he ran in the Toronto Waterfront Marathon becoming the only person in the world over 100 years old to compete and finish such a feat.

Because of health complications, Singh did not start walking until he was five years old, but once he started he never stopped. Amazingly, he started running competitively at the age of 89 after witnessing the death of his son on a construction site. From that moment, he had a new perspective and outlook on life. Singh has said of the grueling race, "The first 20 miles are not that difficult. As for the last six miles, I run while talking to God."

His resolve and determination remind us that it is never too late to start something. Regardless of your physical limitations, age, finances, or lot in life, with the help of God you can start and finish your race.

DAILY SCRIPTURE READING: Genesis 30-31

JANUARY 11
THE GOD WHO DOESN'T SLEEP

"God invites us to take a holiday, to stop being God for awhile, and let him be God." –Simon Tugwell

Occasionally while I am reading it happens. My mind will drift far from the page. Before I realize it my eyelids become very heavy, and I find myself in a struggle to stay awake. I will try to stir myself by blinking but within just a few seconds I am nodding back into the dark recesses of slumber. I go back and forth resisting and succumbing, resisting and succumbing until I finally give in, put the book aside and drift off. Sometimes the urge is so strong, and my will is so weak, that even if I wanted to I couldn't fight off the sleep.

God doesn't have that problem. He never has, and He never will.

His eyes never grow heavy, His Spirit never gets tired, His mind never drifts. The psalmist said, "He will not suffer thy foot to be moved: he that keepeth thee will not slumber. Behold, he that keepeth Israel shall neither slumber nor sleep" (Psalm 121:3-4).

As a sleeping child finds solace in the arms of his father, even so, we as children of the living God, should find rest in knowing that God continually watches over us. We need not worry if He is taking a heavenly break or a celestial nap. He continually guards and protects His children. I can sleep safely each night knowing that my God never does!

DAILY SCRIPTURE READING: Genesis 32-34

JANUARY 12
NO EXCUSES

"Some men have thousands of reasons why they cannot do what they want, when all they need is one reason why they can." –Willis Whitney

Kyle Manard is an extraordinary human being. He came into this world with a rare condition that affects only one in every two thousand births. A congenital amputee, Manard was born with only the upper portion of his arms and legs. Although he faced many challenges while growing up he never allowed those obstacles to limit him.

Manard's parents taught him not to use his handicap as an excuse. As a child he played all types of sports including street hockey and football. It wasn't until sixth grade however that he found his love for wrestling. In middle school he lost all thirty-five of his matches, but when he got to high school he had perfected his craft. During his high school years he wrestled on the varsity team winning thirty-five matches, and only losing sixteen. He qualified for the state championship, and won the first three matches.

Although Manard has a physical condition, the condition has never had him. In 2005, he wrote a book simply entitled, *No Excuses*. To Kyle that title is more than a catchy phrase, it is a way of life.

Excuses abound; only those with a will to overcome can experience victory. Do not use your limitations as an excuse. Move beyond your disabilities realizing that you *can* do all things through Christ.

DAILY SCRIPTURE READING: Genesis 35-37

JANUARY 13
THE HEAVY WEIGHT OF SIN

> *"It is not thy hold on Christ that saves thee -it is Christ that saves thee."* –Charles Spurgeon

After hearing the pastor's fiery sermon, a skeptic approached the man of God after church and said, "Pastor, you say that unsaved people carry a great weight of sin. Well, to be honest with you, I feel absolutely nothing. So tell me, just how heavy is my load of sin? Ten, fifty, a hundred pounds?"

The preacher wisely replied, "Dear sir, if you laid a hundred-pound weight on a corpse, do you think he would feel it?" The man laughed and said, "Of course not –he's dead." The pastor in return said, "My point exactly. Sinners are dead in trespasses and sin; although the load is very great, he doesn't feel it until he is made alive in Christ."

A dead man has no spirit, he has no life; he has no ability to feel, taste, or touch. The same holds true with someone who is lost in sin. He is separated from God and has no life within him. Oh, he may exist, he may work, he may seem to function as best he can, but he is not alive.

Only through the power of the Spirit of God are we quickened. And until that moment, we carry the great weight of sin. No, we may not feel the weight but it is there. Cast those heavy burdens aside; place your faith in Christ, and experience life as never before.

DAILY SCRIPTURE READING: Genesis 38-40

JANUARY 14

THE POWER OF ONE VOICE

"I believe the highest form of passion is that which sees the greater good as its object." –Zig Ziglar

Just one person can make all the difference in the world. There have been times throughout history when major events were determined by the power of one voice. Consider the following:

In 1645, one vote gave Oliver Cromwell control of England

In 1776, one vote gave America the English language instead of German

In 1845, one vote brought the state of Texas into the Union

In 1868, one vote saved President Andrew Johnson from impeachment

In 1875, one vote changed France from a monarchy to a republic

In 1923, one vote gave Adolph Hitler control over the Nazi Party

The same holds true in Scripture. Noah was just one preacher who refused to succumb to the evils of his day. Daniel was just one exile who wouldn't stop praying. Elijah was just one prophet who wouldn't bow a knee to the false god Baal. John the Baptist was just one voice crying in the wilderness.

Sometimes all it takes is just one person with the right convictions to make an eternal difference. Be that voice and make that difference, and trust God to give the victory.

DAILY SCRIPTURE READING: Genesis 41-42

JANUARY 15
THE HOME-FIELD ADVANTAGE

"Each day of our lives we make deposits into the memory banks of our children." –Chuck Swindoll

Imagine just for a moment a stadium filled with thousands of cheering fans. Can you see the banners? Do you hear the applause and the music? Can you sense the excitement? The place is energized with an electric charge. Those gathered have come out to cheer on their team to victory. Every coach wants it and every player works hard to earn it –it is called the home-field advantage.

Home-field advantage is often the determining factor in winning or losing. The home team benefits greatly from the encouragement of the fans, the familiarity of the facility, and the psychological confidence of just being at home. Statistics prove, regardless of the sport, that playing with the home-field advantage typically gives you a greater chance of beating your opponent.

I believe the same holds true with our children. When we raise them in an environment that is encouraging and stable, they are more likely to get the edge in life. They need to know their parents are cheering them on. They need a home that is safe, secure, and spiritual because their opponents are greater, stronger, and tougher than ever before. Raise the banners, crank up the music, stand in ovation, and cheer them on to victory. Give your children the home-field advantage!

DAILY SCRIPTURE READING: Genesis 43-45

JANUARY 16

THE COVERING OF LOVE

"True love is willing to give at any price regardless of reciprocation." –Kenneth Kuykendall

During a blizzard storm in South Wales, England, a young mother and her baby were making their way across some foothills when she was overtaken by the frigid storm. Failing to reach her destination, a group of searchers found her frozen body with the baby tightly wrapped underneath her; the child was warm and still alive. The mother had taken off her outer garments and covered her child from the cold.

The baby grew up to be David Lloyd George, Britain's prime minister and one of the greatest statesmen in England. His political and social greatness was made possible because his mother covered him in love.

Love is the greatest of all virtues. True love is selfless and sacrificial. True love is willing to give at any price regardless of reciprocation. The apostle Paul said, "And now abideth faith, hope, and charity, these three; but the greatest of these is charity" (1 Corinthians 13:13).

True love was displayed officially at Calvary when Christ died in our place. Our burden of sin was laid upon Him as He covered us in grace. He not only took our sin, He took our sin away. This "covering" affords us the life of blessing and honor. Much like David Lloyd George, our achievements in life can only be attributed to the covering of God's love.

DAILY SCRIPTURE READING: Genesis 46-47

JANUARY 17
WINNING IN TRANSITION

"To see far is one thing;
going there is another." –Constantin Brancusi

In high school I was on the track and field team. Each year I ran the 4 X 100 relay race. In this particular race, four individuals on each team are required to run 100 meters each while passing the baton one to another at certain points. These "exchange zones" are designated spots in the race and on the track where the transitions are made.

One of the fundamental components of this race is learning how to time your exchanges. It doesn't matter if you are the fastest kid in school; if you don't do well in the transitions you don't win the race.

The same holds true in life. The success of your race is determined by how well you handle the transitions. Let's admit it, life is constantly moving and changing. Kids grow up, careers get altered, the economy fluctuates, people move on, ministries get modified –sometimes it feels like we live in the "exchange zones."

Transitions are difficult, but sometimes they are necessary. If you are going through a life-changing transition, remember that God doesn't change. Anchor your hope in Him, and lean upon Him for guidance and direction. He is cheering you on.

DAILY SCRIPTURE READING: Genesis 48-50

JANUARY 18
QUARTER FRIENDSHIP

*"Friendship is like money-
easier made than kept."* –Samuel Butler

You don't have to be a mathematical genius to know that one hundred pennies and four quarters both equal one dollar. Even though they are same amount, I would much rather have the four quarters. Quarters are more widely accepted, they are easier to carry, and they have more value per piece.

Think about the same concept when it comes to friendship. Would you rather have one hundred "penny" friends, or four "quarter" friends?

In this day of social media, we seemingly have thousands of "friends" and "followers." We hear about their menial daily activities, we see their pictures, we know their moods, likes, dislikes, and weird little quirks. But in all reality, we do not really know them at all.

Friendship involves more than accepting a request through an email. Friendship takes work. Friendship requires honesty, connection, trust, and sacrifice. True friendship is not cheap. Jesus said, "Greater love hath no man than this, that a man lay down his life for his friends."

Don't get me wrong I appreciate every single penny I have ever owned; but if I had my choice, I prefer the quarters. It doesn't take as many of them to get the job done.

DAILY SCRIPTURE READING: Exodus 1-3

JANUARY 19

GO SOMEWHERE WITH GOD

"Our problem is not too little time, but making better use of the time we have." –Oswald Chambers

Studies conducted by the U.S. Census Bureau show that Americans are spending more time in their vehicles than ever before. The daily commute for the average American translates into about one hundred hours of driving time each year. To put that in perspective, we are driving more hours than we spend on vacation. What do we do with that time? How can we be productive during those frustrating hours of commute? Here are a few suggestions:

Pray. You certainly do not want to confine your prayer life solely on the road, but what a great opportunity it is to talk with God. By the way, you may not want to close your eyes!

Listen to Christian Resources. Whether it is music, preaching, or audio books, you can use that time to grow in your walk with the Lord.

Catch up on Bible Time. There are plenty of programs that will read the Bible to you. If you missed your devotion that morning, catch up while going down the road.

Worship. Use that time to worship the Lord. You do not have to be in a sanctuary to have church. Sing to the Lord; honor Him with your lips. Use your drive time as a means to go somewhere with God!

DAILY SCRIPTURE READING: Exodus 4-6

JANUARY 20
A LETTER FROM GOD

"Christ veiled His deity, but He did not void it." –A.W. Tozer

According to Hebrews 1:2, Christ Jesus is the "express image" of God. This concept can be illustrated through the ancient practice of sealing a letter. Whenever a king would send an official document to another land he would always take his signet ring, dip it in ink, and press the image of his ring upon the letter. The king's mark would be the official token of his authentication and approval of the correspondence. Having the mark upon the letter was just as authoritative and official as if the king were present himself.

Christ is the Word of God who became flesh and dwelled among us. The Great God of Glory sent His Son, who bore the mark of the King. Being the "express image" of God, Jesus showed the world a glimpse of God's Person.

When we encounter Christ we encounter the divine. Christ was God's official and final "letter" to the world. The writer of Hebrews records, "God, who at sundry times and in divers manners spake in time past unto the fathers by the prophets, Hath in these last days spoken unto us by His Son." Christ is not only the mark of the King, He is also the message of the King. Now that's a letter worth reading!

DAILY SCRIPTURE READING: Exodus 7-9

JANUARY 21
SEEK AFTER WISDOM

"One of the wisest things you can do is ask the Lord for wisdom." –Kenneth Kuykendall

Suppose God offered you anything you wanted; what would you chose? Money, fortune, fame, security? Popularity, prominence, charisma, happiness? Suppose you could have all of these things if you only asked for one thing.

The Lord gave Solomon the proverbial blank check. He could have cashed it in for anything his heart desired; but the one thing Solomon asked for was wisdom. As a result, God not only gave Solomon wisdom, He gave him everything that accompanies wisdom. Solomon received world-wide fame along with an incomparable empire.

Ken Blanchard says of wisdom, "It (wisdom) is the application of knowledge, discernment, insight, experience, and judgment to make good decisions when the answer may not be obvious." Wisdom comes from our experiences, our mistakes, our understanding of Scripture, and our hunger for truth. Ultimately wisdom comes from God. James said, "If any of you lack wisdom, let him ask of God, that giveth to all men liberally" (James 1:5). True wisdom understands what God wants accomplished in any given circumstance. One of the wisest things you can do is ask the Lord for wisdom. Seek after wisdom; there is no telling what else you will find!

DAILY SCRIPTURE READING: Exodus 10-12

JANUARY 22

LEARNING TO BE CONTENT

"If your contentment is not in the Lord you will never be happy. If it is in the Lord you will never be happier." –Kenneth Kuykendall

One of the most fascinating comments made by the Apostle Paul is found in Philippians 4:11, "I have *learned* in whatsoever state I am, therewith to be content." Obviously these words were not recorded by Paul, the young, eager zealot. No, they were written by Paul, the seasoned veteran who was coming into the wintry season of ministry and life. The contentment Paul discovered was a wonderful find, but his discovery was not an overnight revelation.

Paul said it was something he learned. I am sure the first few times he was cast into prison he found little contentment. By his own admission he prayed three times for the thorn to be taken away. One would assume that Paul didn't necessarily like the beatings, the persecution, and the hardships, at least initially. But through the adversities he learned something about contentment –it is not found in the absence of trouble, rather is it found in the presence of God. Contentment is something that flows from above and then from within.

His struggles did not restrict his contentment, and his successes did not merit his contentment. His contentment was something learned after many years of leaning on and trusting in Christ. If your contentment is not in the Lord you will never be happy. If it is in the Lord you will never be happier.

DAILY SCRIPTURE READING: Exodus 13-15

JANUARY 23
HE TOOK MY PLACE

"God is none other than the Savior of our wretchedness. So we can only know God well by knowing our iniquities." –Blaise Pascal

Barabbas was not a good man. On the contrary, he was a rebel, a murderer, a robber, a notable prisoner. Yet, the crowd cried out for his release from jail. In return, they wanted Jesus crucified. The religious mob stood before Pilate that day and demanded the freedom of a wicked man in exchange for the life of Christ.

The context of their evil request stood in light of Passover. The Levitical law ordered the high priest to select two goats from the fold. One animal would be sacrificed while the other was set free in the wilderness by a "fit man." When Barabbas was released from prison he stood in type and shadow of the freedom we receive in the death of Jesus Christ. As a matter of fact, the name Barabbas means, "the son of *a* father." Quite literally Barabbas stood as any and every man before God.

Jesus, the Son of *the* Father took our place at Calvary. He was innocent, righteous, and holy; yet like Barabbas, we were guilty, condemned, and sentenced to die. The spotless Lamb of God became the substitution for every "son of the father." He died to release us from the bondage and burden of sin. As someone has anonymously said, "The life Christ lived qualified Him for the death He died, and the death He died qualifies us for the life we live."

DAILY SCRIPTURE READING: Exodus 16-18

JANUARY 24
INFLUENCE YOUR WORLD

"The only inheritance that a man will leave that has eternal value is his influence." –Larry Dobbs

Whether you realize it or not-you have it. It may not be with a large circle of people or on a decorated platform, but it is there. It may not be evident among the masses or recognizable among the elite but it looms in the shadows of your day to day activities. It is called influence, and you have more of it than you think.

In his book *Spiritual Influence*, Mel Lawrenz incisively states, "God uses millions of no-name influencers every day in the simplest selfless acts of service. They are the teachers whose names will never be in the newspaper, pastors who will never author a book, managers who will never be profiled in a magazine, artists whose work is buried in layers of collaboration, writers whose sphere of influence is a few dozen people who read their blogs. But they are the army that makes things happen. To them devotion is its own reward. For them influence is a continual act of giving, nothing more complicated than that."

Lawrenz hits the nail on the head. You don't have to become a household name to change the house. You don't have to have your name out on the marquee to change the marquee. Small people doing small things change the world. Recognize your sphere of influence, regardless of its size, and do something to make a difference.

DAILY SCRIPTURE READING: Exodus 19-21

JANUARY 25
SEASONED WITH GRACE

"People are more apt to hear what we have to say if what we say is seasoned with grace." –Kenneth Kuykendall

The apostle Paul was a brilliant *theologian*. He was the recipient of divine revelation. His mind, his pen, and his life oozed doctrine. He was also a mighty *preacher*. Everywhere he went people were mesmerized by his authoritative and captivating style. He preached in the "power and demonstration" of the Holy Ghost. Furthermore, Paul was a *missionary*. His adventurous and courageous spirit, combined with his heavenly calling, led him from lowly prisons to lofty palaces. His heart was the heart of a man on a mission. He loved the local church and spent most of his life building and encouraging it.

The list could go on and on. Paul literally was all things to all men. But one of the things we often overlook about Paul was that he was a gracious man. If you study the salutations and benedictions of his epistles, you will not find the greetings of a cold, rigid theologian; neither will you find an over-the-top rhetoric approach from a flashy evangelist. Instead you find his speech to be courteous, thoughtful, and kind.

People were drawn to Paul's message, but they also connected with his manners. We should take note of his pleasant etiquette. People are more apt to hear what we have to say if what we say is seasoned with grace.

DAILY SCRIPTURE READING: Exodus 22-24

JANUARY 26

SOLACE IN THE STORM

"Let God's promises shine on your problems." –Corrie Ten Boom

Not long ago a severe thunderstorm came through our community. My family gathered in the living room and watched the damage of the massive storm unfold on television. Lightning crashed all around us, the sirens sounded at the nearby fire stations, and the meteorologist warned all of his viewers to take immediate cover.

Knowing that we could not panic, my wife and I kept our composure in front of our children. The weather was relentless that evening but surprisingly my children were not bothered at all by the storm. They found strength and security in my response. The storm was more dangerous than they realized, but by keeping their attention on us, they were able to go through it without any terror or alarm.

As children of God we too can fearlessly face the storm when we consider the strength and security of our heavenly Father. As long as Peter kept his eyes on the Lord he was able to operate in faith; it was only when he took his eyes off the Lord he became frightened by the storm.

The storm may be stronger than you, but it is not stronger than God. Keep your eyes on the Lord and you may not even realize it is raining!

DAILY SCRIPTURE READING: Exodus 25-27

JANUARY 27
RESPONDING IN FIERY TRIALS

"When a man has put a limit on what he will do, he has put a limit on what he can do." –Charles Schwab

William Carey, the father of modern missions, spent years in India learning indigenous languages and translating the Bible in Sanskrit. But on March 11, 1812 he lost most of his literary work to a fire in his print shop. Carey had a wide collection of items he had personally written. The fire consumed ten different translations of the Bible, two grammar books, a large supply of dictionaries, deeds, and accounting books, and most unfortunately, his completed Sanskrit dictionary.

After the fire, Carey was faced with the daunting task of reproducing his material. Instead of whining, he started writing. Line by line, page by page, book by book. Carey himself said of his work, "It is easier to walk a road the second time." At the end of his ministry, William Carey had translated the Bible, either in whole or part, into forty-four different languages.

Instead of getting down, Carey got up and did something about his unfortunate situation. Fred Smith said, "The energy needed to retreat might have been just the amount of energy to succeed." What you have at the end of life will be determined by how you responded during and after the fiery trials of faith.

DAILY SCRIPTURE READING: Exodus 28-29

JANUARY 28

SMALL MOUNTAINS

"Wherefore let him that thinketh he standeth take heed lest he fall." –The Apostle Paul

Years ago a well-trained mountain climber was honored by his many years of exploratory work. He had climbed the world's most challenging mountains and faced some of the most grueling terrains you could imagine. His colleagues and friends convinced him to extend his knowledge to the next generation by instructing and equipping others.

He agreed to head up a new training program in which he would teach amateur rock climbers the basic techniques. Not long after the program started he led a few students up a rock wall. Just forty feet from the ground he lost his footing and plummeted to his death.

This great climber had traveled all over the world and conquered some of the fiercest mountains, yet in the most elementary climb he stumbled. His death serves as a sober reminder: even the most experienced and trained people can lose their balance when climbing the smallest of mountains.

Mountain climbing is no easy task. Financial, emotional, and spiritual hills, even for the most experienced climbers, can be dangerous. Oftentimes the smallest trials present the biggest troubles. Paul said, "Wherefore let him that thinketh he standeth take heed lest he fall."

DAILY SCRIPTURE READING: Exodus 30-32

JANUARY 29
A GATHERING IN THE CLOUDS

"A true Christian has hope when he looks ahead, the worldly man has none." –J.C. Ryle

The older I get the more people I know in heaven. I believe there comes a time in a person's life when he actually has more loved ones in eternity than he does on earth. We have all walked away from the grave with a feeling of sorrow and sadness, but never hopelessness, if the person was saved.

We have the promise from God's Word of a glorious reunion. The apostle Paul gave us comforting words when we said, "For the Lord himself shall descend from heaven with a shout, with the voice of the archangel, and with the trump of God: and the dead in Christ shall rise first: Then we which are alive and remain shall be **caught up together with them** in the clouds, to meet the Lord in the air: and so shall we ever be with the Lord" (1 Thessalonians 4:16-17).

When Christ returns there will be saints of God that return with Him, and there will also be saints of God alive on the earth. We which are alive will be "caught up together with them in the clouds." We will be with our loved ones again. We will see them again. We will know them again; but we will know them without sin and imperfections. We will see them without sickness, pain, and sorrow. And the best part, we will join them in the clouds to meet the Lord. What a happy, glad reunion day!

DAILY SCRIPTURE READING: Exodus 33-35

JANUARY 30

DON'T LET THE DEVIL STOP YOU

*"God wants us to worship Him; He doesn't
need us to, He just wants us to."* –A.W. Tozer

After the Lord raised her brother from the dead, Mary made her way once again to the feet of Jesus. Three times in Scripture Mary was found at His feet. The first two times she wanted to get something from the Lord, this time she wanted to give something to the Lord –herself.

She broke open her alabaster box, and poured out the costly spikenard upon the Lord. Taking her hair, she wiped His feet as a memorial for His death. She exchanged her glory (which was her hair), for the glory of Christ. For many days after, she would be able to smell the fragrance of worship upon her life.

In the midst of her adulation, Judas criticized her efforts. He condemned her for spending her fortune on Christ, and suggested she should have given it to the poor. Judas, the consummate critic, cared not for the poor, but was a thief, and wanted the money for himself.

Whenever you worship the Lord, there will always be a thief somewhere around who tries to take away your investment of worship. They will criticize, evaluate, and question your motives. Give no thought to their evaluation. Break open your box and glorify your God. Don't let the devil stop you.

DAILY SCRIPTURE READING: Exodus 36-38

JANUARY 31
MISSING THE MARK IN MINISTRY

"Dealing with failure is not the occasional distraction of our mission; it is our mission." –Mel Lawrenz

Every year thousands of preachers, pastors, and evangelists leave their calling. It is true –God may redirect some men into different locations and fields at various times. On occasion God will close and open the doors of ministry. But many leave with the intent to only go through one more door, and that is the door out in the vestibule. While ministry is the greatest privilege of a man's life, it is also difficult. If you want to truly miss the mark in ministry and just involve yourself in these frustrating endeavors:

1. Do It All By Yourself. Andrew Carnegie said, "No one will make a great leader who wants to do it all himself or get all the credit for doing it." Get some help quick if you are doing it all alone.

2. Compare Your Ministry with Others. Our measure of success should not be other ministries it should be our obedience to the Word of God. Base your ministry upon Scripture and leave the results to God.

3. Expect Immediate Results. A lot of ministers want 20-year results in 20 months. The law of harvest doesn't work in speed or convenience.

4. Quit During Hard Times. Never make final decisions in moments of frustrations. Fred Smith said, "The energy needed to retreat might have been just the amount of energy to succeed."

DAILY SCRIPTURE READING: Exodus 39-40

FEBRUARY

FEBRUARY 1
BEYOND THE PROPERTY LINE

"You may find hundreds of faultfinders among professed Christians; but all their criticism will not lead one soul to Christ." –D.L. Moody

George Beverly Shea was the lead singer and composer of the Billy Graham crusades for years. He once told a story about the wheat fields of his home town. As a boy he could remember the time of the harvest and the crops being very large. He said, "When the wheat gets high and the fields are ripe with the harvest, you could not even see the fences that divided the properties. The same holds true for the spiritual harvest. Because the field is ripe, we must put aside our petty differences that may divide us, and get to work."

Can you see the old wheat fields of Shea's home town? Imagine the fading property lines as the stalk ripens. The crop doesn't know the boundaries; it just waits to be harvested. The same holds true with the lost and dying world. They do not know our various standards, convictions, and preferences. How can we expect them to know the diverse doctrines of denominations? They are just waiting for someone to tell them of Jesus.

No wonder the Lord said, "Lift up your eyes, and look upon the fields; for they are white already for harvest." As the old-timers used to say, "Let's keep the main thing, the main thing!" The harvest is waiting.

DAILY SCRIPTURE READING: Leviticus 1-4

FEBRUARY 2

GOD IS NOT FAIR

"There are always uncertainties ahead, but there is always one certainty-God's will is good." –Vernon Paterson

In the midst of national tragedy or personal conflict, people question the love, goodness, and sovereignty of God. We have all heard people say "God's not fair!" And the truth is, God is not fair; and for one, I am glad!

If God was always fair I would be condemned in sin. If God judged me solely on my righteousness I would be destined for hell. If the Lord based my worth on my own goodness, I could never be loved by a holy God. So I praise the Lord that He is not always fair.

Instead, God is always merciful and kind. I do not have the authority to explain every national tragedy or personal calamity. I do know that God punishes the wicked, and, as a loving Father, He chastises His children. I do know there is a high price to be paid for sin; but even in the midst of judgment, God always extends grace, and that certainly doesn't seem fair.

He makes His mercy new every morning. He extends the invitation to know Him, to come to Him, to experience Him. He stands on our behalf, He cleanses us from all unrighteousness, He bestows daily benefits, He sets His affection upon us. So when you hear someone say "God is not fair" just tell them God is too good to always be fair.

DAILY SCRIPTURE READING: Leviticus 5-7

FEBRUARY 3

SPIRITUAL SANITATION GRADE

"The one who calls you to a life of righteousness is the one, who by our consent, lives that life through you." –Major Ian Thomas

Recently my family and I were in line at a drive-through restaurant. We placed our order and drove up to the window. Just before it was time to pay the cashier, we noticed they had openly placed their sanitation grade for all the drivers to see. When we saw the low-score of 72 we were somewhat disgusted. I didn't want to inconvenience the workers by driving off, but at the same time I didn't want to buy food from a restaurant in such poor-working conditions. I kindly told the cashier to cancel our order and told her the reason why.

As I drove away I thought about my own sanitation grade. Do I live in such a way that makes people want to drive-off? Is my spirit inviting? Is my heart clean? Do others see the grace of God at work in my life?

I thank God we are not assigned a grade to be displayed before the world; but in reality, we are to exhibit the fruit of the Spirit in our lives. People are watching us, and by our actions and reactions they determine if they want what we have.

Whether we realize it or not, many people make decisions about Christ by the way we display Him. Live pure, live clean, live holy and you'll be able to serve all those who come through your line.

DAILY SCRIPTURE READING: Leviticus 8-10

FEBRUARY 4

WILLING TO DIE

"The cross is not just something done by us, it is something done for us." –Kenneth Kuykendall

A young girl was diagnosed with a rare blood condition and needed a transfusion. The only one in her family with the same blood type was her little six-year old brother. His mom and dad sat him down and told him his sister needed some of his blood and asked if he would be willing to give it to her. The little boy hesitated somewhat, but after a few minutes consented to help his big sister.

They took him to the doctor the next day to get things ready for the procedure. Just before they started drawing his blood, the little boy told his parents, "Before they kill me, tell my sister I love her."

Mistakenly, he thought his parents asked him to lay down his life so that his sister could live. Loving her so much, he was willing to pay the ultimate price.

You and I needed a blood transfusion. We were diagnosed with the awful disease of sin. The only hope we had was for Christ, the Son of God to give His blood. In love and grace He laid down His life for our sins so that we could have everlasting life. Christ was not forced or coerced into dying on the cross. What He did for us, He did willingly.

DAILY SCRIPTURE READING: Leviticus 11-13

FEBRUARY 5
HOME IS WHERE THE CHURCH IS

"The early church was in the upper room agonizing, the modern church is in the supper room organizing." –Vance Havner

It has been said that everyone needs three homes. First, we need an **eternal home**. Our deed to this home is secured with the payment of Christ's own blood. Then we need an **earthly home**. No matter if it is a mansion on the hilltop or a cabin in the valley, home is that special place where we spend time with family. Finally, we need an **extended home**. Our extended home is none other than the local church.

Every born-again believer needs to assemble himself with a local congregation. We are to unite our lives with the dynamic power of the church in order to carry out the orders of the Great Commission. Church is the launching pad for ministry. It is where we get instruction for life. It is where we connect for worship. It is where we administer the gifts given to us by the Holy Spirit of God.

There are many today who try to undermine the relevancy of the church; but the writer of Hebrews tells us, "Not forsaking the assembling of ourselves together, as the manner of some is; but exhorting one another, so much the more, as ye see that day approaching" (Hebrews 10:25). The closer we get to our eternal home, the more faithful we should be to our extended home.

DAILY SCRIPTURE READING: Leviticus 14-15

FEBRUARY 6

DON'T ALWAYS TRUST YOURSELF

"The reason why many men of God experience moral failure is because they wrongly assess their strength." –Kenneth Kuykendall

Hundreds of ministries fail each year because of the blurred lines of accountability. Thousands of marriages are destroyed routinely because lines in the proverbial sand are not drawn. We all need accountability systems in place to protect and safeguard our lives. "If we don't have proper and reasonable lines of accountability, then our only guide will be the expectations we put on ourselves," said Mel Lawrenz, "and we should not trust ourselves that much."

"We should not trust ourselves that much" is an understatement. I believe the reason many men of God experience moral failure is because they wrongly assess their strength. They measure their spiritual grit by personality, success, degree, influence, and popularity. As a result, pride permeates the heart and the seeds of temptation germinate in the soul. Delusion sets in and convinces us that we can trust our flesh. Joseph, when tempted in the Old Testament, ran out of Potiphar's house, not because he was spiritual, but because he recognized his own carnality: we all should do the same.

Keep safeguards in place and hold yourself accountable to those particular boundaries. And remember not to "trust yourself that much."

DAILY SCRIPTURE READING: Leviticus 16-18

FEBRUARY 7

USE THE DELETE BUTTON

"The men who try to do something and fail are infinitely better than those who try nothing and succeed." –Theodore Roosevelt

Most of the programs we watch in our home have been recorded by the DVR. My children have a tendency of watching the same old shows multiple times. Not long ago they were watching a particular scene of this fellow who accidentally fell down some stairs. They laughed and laughed, and just kept rewinding it over and over. Twenty minutes passed of them watching, rewinding, laughing…watching, rewinding, laughing.

I think many believers do the same thing. We have a tendency to play over and over again in our minds certain events…especially those events of us falling. I have gone to bed many nights trying to process the events of the day. I wrestle with the past. I grapple with regrets. I entangle my thoughts with the failures of days gone by. I constantly rewind and review those embarrassing moments of malaise.

It is then I realize that God has a "delete" button, and we should familiarize ourselves with it. He doesn't keep our failures archived so that we can continually be defeated. Instead, He shows us the error of our way and gets us back on the right path. So I will just agree with Paul, I will forget those things behind me, and press toward the mark; and from time to time I will use the delete button.

DAILY SCRIPTURE READING: Leviticus 19-21

FEBRUARY 8

THE GREATEST ADVENTURE

"Every man's life starts and ends the same way. It is only the details that distinguish one man from another." –Ernest Hemingway

In his early twenties, Ernest Hemingway started his career as a novelist. Much of his writing came from an adventure-packed life. Someone said of Hemingway that he was able to pack ten lives into one. He had a love for bullfighting, big-game hunting, deep-sea fishing, and an ongoing fascination with war. He lived in Spain, Paris, Key West, Cuba, and Idaho. From the outside looking in you might think the prolific writer lived a full life...Hemingway would not agree.

On the contrary, he spent much of his life trying to fill an ever-expanding void. He dealt with severe depression and struggled with alcoholism most of his adult life. He had four marriages, all of which suffered from his obsession with hedonism and self-fulfillment. At the same time he received the Nobel and Pulitzer prizes, he was also receiving electroshock treatments for his anxiety and paranoia. His life ended tragically with a self-inflicted gunshot wound to the head.

Sadly, Hemingway reminds us that living an adventurous life is not the same as living a fulfilling life. Having the applause of man is not the same as having the peace of God. The greatest adventure one can experience is the adventure of finding the Lord. Knowing Him is the essence of living.

DAILY SCRIPTURE READING: Leviticus 22-23

FEBRUARY 9
LOOKING FOR COWS

"Our heavenly Father never takes anything from His children unless He means to give them something better." –George Mueller

Years ago Harry Ironside was lecturing at a well-known seminary. The school was in great need of financial assistance and asked Ironside to offer a special prayer to the Lord for provision. Ironside offered a short but powerful prayer, "Dear Lord, you own the cattle of a thousand hills, please sell some of those cattle to help us meet this need."

It wasn't long after the prayer meeting that a check for $10,000 came to the school. It was sent by a man who had no idea of the school's financial distress; he simply said the gift was the result of him selling some of his cattle.

As the old-time preachers used to say, "The Lord owns the cattle of a thousand hills; and every now and then He is known to give me a heifer or two!" Simply put –God always provides. It may not be in our timing, or by our methods, but He always comes through!

Paul said, "But my God shall supply all your need according to his riches in glory by Christ Jesus" (Philippians 4:19). God knows our needs, and He knows how to meet those needs. If you have a need today, call upon Jehovah-Jireh, and expect a cow or two to show up somewhere in your life!

DAILY SCRIPTURE READING: Leviticus 24-25

FEBRUARY 10

TAKE THE PLUNGE

"Those who don't have the courage to take risks, and those who do, experience the same amount of fear in life." –John Maxwell

During the Vietnam War, General George Westmoreland approached some of his paratroopers and asked them about their jumps. One fellow in particular said, "Sir, it is the greatest experience of my life. I love making the jumps!" Another fellow replied, "There is nothing else I would rather do." The general came to another young man and asked, "Son, do you like making the jumps?" The boy replied, "No sir, not particularly, I just like being around the people who love to jump."

"Courage is contagious" said Billy Graham, "when a brave man stands, the spines of others are stiffened." There is something infectious about being around people who are fearless. They stir us to move; they motivate us to attempt the difficult; they stimulate the stagnant.

Winston Churchill said, "Courage is the first of human qualities, because it is the only quality that guarantees all the others." Courage moves us into unchartered waters; it unleashed a sense of adventure and discovery in our hearts. It gives us the drive and zeal to move beyond our own limitations and trust God for the impossible.

Get around someone with courage and see if it doesn't rub off. Before you know it, you just might be taking the plunge!

DAILY SCRIPTURE READING: Leviticus 26-27

FEBRUARY 11
NO-NAME JERSEYS

"When it gets down to it, the name on the back of the jersey is not as important as the name on the front." –Kenneth Kuykendall

During his tenure at Notre Dame, head coach Lou Holtz would not permit his players to stitch their names on the back of the jerseys. When asked about this particular policy, Holtz replied, "At Notre Dame, we believe the interlocking ND is all the identification you need. If your priority is the team rather than yourself, what else do you need?"

If this principle of teamwork is true in the sports world, it is certainly true for believers in a local church. Churches experience division when individuals place more priority on what they want rather than what is good for the "team."

What binds us together as believers is the blood of Jesus Christ. The apostle Paul said, "But now in Christ Jesus ye who sometimes were far off are made nigh by the blood of Christ...And that he might reconcile both unto God in one body by the cross, having slain the enmity thereby: And came and preached peace to you which were far off, and to them that were nigh" (Ephesians 2:15-17). We are united in Christ.

When it gets down to it, the name on the back of the jersey is not as important as the name of the front. Victory comes when we lose our identity and unite under His name. He must increase, we must decrease.

DAILY SCRIPTURE READING: Numbers 1-2

FEBRUARY 12
POPULARITY AND TRUTH

"Truth is so obscure in these times, and falsehood so established, that unless we love the truth, we cannot know it." –Blaise Pascal

The crowd cheered enthusiastically when Jesus came riding on a colt into Jerusalem. They waved palm branches and shouted, "Hosanna, in the highest" saluting Christ as their king; it was the peak of His popularity. However, just a few days later, this very crowd was shouting, "Crucify him! Crucify him!"

Popularity is a dangerous thing. Some people who love and adore you in one breath, will curse and condemn you in the next. Christ's popularity varied. At times, multitudes would follow Him into the most barren of deserts just to hear His words, and then at others times, He would have masses leave because of His teachings. He did not base His doctrine on the opinion polls of man, and neither should we.

There is a tendency in this culture to please and appease everyone. Whether we admit it or not, we liked to be liked, we loved to be loved. But if our motivation for ministry is the applause of the audience we are offending the most important person –our Lord.

We must stand for truth. Truth, regardless of its acceptance. Truth, regardless of its likeability. Truth, regardless of it popularity. Popularity comes and goes with the crowd, but truth abides forever.

DAILY SCRIPTURE READING: Numbers 3-4

FEBRUARY 13
THE SWEETNESS OF GOD'S WORD

"A daily, prolonged thoughtful bath in the Word of God is the only thing that will keep a life clean." –R.A. Torrey

In his book *Christlike*, Bill Hull describes how Jewish rabbis influence their students to read the Word of God. He notes, "They put honey on the fingers of their young male students and have them smear it on a tablet. The boys are then instructed to lick the tablet to taste the sweetness of the Torah, the Law of God. Taking in the Word of God is to be a total sensory experience because it is to change everything about us, from head to toe."

In Psalm 19:10 the psalmist spoke of the sweetness of God's Word, "More to be desired are they than gold, yea, than much fine gold: sweeter also than honey and the honeycomb." And again in Psalm 119:103, "How sweet are thy words unto my taste, yea, sweeter than the honey to my mouth."

R.A. Torrey said, "Any day we neglect to feed on the Word of God, we leave an open door through which Satan is sure to enter our hearts and lives." God has given us His Word not only for instruction and direction, but for joy and gladness. The truths discovered in the Bible will stimulate your mind, strengthen you spirit, satisfy your thirst, stir your heart, and sanctify your body. Sift through the pages and taste His goodness. God has spread a table in every jot and tittle. Delight in His Word and His Word will delight you.

DAILY SCRIPTURE READING: Numbers 5-6

FEBRUARY 14
COURAGE, PATIENCE, AND LOVE

"Love is not a silly sentiment or an adolescent infatuation. Love is the gutsiest and boldest of human initiatives." –Mel Lawrenz

I remember how anxious I felt on that Valentine's Day in 2000. The ring was purchased, the reservations at the famous Sundial restaurant were made; all I needed was the courage to ask my soon-to-be wife the question of a lifetime. I was nervous, not from riding in a glass elevator 73 stories above Atlanta, or from fear that she would say "no" but from the reality of the question. This one question would forever change both of our lives.

As we sat in the spinning, panoramic complex I prepared myself. The mood seemed right and the timing was perfect. Just as I reached for the ring, the fellow sitting at a nearby table bowed his knee to the ground and made a subtle commotion. He too came with a ring and stole my thunder as he asked his date for a hand in marriage. Not wanting to be a copy-cat proposer I put the ring back in my coat pocket and finished the meal.

Later that evening on a carriage ride through historic Atlanta, I took Heather's hand, with no one watching but God, and asked the question. She said "yes" and God has been writing our story ever since. I didn't realize it that evening but as I look back I understand something about love- it takes courage and patience to demonstrate it. As Mel Lawrenz says, "Love is not a silly sentiment or adolescent infatuation; love is the gutsiest and boldest of human initiatives."

DAILY SCRIPTURE READING: Numbers 7

FEBRUARY 15
THE HOLY SPIRIT TINKERS

"God is the only one who can separate the true from the false, the only one who can purify the motives of the heart." –Richard Foster

When it comes to mechanical knowledge of vehicles, I have very little. I understand the basic concept of filling up the gas tank; and if need be, I could perhaps change the oil, as long as I have the owner's manual nearby. I should have more understanding than what I do seeing that my dad is a "shade-tree mechanic." The term "shade-tree mechanic" simply means what it sounds like –parking a car under a tree, and working on it. Before the computerization of vehicles, people used to actually work on their own cars and trucks more often than they do now.

There have been many times something would go wrong in my vehicle and dad would come over and start looking things over. He would lift up the hood, jiggle some wires or belts, fiddle around, and within a few minutes have the problem figured out. He knew where and how to tinker.

The Holy Spirit works the same way. When we are having trouble getting our engine started, when we fail to move forward, He begins tinkering under our hood. He knows what parts are stalled-out or broken. Within moments He has pin-pointed the problem and starts working to get the issue resolved. He alone can reveal the "mechanical glitches" of our spirituality. Allow Him to tinker, so you can get back on the road.

DAILY SCRIPTURE READING: Numbers 8-10

FEBRUARY 16

WALKING ON MARBLE

"You cannot measure your eternal value by the worth or collection of your earthly vessels." –Kenneth Kuykendall

At the height of Charles Spurgeon's ministry, he was persuaded by a wealthy business man to tour an expensive, palatial home. Walking through the corridors of the palace, the owner showed Spurgeon his Italian marble floors. He tried to convince the prince of preachers that it was the best money could buy. In his typical convicting style, Spurgeon replied, "These are the things that make it hard to die."

Spurgeon's remark was a rebuke against the desire for worldly possessions. When a man spends his life pursuing the things of this world, he will often do so at the expense of missing the next world, therefore making it hard to die.

You cannot measure your eternal value by the worth or collection of your earthly vessels. The Lord declared, "For a man's life consisteth not in the abundance of the things he possesseth" (Luke 12:15). All that we possess in this life will one day fade away. The only thing that will last eternally is your relationship with God. Therefore, we are instructed to "set our affection on things above, not on things below."

Your feet may never touch Italian marble floors, but if you live and die in faith they will one day walk on the heavenly street of gold.

DAILY SCRIPTURE READING: Numbers 11-13

FEBRUARY 17

PROBLEMS WITH THE PILE ON

"Defeat may serve as well as victory to shake the soul and let the glory out." –Sam Ervin Jr.

I played defense three out of four years of high school football. One of the fundamental principles in playing defense is the importance of group tackles. When your teammate grabs hold of the guy with the ball, you are to run to the place of action and "pile on." "Pile on" was actually a term our coaches used frequently. There were times when five or six of us would pile on one fellow –it is called good defense.

I have to admit, there have been times I have been on the other end of the pile; have you? Have you ever felt like life and all of its problems just kept piling on? Something causes you to stumble and before you know it, you are down on the ground; the devil cries out "Pile on!" Financial hardship hits your life and you go to bed with worries; the devil cries out "Pile on!" You have stress beyond imagination at work and you wonder if you should be somewhere else; the devil cries "Pile on!"

I remember those fellows at the bottom of the pile. The only thing that saved them from being crushed was a whistle. Somewhere on the sidelines the referee would came to their aid. He didn't always stop the "pile on" from happening, he just prevented them from being killed by it. Our heavenly Father does the same. He knows when we have had enough, and He uses His power to relieve us from the weight of the pile on.

DAILY SCRIPTURE READING: Numbers 14-15

FEBRUARY 18

RELIGION IN ITS PUREST FORM

"If we love the world the way Jesus loved the world, we would never love the world the way we shouldn't love the world." –Vance Havner

I find it interesting that the Book from which our religion is established only used the word "religion" five times. Four out of those five times it is used to describe the structure and system of Judaism. Only in the book of James do we get a true, working definition of the word: "Pure religion and undefiled before God and the Father is this, To visit the fatherless and widows in their affliction, *and* to keep himself unspotted from the world" (James 1:27).

True religion can be summed up in two words: compassion and consecration. We are to go into the world to care and take care of others while at the same time we are to prevent the world from soiling our lives. This is a unique balance of changing the world while not allowing the world to change us. Vance Havner said it like this, "If we love the world the way Jesus loved the world, we would never love the world the way we shouldn't love the world." Read that again slowly.

Believers who are saved by the grace of God should submit themselves to this brand of religion. We are to make a difference in the world while being different from the world. This is religion in its purest form. Now, how religious are you?

DAILY SCRIPTURE READING: Numbers 16-17

FEBRUARY 19

THE PROMISE OF REUNION

"In our mourning, God gives the hope of another morning." –Kenneth Kuykendall

Famed theologian and pastor F.B. Meyer spent most of his life serving in churches in England. From time to time he would make trips to North America for evangelistic crusades, seminars, and meetings. During his last few days of travel, Meyer wrote a friend and colleague with these touching words:

"I have just heard, to my great surprise, that I have but a few days to live. It may be that before this reaches, I shall have entered into the palace. Don't trouble to write me. We shall meet again in the morning."

A few days later, Meyer passed away, but not without the promise of reunion. Meyer understood that his end was really just his beginning. You see, in our mourning God gives the hope of another morning.

We live in this tabernacle now made of clay, and when it is dissolved we have another home prepared not made with hands. Meyer referred to it as his palace; Christ called it a mansion, but we can call it home if we have been saved by grace. Yes, weeping may endure for the night, but joy comes in the morning. The sting of death is very real, but the promise of morning outshines the gloom from that dreary valley. No correspondence will be needed in heaven, for there we will see each other face to face.

DAILY SCRIPTURE READING: Numbers 18-20

FEBRUARY 20

THE LAW OF INTENTION

---

*"When your holiness becomes tarnished,
let your happiness become dim."* –A.W. Tozer

In his book, *A Serious Call to a Devout and Holy Life*, William Law concluded that people fail to embrace holiness because they lack the intention of doing so. He suggested, "The reason why you see no real mortification or self-denial, no eminent charity, no profound humility, no heavenly affection, no true contempt of the world, no Christian meekness, no sincere zeal, no eminent piety in the common lives of Christians, is this, because they do not so much as intend to be exact and exemplary in these virtues."

I have heard people excuse their unrighteous living because they say the Christian life is too difficult. Yet these same people work difficult jobs, maintain difficult schedules, and work fervently to solve difficult problems. They are able to overcome the difficulties because it is their intention.

Yes, living holy is difficult at times, but it is possible through and in our position and relationship with Jesus Christ. Holiness has become almost a taboo subject in our culture, but God still requires it. We are to "be holy, even as He is holy." Unless you intend to live holy, you will never attempt to be holy; and thus living without it, you'll never know the joy of living with it.

DAILY SCRIPTURE READING: Numbers 21-22

FEBRUARY 21
THE IMPORTANCE OF PRUNING

"It is simply absurd to say you believe, or even want to believe in Him, if you do not do anything he tells you." –George MacDonald

Every gardener understands the importance and value of pruning. The unproductive growth of a plant will take away nutrients and choke out the productive growth. Without proper pruning, the entire harvest will suffer thus producing fruit that is not eatable or desirable.

Jesus spoke of this process in the fifteenth chapter of John. He said, "Every branch in me that beareth not fruit he taketh away: and every branch that beareth fruit, he purgeth it, that it may bring forth more fruit" (John 15:2).

We must all admit there are areas in our lives that need pruning. What we often fail to realize is that without pruning, we actually hinder our growth in the Lord. There may be some temporal pleasure in vices, habits, and addictions; but that fleeting pleasure hinders you from a life of joy and contentment. Much like the unproductive branches, they sap the spiritual nutrients and cause your fruit to be wilted and unhealthy.

Take out the spiritual shears and start cutting off those lifeless, droopy vines. Don't feed them any longer. Don't allow them to keep robbing you of the joy that is in Christ. Recognize what they are doing to your fruit, your faith, and your future, and get to hacking.

DAILY SCRIPTURE READING: Numbers 23-25

FEBRUARY 22

THE MOST IMPORTANT PART

"Our Lord has written the promise of resurrection, not in books alone, but in every leaf of springtime." –Martin Luther

Curtis Hutson used to tell a story about a man who stood looking at a picture of Christ in a gallery store. The picture depicted Jesus on the cross with the Roman soldier standing by. A young boy came up to the man and started explaining the picture.

He said, "Mister, that's Jesus on the cross." The man didn't say a word; he just kept staring at the picture. The boy went on, "Sir, you see those soldiers, they killed Jesus." Still, the man was silent. The boy kept explaining, "And those disciples kneeling down, they took the body and buried the Lord." Not saying a word, the man simply walked away.

After walking a block down the road the man heard the pounding steps of the young lad. Finally catching up with the man, the boy exclaimed, "Mister, I forgot to tell you the most important part, Jesus came out of the grave! And He is alive!"

That is certainly the most important part. Without the resurrection, all hope would be lost. Our faith would be vain. Our preaching would just be idle chatter. Our destiny would be doomed. But Christ is alive! And that one life-changing fact is worth running down the street to tell mankind the good news of Jesus Christ!

DAILY SCRIPTURE READING: Numbers 26-27

FEBRUARY 23

THE NOBILITY OF SERVICE

"Obedience is the only sound objective of a Christian spirituality." –Dallas Willard

One of my favorite quotes on service is by T.W. Manson. He said, "In the kingdom of God, service is not a stepping stone to nobility- it is nobility, the only kind that is recognized." Service and humility is foreign to our culture. Today's brand of Christianity is geared more toward accumulation than distribution. Most of the effort in Christendom these days is about what we get over what we give.

We determine our ministerial well-being by corporate standards rather than Christ-like service. We want, as the mother of James and John wanted for her sons, to be seated in glory and recognition without drinking the cup of suffering and humility. But glory never comes in that order. True glory is actually discovered through humble service.

Do you live in continual service to the Master? Have you bowed with Him in the upper room to wash the feet of others? Have you touched the leprous brow to extend healing and grace? Have you spoken words of kindness to the downtrodden and sinful? God is not looking for stars, just servants who will be transformed into the image of Christ- that's the greatest move toward nobility you can experience.

DAILY SCRIPTURE READING: Numbers 28-30

FEBRUARY 24

THE CITY OF REFUGE

"Peace is the continual rehearsal of standing in the right spot in the grand order of things-not lower or higher." –Mel Lawrenz

According to the Mosaic Law, anyone who committed murder was subject to execution. However, the Lord established various "cities of refuge" for those who killed someone unintentionally. These cities were part of the distribution of the Promised Land given to the Twelve Tribes of Israel. God set these cities aside to which the murderer could flee. Within the boundaries of that particular city, he would be safe from any avenger –at least until the case went to trial.

These cities provided a safe-haven, a place of security during troubled times. They were indeed cities of refuge.

In Scripture, the word "refuge" was synonymous with these cities. There is no doubt King David alluded to these particular regions when he said, "God is our refuge and strength, a very present help in trouble" (Psalm 46:1).

There were times David could not make it to the cities established by the law, but he could go to God. Indeed, the Lord is our rock, our shield, our fortress, our high tower, and our strength. His provision is discovered in His presence. Run to God, abide in His company, and experience His peace during troubled times.

DAILY SCRIPTURE READING: Numbers 31-32

FEBRUARY 25

THE VALUE OF A CROWN

"Those who pursue the will of God will not always get what they want; but the will always want what they get." –Zig Ziglar

As a father I love giving gifts to my children, especially surprise gifts. I love the look on their faces when I give something unexpected. I also like to receive gifts from my children. I have a wide-collection of ties I have never worn, pens I have never used, and various plastic instruments they have purchased from school fund-raising events. I hold these gifts near to my heart, not because of their intrinsic value but because of the people who gave them to me.

Their gifts are simply reminders of the greater gift –themselves.

When you and I stand before our Holy God, we may or may not receive various crowns (I like to think that I will have one or two). Those gifts, unlike ties and pens, will have eternal value. What will make the gift so special, again, is the One Who gives it. The true reward is not so much receiving a crown, but receiving it from our Lord and Savior.

We will stand before His thrown and salute Him as the King of kings, and the Lord of lords. There we have no earthly merit to claim. Our song will be one of grace and mercy. The value of the crown is not found in the ones who received it, but rather in the One Who gave it.

DAILY SCRIPTURE READING: Numbers 33-34

FEBRUARY 26

UNION AND COMMUNION

"Our union with Christ is a divine work, our communion is a personal responsibility." –Kenneth Kuykendall

Our relationship with the Lord can be described in two words: union and communion. Our union with Christ took place at conversion. We were forever united in the family of God through the blood of the Lamb. Our union can never be altered, changed, or undone.

Our communion with Christ speaks of the condition of that relationship. Our union in Christ can never be changed, but our communion with Christ fluctuates. Communion is based upon our obedience, holiness, and willingness to spend time with Him. Our union with Christ is a divine work; communion is a personal responsibility.

It is possible to have union with the Lord and have very little communion. Consider the bond of marriage. You can't be any less or any more married (this is your union), but you can have a stronger or weaker marriage (this is your communion).

The same holds true in your relationship with Christ. You can't be any more or any less saved than you already are; but you can have more or less joy in the relationship. The difference in a strong communion and a weak communion is the time, energy, and effort you put into the relationship. Rejoice in your union, but be committed in your communion.

DAILY SCRIPTURE READING: Numbers 35-36

FEBRUARY 27

SHAKE IT OFF

"I have been around religious circles for a long time and have never heard the word resent used by a victorious man." –A.W. Tozer

When the Lord commissioned His disciples to go and preach the gospel of the kingdom He said not everyone would receive it. He told them, "And whosoever shall not receive you, nor hear your words, when ye depart out of that house or city, shake off the dust of your feet" (Matthew 10:14).

In the service of the Lord there will be times of rejection. There will be people who adamantly refuse our message. They will scoff at our preaching, they will decline to open the door, and even rebuke our efforts. In essence, they are not really denouncing us as much as they are denouncing Christ. It is certain, no one likes rejection, but there are times we must simply shake it off.

Jesus said to shake off the dust from your feet as a testimony against them. In other words, "Get over it, get beyond it, and go on down the road to the next stop." How often do we allow others to hinder us in the service of the Lord? Hurt feelings, bitterness, resentment, pride…just shake it off. If they rejected Christ (and they did) we shouldn't expect anything more in our own lives. Be faithful, be steadfast, be adamant, and just shake it off.

DAILY SCRIPTURE READING: Deuteronomy 1-2

FEBRUARY 28

POWER WITH NO PURPOSE

"Therefore I take pleasures in infirmities... for when I am weak then an I strong." –The Apostle Paul

I recently watched a body-building competition on a sports channel. The men walked out on stage looking like chiseled statues made of stone. They posed and flexed their muscles as judges examined their definition, tone, and body weight. Though initially impressed with their power, I began to wonder how their strength was utilized. Think about it, how often will they use their muscle in day-to-day living? Outside of creating an extraordinary physique, what is the purpose of their power?

These well-oiled body-builders remind me of Christians who want to appear strong before the spiritual judges, but never really use their strength for any real cause or purpose. Too often we flex our religious muscles in an attempt to gain the applause of those who judge us. We work out, we sweat, and we dedicate our lives for the recognition and acknowledgment of others. Like well-oiled performers on a stage we prance around hoping someone will identify our effort.

What we need are some men and women who are strong in the Lord and the power of His might –some believers who not only hearers but doers of His Word. Instead of prancing around on stage or standing in judgment of those who are, we should seek to operate in the power of His strength.

DAILY SCRIPTURE READING: Deuteronomy 3-4

MARCH

MARCH 1
HE WILL CARRY ME

"One of the realities of life is if you cannot trust a person at any point, you cannot truly trust him at all points." –Cheryl Biehl

French acrobat Charles Blondin was a legend in his time. In 1859, he crossed the entire width of Niagara Falls on a tightrope. During his prime he walked the tightrope with a wheelbarrow, another time blindfolded, and once even on stilts. Perhaps the most amazing feat of his life was when he walked the rope while carrying another man on his back.

What is so amazing is not that he was able to carry the man, but that he was able to convince the man to let him carry him. That my friend is what you call trust. This unidentified fellow didn't just believe, in theory, that Blondin was able to carry him; he put his faith to the test.

What a beautiful picture of our relationship of faith in Jesus Christ. Faith is an action word. It moves beyond religious rhetoric and theory. Genuine faith climbs on the back of the Savior and believes fully that He is able to sustain and support us.

A.W. Tozer said, "How completely satisfying to turn from our limitations to a God Who has none." You and I could never cross the great span between earth and heaven, man and God; but we can trust in Jesus Christ to carry us all the way to glory by His power and strength.

DAILY SCRIPTURE READING: Deuteronomy 5-7

MARCH 2

GOD IS A SLOW DRIVER

"I don't like hearing that I need patience. And I know why: because I don't like being patient." –Mel Lawrenz

Traffic jams, crowded doctor offices, and long lines at the grocery store far too often expose my impatience. There is nothing about waiting that I enjoy, but it is an inevitable part of life. Someone has rightly said: "If the request is wrong, God says "No." If the timing is wrong, God says "Slow." If I am wrong, God says "Grow." But if all three are right, God says "Go." That sounds good in theory, but my biggest problem is that I rarely have all three (requests, timing, and self) in sync with each other. So the inevitable occurs…I have to wait.

Sometimes it feels as though God is a Sunday-afternoon driver; He is taking His sweet time; all the while, I am in the car behind him with the psalmist David in the backseat asking, "How long? How long, O God?" (Psalm 13). Have you ever wanted God to just hurry up?

God doesn't just want you to get to a desired location; He wants you to enjoy the ride. To the slow Sunday-afternoon driver, the journey is just as important as the destination. God may be going slower than you would like because He wants you to see something you have never seen. Stop honking the horn and flashing the lights, God is not only taking you to where you need to go, He wants you to enjoy where you are. Keep following Him.

DAILY SCRIPTURE READING: Deuteronomy 8-10

MARCH 3
WHILE YOU WAIT

"We are not to idly sit by while we wait; we are to be actively engaged in seeking God's will." –Kenneth Kuykendall

The prophet Isaiah said, "But they that WAIT upon the LORD shall renew their strength; they shall mount up with wings as eagles; they shall run, and not be weary; and they shall walk, and not be faint" (Isaiah 40:31). We tend to think that while we are waiting we are supposed to be doing nothing –that is simply not true.

The word WAIT in the passage has two implications. It means to look (literally to watch with anticipation), but it also means to labor (literally to gather, collect, or be profitable for someone else). We are not to idly sit by while we wait; we are to be actively engaged in seeking God's will. Here are four things to do while you WAIT:

W. Worship the Lord. When Job waited for his restoration, he fell to the ground and worshipped His Creator.

A. Align Your Heart with God's. Moses waited 40 years in the wilderness before God spoke to him from the burning bush. During that time God was molding and shaping the heart of His servant.

I. Involve Yourself in Service. Jacob served his father-in-law for 14 years so that he could marry Rebekah.

T. Trust in His Plan. Joseph spent years in the prison before he found his place in the palace. While he waited, he trusted that God was working.

DAILY SCRIPTURE READING: Deuteronomy 11-13

MARCH 4
THE BEAUTY OF THE BUTTERFLY

"The secret to happiness is the consistency to pursue." –Harry Banks

A young boy visited his grandfather's butterfly farm and was amazed at what he learned. His grandfather showed him the cocoons and told the young boy about the transformation process. The grandson noticed a particular cocoon where a butterfly was struggling to get out. While his grandfather was not looking he took a small twig and released the insect from its tight quarters. A beautiful butterfly sprang forth in life but quickly fell to the ground and died.

The young boy tearfully asked his grandfather why the butterfly didn't survive. The grandfather said, "You let him out too soon. His struggle is what makes him strong. If he does not fight his way out, he will not have the strength to survive."

It is our travail that gives way to our triumph. Too often we ask the Lord to release us from our burdens, when in reality, those very burdens are being used by God to develop patience, devotion, and strength. It is the struggle that makes us strong. Keep fighting and believing your way through; on the other side you will break forth in liberty and freedom from that adverse circumstance as a beautiful testimony of God's transforming power and grace.

DAILY SCRIPTURE READING: Deuteronomy 14-16

MARCH 5

A BOOK LIKE NONE OTHER

"There is absolutely no shortcut to holiness that bypasses or gives little priority to a consistent intake of the Bible." –Jerry Bridges

When asked what book he would like to have if stranded on a desert island, G.K. Chesterton cleverly replied, *"Thomas' Guide to Practical Ship Building."* He said he could not imagine himself in that kind of circumstance but if such an occasion arrived he would like to at least have a chance to get home.

Although Chesterston's answer seems logical and quite witty, there is another book that would be far more helpful –the Holy Bible. As John Quincy Adams said, "The Bible is the book of all others, to be read at all ages, and in all conditions of human life." (Even on a stranded island).

The Bible indeed is for all conditions of human life. The Word of God has an answer for every question we face. It has light for our darkened paths. It is a sword and shield for the war-torn soldier. It is a cool drink of water for the dry, parched soul.

The Bible is the only book that reads the reader. It provides nourishment, direction, inspiration, comfort, and rebuke. It is alive. *Thomas' Guide to Practical Ship Building* may give instruction on to how to escape a desert island, but the Holy Bible gives instruction on how to get to our heavenly home.

DAILY SCRIPTURE READING: Deuteronomy 17-20

MARCH 6

A PLACE LIKE NONE OTHER

"I was glad when they said unto me, Let us go into the house of the LORD." –King David

There are very few things I enjoy more than spending time with my family on vacation. We love going to places we have never been and experiencing different environments and cultures. Out of all the places we travel though, no other place is as precious as the House of God.

The psalmist David said, "For a day in thy courts is better than a thousand. I had rather be a doorkeeper in the house of God, than to dwell in the tents of wickedness" (Psalm 84:10). One thousand days is close to three years. One can see a lot in three years; if given enough effort, you could quite possibly see the entire world. But the entire world, with its majestic scenery and glorious landscape cannot compare to one day in the House of God! David had great admiration and affection toward God's House. To him it was a place of rest, refuge, rejoicing, and redemption. He did not go to God's House out of obligation or religious routine; he went to find solace and strength for his soul. He went to meet God and grow in holiness.

We should not grudgingly come into the House of God with a thousand other things (or places) on our mind. When we enter His courts, we should do so with praise and thanksgiving. We have come to meet the King!

DAILY SCRIPTURE READING: Deuteronomy 21-23

MARCH 7
A FRIEND LIKE NONE OTHER

"Ye are my friends, if ye do whatsoever I command you." –Jesus Christ

Proverbs 18:24 declares, "A man that hath friends must show himself friendly: And there is a friend that sticketh closer than a brother." They say that "blood is thicker than water" but there is a type of friendship, Solomon concluded, that is actually thicker than blood. It is the kind of friendship Jesus referred to in John 15:13, "Greater love hath no man than this that a man lay down his life for his friends."

Self-denying, sacrificial love is the greatest virtue of any friendship. Paul said this kind of love is actually greater than faith and hope (1 Corinthians 13). Jesus Christ is this kind of friend.

He never refuses you. You can talk with Him any hour of the day (or night). He only gives you good counsel and advice. He is not self-serving. He bestows daily blessings and benefits in your life. He is reliable, dependable, and trustworthy. He doesn't talk behind your back. He doesn't leave you during hard times. He is a physician, a counselor, a shepherd, a Savior. He's THE Friend that sticketh closer than a brother.

Joseph Scriven perhaps said it best in his classic hymn, "What a friend we have in Jesus, all our sins and grief to bear! What a privilege to carry, everything to God in prayer!" Indeed, He is a Friend like none other!

DAILY SCRIPTURE READING: Deuteronomy 24-27

MARCH 8

A LIFE LIKE NONE OTHER

"Ordinary disciples telling ordinary people about an extraordinary Savior is the heartbeat of the Commission." –Kenneth Kuykendall

When Jesus commissioned His disciples into the world His intent was to evangelize the nations. Just a handful of men revolutionized the surrounding community and ultimately the world at large. These men were not scholarly or brought up through rabbinical training. On the contrary, they were "unlearned and ignorant men." But they were willing.

In his book, *Follow Me*, David Platt asks, "How is your life going to impact every nation, tribe, tongue and people in the world?" He answers, "This is not a question for extraordinary missionaries; this is a question for ordinary disciples." Ordinary disciples telling ordinary people about an extraordinary Savior is the very heart of the Great Commission.

The idea that one individual can impact the world seems daunting and quite impossible. But when we give our time, money, prayers, and effort to the propagation of the gospel, God multiplies our efforts in ways we cannot measure. One dollar, one testimony, one mission trip, one life can change the world. How is your life reaching the nations? How much of your budget goes toward spreading the gospel? How many people have you told about Jesus this year? You don't have to be extraordinary; you just have to be obedient.

DAILY SCRIPTURE READING: Deuteronomy 28-29

MARCH 9

EXERCISE TO BE HOLY

"The greatest need of my people is my own holiness." –Robert Murray M'Cheyne

When the apostle Paul wrote Timothy, he instructed his young protégé to "exercise thyself rather unto godliness" (1 Timothy 4:7). Paul was familiar with the Olympics of his day, and referred to the games quite often in his writings. But instead of training the body, Paul taught Timothy to train the spirit. He was to exercise his life in a direction of godliness.

Bill Hull states, "Training to be holy is very different from trying to be holy. Trying to be holy doesn't work, training does." To exercise godliness you must be deliberate. One does not "accidentally" work-out. No one mistakenly lifts weights or jogs three miles. The same principle holds true when it comes to our spirituality.

To be godly we must train ourselves. We must have an intentional program, a set of core values and a strong will to live within the parameters of the Word of God. We must stick to a daily regime of prayer, meditation, and spiritual disciplines. Horatius Bonar stated, "Holiness is not measured by one great heroic act of mighty martyrdom…it is the small things that a holy life is made of." We grow strong spiritually the same way we grow strong physically, by exercising a little every day.

DAILY SCRIPTURE READING: Deuteronomy 30-31

MARCH 10

DIRTY TOWELS

"When we fail to assume the position of a servant, we work from the premise that we are better than Christ." –Kenneth Kuykendall

The dusty streets of Palestine combined with the open-toe sandals of the day made for high employment among servants. Those who entered into the homes of friends and family were typically greeted by a welcoming bond-slave. The servant would wash the feet of the guests as a gesture of hospitality. Though it was a delightful experience for the visitor, it was a demeaning position for the servant.

You might even say it was a little gross.

The towel of a servant is a constant reminder that things are going to get a little dirty. Even as the feet of the disciples were soiled, you and I should expect to encounter people in our lives and ministries who have dirty feet. A *clean* towel is a misnomer.

People are dirty by nature. We enter into the world that way. A child, if left unattended at birth, will die in its natural condition. The filth of our physicality is just a mirror of the soul. As the feet become unclean by the dust of the earth, the soul too is stained by the elements of the world. People need to be touched with our towels; they need to be served with a gracious and loving spirit. You see, only dirty people need towels-to expect anything more out of them is hypocrisy.

DAILY SCRIPTURE READING: Deuteronomy 32-34

MARCH 11
THAT IS WHY WE ARE HERE

"The New Testament never teaches us to build a place for people to come; it commands us to give our lives going to people." –David Platt

A few years ago we had some major trouble with one of the heating units in our home. I had to call the mechanic on three different occasions with various issues. The last time I called him it was late in the evening, but he promptly came out and took care of the problem. When he arrived I apologized about the inconvenient hour to which he replied, "Sir, we would be out of business if you didn't have these problems, that is why we are here."

Sometimes I think as a church we have forgotten why we are here. Many times we are repulsed by sinners and their ways. We are quick to judge their sin and evaluate their indifference to God; but hasn't the Lord called us to be the salt and the light? Should we not, with the same compassion of Christ, reach out to those who are lost and doomed for hell?

This is why we are in business; this is why we are here. We are to speak with the words of Christ, love with the heart of Christ, and minister with the hands of Christ. Our business is lost sinners and I think sometimes we have reduced our calling to nothing more than social encounters in religious buildings. We are to make "house calls" to the world even if it is inconvenient to our schedule. That is why we are here.

DAILY SCRIPTURE READING: Joshua 1-4

MARCH 12

OFF TARGET

"Stand fast therefore in the liberty wherewith Christ hath made us free." –The Apostle Paul

During the 2004 Olympics, archer Matt Emmons was one shot away from a gold medal. He was competing in the 50-meter three position rifle event and was in perfect position to claim victory. He didn't even need a bulls-eye; all he needed to do was hit the target to win the gold. However, standing in lane two, Emmons took a shot at the target in the third lane. His shot was dead on, the only problem, it hit the wrong target. He received zero points and landed in eighth place.

I have had some "Matt Emmons'-moments." There have been moments when I have missed the mark. I had the right aim, the right ability, and the right precision, but was still off target. In those moments I am always reminded of my humanity, my sin, my pride, my flesh, but also my Savior.

You see, like Emmons, we have all "fallen short of the glory of God." We have all missed the mark from time to time. But in the midst of our imperfections, weaknesses, and fatal mistakes stands a Savior who reminds us of His righteousness. We do not have to be perfect because He is perfect. Our standing is in Christ; therefore we must stand in Him. Through Him we become the righteousness of God. I do not have to always be "on target" because through Him I have already won the gold!

DAILY SCRIPTURE READING: Joshua 5-8

MARCH 13

RESPONSIBILITY AND DEPENDENCE

"While therefore we grow in the Christian life by divine grace, it is our duty to grow in grace." –George W. Bethune

In his book *The Practice of Godliness*, Jerry Bridges speaks of the "Spiritual Principle of Responsibility and Dependence." Many believe that the Christian is supposed to live one way or the other, either a life of responsibility, or a life of dependence.

As frail, finite, fallen creatures we are to depend upon the power, the mercy, and the Spirit of God to develop holy lives. In the transaction of grace we cannot depend upon our own virtue or righteousness. However, we are not mechanical robots without a free-will. We cannot assume that godliness will just somehow occur without us ever putting forth an effort. So, do we become holy through total dependence upon the Lord, or do we become holy through personal obligation? The answer –both.

"Though the power of godly character comes from Christ" Bridges contends, "the responsibility for developing and displaying the character is ours." Walking in holiness ultimately involves two strides-one stride of dependence, the other stride of responsibility. Only by the unmerited favor *of God* can we pursue a godly life, but in order to obtain *we* must pursue. Perhaps the psalmist said it best, "As the hart panteth after the waterbrooks; so panteth my soul after thee, O God." Depend upon God responsibly.

DAILY SCRIPTURE READING: Joshua 9-11

MARCH 14

ARE YOU IN THE CROWD?

"The early church was in the upper room agonizing, the modern church is the in the supper room organizing." –Unknown

Jesus was never impressed with large crowds. Most of the people who followed Him in the early part of His ministry did so because they received something of the Lord (bread and fish, healing, words of life). As a matter of fact, whenever Jesus looked upon the multitudes He saw them as lost, aimless sheep. .

However, the crowds started thinning out when the Lord demanded commitment and faithfulness. When Jesus said, "Let the dead bury the dead" and "No man, putting his hand to the plow, looking back, is fit for the kingdom" some started questioning Him. When He said, "Drink my blood and eat my flesh" many turned away and said, "This is a hard saying." When Jesus declared, "The foxes have holes, and the birds of the air have nests, but the Son of man hath no place to lay his head" still others went home. You see, at that point, it was no longer about what they received from Christ; it was about what they had to give up for Christ.

Pop-culture Christianity is looking to fill the stadiums, and pack the pews, but Jesus is not looking for a crowd, He is looking for commitment. It is easy to follow Christ when nothing is required and the blessings flow from above. But there comes a time when His true disciples follow Him simply because of Who He is.

DAILY SCRIPTURE READING: Joshua 12-15

MARCH 15
LAS VEGAS LETDOWN

"I have found a friend in Jesus, He's everything to me. He's the fairest of ten thousand to my soul." –Charles W. Fry

An elderly missionary returned to the United States after being on foreign soil for over thirty years. Arriving in California he boarded a bus to the Midwest to stay with his daughter. The first stop was in Las Vegas. He decided to stay over to view the sights and sounds of the city.

As he walked down the streets he heard the loud music, saw the grand hotels, and was disoriented by all the flashing lights. He heard the clinking of the slot machines, saw the advertisements of famous celebrities, and witnessed thousands of people drinking and laughing. Overwhelmed by the parties, people, and promiscuity he went back into his hotel room, opened the curtain to view the city, and cried out in prayer, "God, I thank you that I haven't seen anything I want more than you."

The world has nothing to offer the child of God. The songwriter Rhea Miller said, "I'd rather have Jesus than silver and gold; I'd rather be His than have riches untold. I'd rather have Jesus than houses or lands; I'd rather be led by His nail-pierced hand." A life committed to service and surrender will never be satisfied with the glitz and glamour of this world. The lights will fade, the music will cease, and the riches will diminish. Anything less than Jesus is a letdown.

DAILY SCRIPTURE READING: Joshua 16-18

MARCH 16

WITH APPROVED CREDIT

"For by grace are ye saved through faith." –The Apostle Paul

Have you ever seen those loud, obnoxious, too-good-to-be true car commercials that offer you a great price with the lowest rate possible? They advertise an unbelievable deal and declare that anyone can buy a car from them. However, at the end of the commercial, usually at the bottom of the screen in small writing, appears a disclaimer-"With approved credit."

What they are offering really is not to everyone. Only those who qualify according to their standards have the opportunity to get in on the offer.

Jesus never made such a contingency. When Jesus said "Come unto me" He was speaking to everyone. When Jesus said, "For God so loved the world" He was speaking about all men. When Paul declared, "The grace of God hath appeared to all men" that is exactly what he meant.

There are no hidden clauses with the Lord. He doesn't discriminate based upon social standing, religious preferences, or the color of skin. He will not refuse you because of your past. He will not deny you because of your faults. He will not dismiss you because of your mistakes. No, He accepts all applications; no credit or background checks necessary.

DAILY SCRIPTURE READING: Joshua 19-21

MARCH 17
BUILDING THE LIVES OF OTHERS

"When I have any money, I get rid of it as soon as possible, lest it find a way into my heart." –John Wesley

Millard Fuller became a millionaire at the age of twenty-nine. He and his wife had anything and everything the world offered. They lived a life of luxury and comfort until one day Richard came home to an empty house. He found a note from his wife declaring she had left him along with all the niceties of their life.

Millard found her at a nearby hotel where they talked about the emptiness and vanity of their riches. She told him she was cold and indifferent in her heart. At the bedside they both prayed together and made a decision to sell all they had. They committed the rest of their lives to serving the poor. The Fullers soon started an organization to assist their community; it was called Habitat for Humanity. To this date, the organization has provided over 600,000 homes for low-income families, and has helped over three million people around the world.

The Fullers came to terms with the words of Jesus, "He that findeth his life shall lose it, and he that loseth his life for my sake shall find it." In the process of seeking Christ and serving others we are promised to find joy and contentment for ourselves. Billy Graham said it best, "God has given us two hands, one to receive and the other to give." The Fullers would concur, and so would the thousands they have helped.

DAILY SCRIPTURE READING: Joshua 22-24

MARCH 18

THE PUBLICAN BECOMES A PUPIL

"There are two great days in a person's life: the day you were born, and the day you discover why." –John Maxwell

During the days of Christ a rabbi had many stringent requirements for his students. An impressive resume was needed just to be in consideration. The student had to have an extensive working knowledge of Scripture, be in line with the traditional Law, and live an exemplary lifestyle as required by the Sanhedrin. The "application" process was tedious and oftentimes the rabbi would reject those who initially applied. The student became the "identity" of the rabbi; therefore, to safeguard his religious character and moral integrity the rabbi chose carefully and oftentimes selfishly.

So when Jesus called Matthew, who sat at the seat of customs and was a hated tax collector, it must have been shocking to His colleagues. There was no entry exam, no long arduous process of inspection, no fine-tooth combing. Jesus simply said to this poor, insipid man, "Follow me." Matthew was not looking for Jesus, he submitted no application to this Rabbi, but still he was invited. The "publican" became a "pupil."

The Lord is still calling men to follow Him. He invites us to Himself and offers a life-changing adventure. Accept the greatest invitation ever given- the invitation to follow Christ and be His disciple.

DAILY SCRIPTURE READING: Judges 1-2

MARCH 19

THE LOGO OF THE LORD

"The only thing Jesus took pains to show after His resurrection were His scars." –Samuel Zwemer

A business or corporation is usually identified with a slogan or symbol of some sort. The golden arches of McDonalds, the "Just Do It" motto of Nike, the triangular emblem of Mercedes are all iconic in their field of industry. The logo of a company speaks to the style, status, and structure of that particular business.

When it comes to the business of Christianity, what logo do you think best identifies us with Christ?

Contrary to popular teaching it is not a symbol of health, wealth, or even prosperity. It is not a dove, a heart, a smile, or a peace sign. It is a cross. Jesus instructed His disciples to take up the cross and follow Him. Ultimately if we are going to be identified with the Lord our lives must become associated with His death.

The apostle Paul declared, "I am crucified with Christ: nevertheless I live; yet not I, but Christ liveth within me…" (Galatians 2:20). Paul was not ashamed to be identified with the cross of Calvary. It was the logo of his life. It was the symbol of his salvation.

In order to be followers and disciples, in order to be in business for the King we must grab hold of our cross and die daily.

DAILY SCRIPTURE READING: Judges 3-5

MARCH 20

IS YOUR SWORD INCLUDED?

---

*"Faith is only real
in obedience."* –Dietrich Bonhoeffer

In his book *Not a Fan*, author Kyle Idleman tells a story of the Knights of Templar. When they came to the church for baptism they would submit to the ordinance with their swords in hand. However, when they were submerged under the water, they held their swords up not allowing their weapon to go underneath. It was the knights' way of saying, "You can have control of me, but you cannot have my sword."

A lot of believers submit to Jesus in the same fashion. We sing from our hymnbook "I Surrender All" while our heart is saying, "I Surrender Some."

We compartmentalize our lives to the point where we give Jesus portions and segments. We are not against the Lord having our Sundays, but what about our Friday nights? We do not mind singing with our lips in the choir, but how do we speak with those same lips in the workplace? We have no problem watching the preacher for thirty minutes, but what do we watch on the internet?

Like the Knights of Templar we grasp our swords tightly and refuse to relinquish all rights to Jesus. The Lord does not want some of you, He wants all of you –including your sword.

DAILY SCRIPTURE READING: Judges 6-7

MARCH 21

TOMORROW IS A BIG DAY

"There are many people who enter into eternity thinking they were headed for tomorrow." –Kenneth Kuykendall

While preaching in a rural area of Kentucky I stopped at an old country store for gas. The station had a home-made sign advertising their sale on fuel. It said, "Gas $1.00 a gallon, on sale tomorrow." The price caught my attention but then I noticed the sign was worn and faded, and had been there for years. In their home-spun humor they safeguarded themselves against the sale of cheap gas because tomorrow is always the next day.

For a lot of people, tomorrow is going to be a big event. Tomorrow things are going to happen. Tomorrow is when it all goes down. Many will start reading their Bibles –tomorrow. Many are going to witness to their lost neighbor –tomorrow. Others will reconcile difficult relationships –tomorrow. Some will start tithing –tomorrow. Still others will trust Christ as their Savior –tomorrow.

The problem with such procrastination is that tomorrow is not promised to any person. James said, "Whereas ye know not what shall be on the morrow" (James 4:14). There are many people who enter into eternity thinking they were headed for tomorrow. Someone has aptly stated, "If you won't be better tomorrow than you were today, then what do you need tomorrow for?" Therefore, do whatever you need to do today, today.

DAILY SCRIPTURE READING: Judges 8-9

MARCH 22

THE KING OF THE HILL

"And the writing was, JESUS OF NAZARETH THE KING OF THE JEWS." –John 19:19

Do you remember playing "King of the Hill" as a child? I recall a group of neighborhood children gathering at the base of a mound. We would wrestle and brawl our way to the top only to push each other off and over until one solitary champion stood all by himself. Many would show up to play, but there could only be one king.

In his classic hymn, *The Old Rugged Cross*, George Bennard wrote, "On a hill far away stood an old rugged cross, the emblem of suffering and shame; And I love that old cross, for the Dearest and Best, for a world of lost sinners was slain." There on Golgotha's Hill hung our Lord and Savior. Above His head were the words engraved on a wooden plaque of timber, "King of the Jews."

That day at Calvary, the true King of the Hill was crowned. Satan and all the demons of hell tried to prevent His reign, but He rose in victory, and forever secured His title. There are no challengers, there is no rematch, there is no starting over. He alone sits upon the throne as the royal, reigning, regal king. He is the King of the Jews, the King of Israel, the King of righteousness, the King of the ages, the King of heaven, the King of glory, the King of Kings, the Lord of Lords. Indeed, He is the King of the Hill!

DAILY SCRIPTURE READING: Judges 10-12

MARCH 23

DON'T WATER IT DOWN

"So skilled is error at imitating truth that the two are constantly being mistaken for each other." –A.W. Tozer

Pharmacist Robert Courtney is not a name you want to be associated with. Over a nine-year period he diluted the medication of cancer patients. It was estimated that he altered over 98,000 prescriptions, and affected nearly 4,200 patients. Seventeen deaths can be traced back to his diluted formula. He made close to twenty million dollars through his fraudulent behavior, but was finally caught and sentenced to thirty years in prison.

Thousands of sick people trusted Robert Courtney with their lives. He was supposed to be an agent of healing, but instead he was an agent of hate and hurt.

Modern culture wants the church to dilute the truth of God's Word. They say it tastes bad, and is divisive. What they do not realize is that by watering down the truth we are actually killing off a generation in their sins. Like a cancer, sin grows and destroys the soul. The only remedy against it is the truth of Scripture. When we fail to tell people about sin, judgment, and eternal hell, we are, in effect, directing them to a Christless eternity. May we ever proclaim the truth of God's Word; the sin-sick sinner needs not a watered-down version.

DAILY SCRIPTURE READING: Judges 13-15

MARCH 24

HOW DO YOU TREAT JESUS?

"So skilled is error at imitating truth that the two are constantly being mistaken for each other." –A.W. Tozer

In the seventh chapter of the gospel of Luke, Jesus was invited to dinner at the house of Simon the Pharisee. Everything seemed to be normal until the meal was wildly interrupted by an unnamed harlot. Thankful for the grace she discovered in Christ, she bowed herself before the Lord, washed His feet with her tears, anointed His head with oil, and kissed Him.

In that culture a guest was greeted at the door with affection, water, and oil. A kiss was a customary sign of hospitality and kindness. Water was given to wash their feet, and oil was supplied to anoint their head. Simon, who was the actual owner of the home refused to embrace Jesus with such respect and honor; but the harlot esteemed the Lord greatly.

Knowing the heart of Simon, the Lord put forth a parable. He simply said, "There was a certain creditor which had two debtors: the one owed five hundred pence, and the other fifty. And when they had nothing to pay, he frankly forgave them both. Tell me therefore, which of them will love him most? Simon accurately answered, "He to whom he forgave the most." The harlot taught Simon a valuable lesson that day: the way you treat Christ comes from your understanding of His forgiveness. How are you treating the Lord these days?

DAILY SCRIPTURE READING: Judges 16-18

MARCH 25
GREEN GRASS AND THE GOSPEL

"I feel it is my duty to plod on while daylight lasts." –William Carey

I had recently told my wife that we needed to improve our lawn care. It had been several years since we had a company who maintained our weed and feed, and I was going to intentionally look for someone to give me a price. Within an hour of that conversation a local company actually called me to see if we needed service or maintenance.

After a few minutes of explaining our needs, I gave the salesman all of our information; he seemed genuinely surprised that I was so eager to talk with him and give him my business. I then asked him how many calls he had made on this one particular day, and how many contracts he secured. He just laughed, and said, "Well sir, you are the first one out of thousands of phone calls." Ironically enough he called at the right time and found someone who was looking for what he had to offer.

The same holds true in soul-winning. In this generation you may witness to thousands of people and knock on hundreds of doors and never get any response. Fulfilling the Great Commission can become tedious and discouraging if you consider the typical reply of those you try to reach. But if you keep on working, you are bound to find someone who realizes you have something they need. As a matter of fact, that person may have been waiting for your call, your tract, or your timely word.

DAILY SCRIPTURE READING: Judges 19-21

MARCH 26

THE VALUE OF EACH VERSE

"The Bible is the Sword of the Spirit, but the Spirit cannot give you a weapon you've not stored in the armory of your mind." –D. Whitney

Suppose I offered you a thousand dollars in exchange for any and every verse you memorized in the Bible. No gimmicks, no strings, no contingencies involved; for every verse you memorized and quoted you would receive cash money. I believe it is safe to assume that most people would take a stab at it. As a matter of fact, I believe most people would be motivated to learn many verses every single day.

Obviously I cannot offer you such a proposition, but I can do you one better. The value of each verse of Scripture is far greater than a thousand dollars. Solomon said in Proverbs 3:13-16, "Happy is the man that findeth wisdom, and the man that getteth understanding. For the merchandise of it is better than the merchandise of silver, and the gain thereof than fine gold. She is more precious than rubies: and all the things thou canst desire are not to be compared unto her. Length of days is in her right hand; and in her left hand riches and honor."

Many find themselves living in spiritual poverty because they fail to access the wealth of knowledge and wisdom in Scripture. God has given us sixty six books by which to live. Every verse contains spiritual nuggets of truth. Open the Bible, read it, memorize it; and in exchange God will give you treasures more valuable than monetary gain.

DAILY SCRIPTURE READING: Ruth 1-4

MARCH 27

START WHERE YOU ARE

---

*"It is His business to lead, command, send, and call…
it is your business to obey, follow, move, respond."* –Jim Elliot

I use my GPS often in my travels. With the advancement of technology most people these days have them on their phones. At any given time you can discover where you are and where you need to go. Within seconds you can have detailed directions to any place in the world. The particular version I have on my phone always asks me if I want to start from my "current location." It's as though it is saying, "You can get to where you want to go from right where you are. You can start right here, you can start right now. Just trust me, and I will show you the way."

If we trusted the Lord the same way we trust our GPS, life would be less complicated. God has a plan for your life –I realize that sounds cliché and overused, but it is a reality. Many people fail to embrace His plan because they do not realize the starting point. Right here, right now, God is inviting all of us to follow Him, to trust Him, to listen to Him.

He has mapped the way, He has scouted the trail, He has charted the course. He has already surveyed the scenery and knows the exact turns you and I should take. Start at your current location and listen to His instruction and guidance. Right here, right now you can begin to trust God. Not only will you get to your desired location, you'll enjoy the trip.

DAILY SCRIPTURE READING: 1 Samuel 1-3

MARCH 28

A HEAVENLY WORD

---

*"We do not make the Bible meaningful,
we discover its meaning."* –Mel Lawrenz

New Mexico has the largest area of radio receivers in the world. It is called the VLA- Very Large Array. These extremely large satellites span thirty-eight miles and have the power to detect energy from millions of light years away. Astronomers from all over the world come to view the images detected by this Very Large Array. We spend billions of dollars a year trying to discover a word, an image, a sound from outer space, all the while; God has already given us a clear authoritative Word from Heaven.

The Bible is God's Word to humanity. We need not look for falling stars, or a celestial uttering. We have been given in complete and final form the very Words of God. Inspired and immutable the Bible teaches us everything God wants us to know.

I sometimes think people would be more apt to believe God if they heard a voice from the clouds, or saw a sign from the cosmos; but in reality, we have something more powerful and eternal. Heaven and earth will pass away, but the smallest part of the smallest letter of the smallest word of God's Book will never fail. When we hold our Bibles, we hold the very Words of God.

DAILY SCRIPTURE READING: 1 Samuel 4-8

MARCH 29

A WARNING ABOUT WEALTH

"It is easier for a camel to go through the eye of the needle, than for a rich man to enter the kingdom of God." –Jesus Christ

Jesus spoke of wealth and riches often during His ministry. Three passages in particular deal with various rich men who struggled to find faith because of their finances. If these men could offer any advice to us today it would be the following:

Beware of the Possession of Riches (Luke 12:13-21). This rich man had such an abundant harvest that he had to tear down his barns to build bigger facilities. Consumed with the possessions of life he failed to prepare his soul. The Lord warned, "...a man's life consisteth not in the abundance of the things which he possesseth."

Beware of the Position of Riches (Mark 10:17-22). This young man was not only rich, he was a ruler. He lived a good, moral, decent life but equated his position with salvation. He refused to relinquish his title for the treasures of heaven, and walked away from true happiness.

Beware of the Pleasure of Riches (Luke 16:19-31). This rich man "fared sumptuously every day." He dressed in the finest clothes and lived a luxurious life, but he did so at the expense of eternity. When he died he lifted his eyes in hell. These three men would warn us to guard our hearts against the love, obsession, and pursuit of money.

DAILY SCRIPTURE READING: 1 Samuel 9-12

MARCH 30
INCONSISTENT EFFORTS

"The hallmark of excellence, the test of greatness is consistency." –Jim Tressel

The greatest detriment to the Christian life is a lack of consistent effort. The easiest thing in the world is to start something. We start our Bible study, our prayer time, our soul-winning programs, our devotions to God; but the hardest thing to do is commit ourselves to these disciplines.

Inconsistency kills our influence and undermines our ability to lead. Whether you are raising children, leading an organization, or coaching a T-ball team, if you are inconsistent in your methods, policies, and philosophies no one will be able to follow you.

Inconsistency hinders our ability to grow in the Lord. A majority of Christians never experience joy in their relationship with Christ because it is confined to sporadic commitment. Jesus gave us the secret to live the Christian life-we are to carry the cross **daily.**

Inconsistency breeds chaos and disorder. From doing the laundry to heading up the business meeting, if there is no consistent pattern in place, the end result will always be confusion and turmoil. Spiritual contentment is found in simple commitment. Don't just start something, stay with it, and finish it. The greatest testimony of faith is grounded in perseverance.

DAILY SCRIPTURE READING: 1 Samuel 13-14

MARCH 31

MISSING PIECES

"For we wrestle not against flesh and blood, but against principalities and powers." –The Apostle Paul

Imagine just for a moment entering into enemy territory. You have been given a special assignment of war by the United States military, and suddenly you find yourself surrounded by dangerous combatants. You are about to engage in conflict when you realize you have no weapon, no plan of action, and no protection at all from the enemy. How confident would you be of victory?

We would not expect triumph under those terms, but why should we expect anything different in spiritual warfare? Let's take a quick test-without peaking, can you name the different pieces of the armor of God? Paul spoke of these garments of warfare in Ephesians 6:10-17. Seriously think about them for a moment. How did you do? Can you name any? One? Two? None?

I believe it is safe to say: if we do not know the different pieces of the armor of God, odds are we are not wearing them. Can we really expect victory in our spiritual battles if we are not prepared for such conflict? Let me give you a special assignment for today; study Ephesians 6 and familiarize yourself with the whole armor of God. Learn them, but more importantly, wear them. Don't go to battle with missing pieces.

DAILY SCRIPTURE READING: 1 Samuel 15-17

APRIL

APRIL 1

SIBLING RIVALRY

"Jealousy takes place at the intersection of insecurity and selfishness." –Kenneth Kuykendall

Martha is your typical overachiever. She loves to keep a list, get things done, and move to the next task. She is always working, always busy, always serving. To say the least, she has a competitive drive. One of her biggest problems is that she is always comparing herself with other people. On the surface she is the queen of accomplishment, but underneath she is insecure and anxious.

Martha has a sister who is completely opposite. Mary is curious, she is inquisitive. She's more interested in building relationships than empires. It's not that Mary is lazy; she has just prioritized her life differently. She seems to be completely oblivious to the competition, but not Martha; she is always looking to outdo her sister. The angst in Martha's heart was finally revealed when she came to Jesus about her sister's apparent apathy toward the kitchen. Jesus, knowing the condition of the calculated sister, called her out, "Martha, Martha, thou art careful and troubled about many things: But the one thing is needful: and Mary hath chosen the good part..."

Too often we miss out on the blessings of God because we are busy comparing our lives with other people. When you value or diminish your worth by the actions of others, you position yourself toward misery. True worth is only discovered at the feet of Jesus.

DAILY SCRIPTURE READING: 1 Samuel 18-20

APRIL 2

THE LAND OF LIMBO

"It is when Christians hardly think of the other world that they have become ineffective in this one." –C.S. Lewis

The Land of Limbo is a miserable place to be. The apostle Paul understood the aggravation of such a place. He, in essence, told the Romans, "Those things I should do, I do not do those things; and those things I should not be doing, those are the things I do." He went on to say that the Spirit opposes the flesh, and the flesh opposes the Spirit-a constant state of limbo (Romans 7).

To Paul, the natural world was appealing to the flesh, but the Spirit of God would not give Him liberty to indulge in its sensuality. On the other hand, the spiritual world escorted him to a right relationship with God, but the flesh constantly hindered him from living in such a state. He seemed to be a resident in the Land of Limbo.

The Land of Limbo has its boundaries between the selfish and the selfless. Its town motto is "Neither flesh nor faith." If you drink from its water you will discover it to be lukewarm, not hot, nor cold. Its streets are paved with apathy and indifference. You may ask, how can we leave such a city? Well, Paul gave us directions out. He said, "I thank God through Jesus Christ our Lord" (Romans 7:25). The only way out of the Land of Limbo is to trust fully and completely the Lord Jesus Christ. Hook your load to His wagon, for He alone can take you out of the Land of Limbo!

DAILY SCRIPTURE READING: 1 Samuel 21-24

APRIL 3

ON THE SHIRT OR IN THE HEART?

"To many people, Christianity is a performance, but for some it is an experience." –Vance Havner

All of my children play baseball, and to be quite boastful, they are all really good. So the other day when my youngest hit a grand-slam homer, needless to say, I was standing and cheering him on. As he rounded third base into home plate, all the parents stood in ovation as he brought his team ahead by three points. One lady in particular stood in front of me cheering and asked a question to her friend, "Who is that kid?"

The proud papa in me wanted to quickly shout out, "That's my boy!" But I was distracted from doing such. I was distracted because the lady had on a team-shirt that had my kid's name on it. I thought to myself, "You have been to all of these games, you wear my son's name on your shirt, and you are even cheering him home; but you do not know him."

Christianity is full of the same kind of people. By association they wear the name of Jesus, they have a "fish" on their vehicle, they even come to church and cheer His name on. But when it gets down to it, they don't really know Christ, and more sadly, Christ doesn't know them. The Lord said, "Not every one that saith unto me, Lord, Lord, shall enter into the kingdom of heaven…and then I will profess unto them, I never knew you, depart from me, ye that work iniquity." Jesus wants to be more than a name on your shirt; He wants to be the Savior of your soul!

DAILY SCRIPTURE READING: 1 Samuel 25-27

APRIL 4

LOUDER THAN YOUR LIPS

"If you have integrity, nothing else matter. If you don't have integrity, nothing else matters." –Alan K. Simpson

A man without integrity is like a person yelling into a bull-horn that is not turned on. No matter how loudly he screams, no one really hears him. Unless your life matches your lips you have no influence, no impact; you make no difference. Ralph Waldo Emerson said, "What you are speaks so loudly that I cannot hear you."

The word "integrity" stems from the Latin derivative *integer*, which means completeness, wholeness. It is a mathematical concept; it implies having all the parts in sync. Ethically speaking, when our life fails to line up with our lips we have a failed *integer,* we are lacking the one component that makes the equation work.

Jesus' rebuke of the Pharisees was from a failed integer. They imposed a non-biblical standard with their words, but their lives failed to comply with the very standards they imposed. Jesus called them hypocrites for their inconsistent behavior.

The truth is our influence is in direct relation to the life we live, not the words we speak. Andrew Carnegie said, "As I grow older I pay less attention to what men say. I just watch what they do." Live louder than your lips.

DAILY SCRIPTURE READING: 1 Samuel 28-31

APRIL 5

DO YOU HAVE A FULL PLATE?

"The reason most major goals are not achieved is that we spend our time doing second things first." –Robert McKain

I try to meet regularly with seasoned men of God. I love to glean from their wisdom and knowledge, and seek advice concerning family, ministry, preaching, and life in general. Not long ago I met with a retired pastor for lunch. In casual conversation he asked about my schedule, my appointments, and my responsibilities. For the next few minutes I shared with him some of the things going on in my life, and then I asked for some practical advice.

Without any reservation he stuck his fork in my roast beef and slung it across the table. Taken back somewhat, I just stared as he tossed a piece of his cornbread in its place. Then he said, "Son, you've got too much on your plate. You want this (pointing to the cornbread), but you just don't have room for it." And with fiery conviction he simply said, "Make room."

Needless to say, I didn't finish the roast beef, but I did leave the table full. He was right. The plate was crowded. Overflowing, really. I walked away that afternoon with a new perspective on an old cliché. I think we accept some responsibilities that God never intended us to have. We assume too many roles, and take on too many tasks. If your plate is crowded, it may be time to throw some food on the table.

DAILY SCRIPTURE READING: 2 Samuel 1-3

APRIL 6

HOW TO GET WISDOM

"The wise man questions himself,
the fool others." –Henri Arnold

Theodore Roosevelt said, "Wisdom is nine-tenths a matter of being wise in time; most of us are wise after the event." It is true; being wise is demonstrated by knowing what to say, or what to do, in a proper context of timing. The problem, as Roosevelt pointed out, is that we rarely connect our mind, heart, and words with the right events –only wisdom affords such an opportunity. But how do we get it?

1. Wisdom comes from Scripture. Without a working knowledge of God's Word you will never understand life in its right context. Scripture gives us a proper world view (God's view).

2. Wisdom comes from failures. The question is not "will we fail?" But rather, "what will we learn when we fail?" Our mistakes afford us the opportunity to know what is right, and also to correct what is wrong.

3. Wisdom comes from learning of others. Solomon said, "Hear ye children, the instruction of a father; and attend to know understanding. (Proverbs 4:1). God has given us teachers and instructors for our benefit.

4. Wisdom comes from desire. Without a thirst for wisdom, it is likely you will not pursue it.

5. Wisdom ultimately comes from God. If any man lacks wisdom, he should seek it from the Lord, for He gives freely to those who ask in faith. If we do not have it, it is not because the Lord fails to give it.

DAILY SCRIPTURE READING: 2 Samuel 4-7

APRIL 7

DON'T SETTLE FOR THE GRAPES

"We run carelessly to the precipice after we have put something before us to prevent us from seeing it." –Blaise Pascal

Kadesh-Barnea will forever be remembered as a place of mediocrity and regret for the children of Israel. It was there that Moses sent out the spies to view the land of Canaan. If you will recall, twelve men were ordered to evaluate the region and bring a report back to Moses. After their adventure, they returned with a single cluster of grapes so large it had to be carried by two men. You could say it was just an appetizer of what God wanted them to have: a land flowing with milk and honey.

Instead of being excited about the promise of God, ten out of the twelve spies were fearful because of the giants in the land. They made a false report of Canaan and refused to enter therein. Those men and their families died instantly and the children of Israel wondered in the wilderness for the next forty years. All of them died before they reached Canaan, only their children and grandchildren gained entrance. The only men who inherited Canaan after the forty years of travel were the two spies who originally had faith in God's Word, Joshua and Caleb.

When we settle for the grapes, it is certain we will miss the main meal. For a majority of Israel, the grapes were enough; but the hunger of Joshua and Caleb could not be satisfied with a mere appetizer. Don't settle for anything less than the perfect will of God for your life.

DAILY SCRIPTURE READING: 2 Samuel 8-12

APRIL 8

THE DEVIL IS A LIE

"Hell is the highest reward that the devil can offer you for being a servant of his." –Billy Sunday

Jesus called Satan the "father of lies." Every falsity told is birthed from the character of the prince of darkness. From the deception of Eve to the temptation of Christ, he sought to destroy man's relationship with God. Today, he still lies to humanity trying to convince us to sin, to doubt, to deny, and to disregard the Lord. Being the "father of lies," he is incapable of telling the truth. Has he ever suggested any of these thoughts to you?

- The Lord really doesn't love you
- You cannot make a difference in the world
- You are not really saved, how can God save someone like you
- Reading your Bible and praying doesn't do anything for you
- People don't want to hear your testimony of salvation
- Your past is too sinful to be involved at church
- You're not capable of taking on that assignment or ministry
- Things will never get better in your life
- Serving the Lord is boring

And the list goes on and on. His words are like quicksand; they paralyze us from moving forward in Christ. Rebuke his lies with the Living Word of God. He may be the father of lies, but your Father is the King of Glory.

DAILY SCRIPTURE READING: 2 Samuel 13-15

APRIL 9

OBJECTS IN THE MIRROR

"Let me entreat all right-hearted believers to look onward and forward to the day of Christ's return." –J.C. Ryle

We've all read the warning posted on the side-view mirror of our vehicles "Objects in Mirror are Closer Than They Appear." This cautionary statement is in place to give us a proper perspective on our surroundings. It serves to remind us of the distance and space of those vehicles around us. What seems to be reality is just a little skewed- therefore, adjust accordingly as you drive.

If we were to look in the mirror of our prophetical surroundings I believe we would see the same warning. Whether we realize it or not, the return of the Lord is closer than it may seem.

The apostle Peter warned that "scoffers" would question the return of Jesus in the last days. The church at large is so busy, so active, moving so quickly down life's highway that we fail to discern the signs of the times. I wonder if we really anticipate His return on a day-to-day basis.

Considering the way people "drive" their lives, it is hard to imagine that His return is in the forefront of our thinking. Whether we are ready for it or not, He is coming back; and when He returns He is sure to stop traffic. Check your spiritual bearings, the climate of the world, and the promise of Scripture- His return is closer than it may appear.

DAILY SCRIPTURE READING: 2 Samuel 16-18

APRIL 10

BEAUTIFUL COFFINS

"For the wages of sin is death; but the gift of God is eternal life through Jesus Christ our Lord." –Romans 6:23

Not long ago I helped a family pick out a coffin for their deceased loved one. As we were escorted into the "showroom" of caskets, the undertaker went into "sales mode." He began pointing out particular features, and addressing particular concerns. As he went down the line of coffins, each one was considered "a beautiful choice."

As he explained the pros and cons of each item, I thought about what Jesus said to the Pharisees, "Woe unto you, scribes and Pharisees, hypocrites! for ye are like unto whited sepulchres, which indeed appear beautiful outward, but are within full of dead *men's* bones" (Matthew 23:27).

Although each casket was beautifully crafted and designed, they were empty; and the only thing promised to occupy the vessel would be the remains of death. Religion, legalism, and the traditions of men are simply beautiful coffins. They have a grand appearance externally, but internally there is no vitality of life. Religion, when applied through the principles of God's Word, and by the channel of grace, is indeed a beautiful thing; but in and of itself it is merely a cold, rigid vessel of bondage and defeat. Christ did not come to give us cold, dead, religion. He came to give us life and life more abundantly!

DAILY SCRIPTURE READING: 2 Samuel 19-21

APRIL 11

TIME ALONE

"Solitude is the furnace of transformation." –Dietrich Bonheoffer

Every time I read through the Gospels I am intrigued by the solitude of Christ. He was constantly being thronged by the masses; He continually engaged the multitudes. He was in high demand everywhere He went. He worked late in the evenings, and rose early in the mornings. He was surrounded by people who sought His attention, His words, and His time. And though He was God, He still understood the importance of dismissing Himself from the commotion of life to a place of seclusion and privacy. Solitude was a frequent part of His schedule. A thorough study of His life proves that He rose early and He rose often to spend time with God in prayer.

We would do ourselves a favorable service if we followed His steps away from the hustle and bustle of every-day living, and allotted a particular time each day in prayer and meditation. Jesus never shunned responsibilities in His quest for solitude; on the contrary, it seemed as though His time alone refreshed Him to engage His responsibilities.

I encourage you today to make time for God. Remove yourself from the loudness of life and allow the still, small voice of God to equip your spirit, renew your mind, and strengthen your faith.

DAILY SCRIPTURE READING: 2 Samuel 22-24

APRIL 12

NO PONIES NEEDED

"There is not in the world a life more sweet and delightful than the continued conversation with God." –Brother Lawrence

The Pony Express was a privately-owned business that carried mail through an organized team of horseback riders in the mid 1800's. Their circuit of travel spanned from St. Joseph, Missouri to Sacramento, California. The cost to send a letter was a pricey $2.50 per ounce. Although this popular concept revolutionized communication it was a short-lived venture. This iconic business was only in operation for sixteen months (April 3, 1860-November 18, 1861). When the telegraph line connected the two cities, the service was no longer needed.

Communication has come a long way since those days. Where it used to take a team of horseback riders to hand-deliver a message over a two-week period, we now can instantly send a message to the other side of the world through email, text messaging, or social media. Those riders would be amazed to see how advanced we've gotten at connecting with others.

However, long before the telegraph or telephone, we were able to tell God: instantly, spontaneously, and without interruption. The priesthood of the believer permits us to gain immediate access to the throne of grace. We can communicate with God anytime, anywhere, at no cost at all. We can talk to Him personally without the aid of a preacher, prophet, priest, or even a pony.

DAILY SCRIPTURE READING: 1 Kings 1-2

APRIL 13

DO YOU HAVE A FAT MIND?

---

*"You are not what you think you are.
What you think, you are."* –Unknown

Someone has rightly observed, "You are what you eat." What we put into our bodies has long-lasting, life-altering effects. Because our culture is inundated with the fast-food mentality, we are the heaviest generation ever in America. If this is true of our bodies, it is equally true of our minds.

There is potentially a lot of "junk food" out there that can cause your mind to be "overweight" and overloaded with the garbage of ungodliness. Websites, magazines, television programs, movies, video games, and the like are designed to captivate our senses and steal away our thinking. We have allowed ourselves to become desensitized to things that are hated by God. As a result, we unknowingly allow our minds to be filled with unhealthy thoughts and notions. Before long, our thoughts become our behavior, and our behavior cultivates our character.

We need filters for our thinking. We need spiritual barriers in place to examine what we allow to enter our minds. That is why the apostle Paul said to think on things that are: true, honest, just, pure, lovely, of a good report, and virtuous. Take the next twenty-four hours and write down all the things you allow in your mind. Those things that are fried up in the grease-pit of the world should be tossed in the trash!

DAILY SCRIPTURE READING: 1 Kings 3-5

APRIL 14

SLEEPING IN CHURCH

"God grows His church by creating disciples who are serious about reflecting the righteousness of God." –David Platt

Have you ever meet someone who slept in church? You probably have a particular person in mind right now that naps frequently at the House of God. It used to personally offend me to look out and see people sleeping while I preached until one day I read in Scripture where Jesus had the same experience.

As a matter of fact, those who slept on Jesus were His closest friends, and it was during the most agonizing hour of His life. Instead of staying awake and staying by His side, they nodded, they blinked, they drifted off in slumber. Their natural state of rest mirrored their spiritual lethargy as they would soon deny their relationship with Christ.

Sleeping in church may sound like a cute and funny notion, but the truth is, those who cannot stay engaged in worship with Christ may find themselves in spiritual trouble after the service is over. They may find themselves walking at a distance with Peter, or turning their hearts away from following Christ. I rarely see people falling sleeping at ball games, concerts, or recreational activities; probably because they are engaged with what is going on. Here is a good remedy for spiritual slumber: make sure your heart is in tune with God's and then intentionally enter His House with a desire to worship Him and hear from His Word.

DAILY SCRIPTURE READING: 1 Kings 6-7

APRIL 15

FISH BEFORE YOU FILE

---

*"The only difference between death
and taxes is an extension."* –Unknown

Many people will be rushing off to the post office today in an attempt to beat the ever-present deadline of filing tax returns. The old cliché of death and taxes is a sobering reminder on April 15th perhaps more than any other day of the year.

Chances are Jesus and His disciples were not scurrying all over Galilee two thousand years ago on this day to pay their taxes, but they did pay. When confronted with the issue of paying tribute, Jesus instructed Peter to cast a hook into the sea and catch a fish. The first fish caught would have a certain amount of money allotted to pay the taxes of both Peter and Jesus. This unusual story in Matthew 17 reminds us of two important financial truths: the first, we are obligated to financially support our country and the second, God always provides for our needs.

If you are like most Americans these days, it is difficult to watch your hard-earned money fall into the hands of politicians who seem to have little interest outside of their own political advancement. But remember, Jesus lived under the hard-pressed rule of Rome, and He said, "Render unto Caesar the things that are Caesars." It is easier to pay taxes when you consider it as an act of obedience to God. God in return proves Himself as Jehovah-Jireh, and supplies in supernatural ways. Fish before you file!

DAILY SCRIPTURE READING: 1 Kings 8-9

APRIL 16

SURFING WITH THE KIDS

"The first and most natural condition of things is for a parent to train up their own children to follow the Lord." –Charles Spurgeon

While on vacation in Navarre Beach, Florida I was entertained early one morning as I watched a father teaching his daughter the fundamentals of surfing. The empty beach and the choppy early-morning waves created a perfect training environment.

The father initially gave his young daughter proper instruction. Before they entered into the water he told her what to expect and how to embrace the board. Once they were in the water it was obvious this was her first attempt at the sport. After several crashes he corrected her technique and told her what she was doing wrong. After forty-five minutes of multiple attempts her dad finally got up on the surf board and showed her how to do it. This seemed to prove successful. After he demonstrated it to her she immediately got on the board and caught her first wave all the way to the shore. This may have been a surfing lesson for the young girl, but it was a life-lesson for me when it comes to parenting.

This man had three fundamental principles in his teaching approach: instruction, correction, and demonstration. Children need our instruction, they also need our correction; but when it seems like they can't get the hang of it, they may need to see us demonstrating it in our own lives. Without a proven example, it is likely they will crash every time.

DAILY SCRIPTURE READING: 1 Kings 10-11

APRIL 17

COUNTERPUNCH CHRISTIANS

"It may not be your fault for getting knocked down; but it will be your fault for not getting back up." –Steve Davis

Some of the greatest boxers in the history of the sport have not been great punchers, they have been great counterpunchers. A counterpunch is exactly what it sounds like: punching someone after being punched. This may sound like an obtuse way of fighting but it actually requires speed, intelligence, and a willingness to endure pain. Knowing when and where to counter is often the difference between victory and defeat.

Have you ever felt like you were in a boxing match with life? A jab here, an uppercut there, and before you know it you are on the ropes wondering when the bell will sound in relief. Overcoming life's greatest opponents: stress, worry, despair, depression, spiritual warfare, busyness, is not always about landing the first punch. If you are like me, you are not looking for a fight, but it somehow seems to find you. To get the upper-hand we must be able to learn how to counterpunch.

Counterpunch with godliness and grace. Retaliate with prayer; strike back with fasting. Land a swift stab of integrity, character, and godliness. Keep hitting back with courage, resilience, and boldness. Counterpunching will not exempt you from being hit, but it just may keep you from throwing in the towel.

DAILY SCRIPTURE READING: 1 Kings 12-14

APRIL 18

THE PURPOSE OF POSSESSIONS

---

*"The world asks, what does a man own—
Christ asks, how does he use it."* –Andrew Murray

You didn't have to remove yourself very far from your bed this morning to realize the blessings of God. They are all around us-His goodness and gifts abound. Have you seen them yet today? Your spouse, your children, your home, your Bible, your vehicle, your clothes, your food, your accommodations, your money, your retirement, your assets and possessions. At every turn, in every room, within every closet, and at every moment we are inundated with the favor of God.

Have you ever wondered why God has blessed in so many ways? Have you ever considered that God has a purpose behind those blessings? He has not just given us good gifts because He is good (although He is infinitely good); He has given us good gifts so that we can use them for His honor and glory. God has a purpose for those possessions. So, how do we honor God with all that He has given? We honor Him by realizing we are simply stewards of His stuff.

We even might consider giving some of it away. I know that seems antithetical to the American Dream, but God has not given abundantly so that we can amass a personal kingdom of wealth and riches. I want to challenge you to take inventory of your blessings, and ask "how can I honor God with what He has abundantly given?" When you find the answer to that question, you'll find the true treasure of your wealth.

DAILY SCRIPTURE READING: 1 Kings 15-17

APRIL 19

WATCH OUT FOR THE CREEPS

"If we would hold fast that which is good, we must not tolerate any doctrine that is not the pure doctrine of Christ's gospel." –J.C. Ryle

In the small epistle of Jude, we are warned to watch out for "the creeps." Actually the verse reads like this, "For there are certain men **crept in** unawares, who were before of old ordained to this condemnation, ungodly men, turning the grace of our God into lasciviousness, and denying the only Lord God, and our Lord Jesus Christ (Jude 4). Notice a few characteristics of these men:

1. They were Subtle. Jude said they crept in unaware. They plotted and planned unknowingly with an agenda. Instead of fighting the church from without, they decided to join the church and destroy it from within.

2. They were Sinful. These were ungodly men according to Jude. Like their father the devil, they were able to transform themselves into the angel of light but they were full of darkness and depravity.

3. They were Sinister. Their goal was to attack and destroy the doctrine of grace. They were false teachers who crafted their words in religious language, but they spoke half-truths, damning men's souls to hell.

4. They were Satanic. They used their appearance, associations, and attributes to gain access into the congregation, but they were indeed messengers of Satan, tares among the wheat. Watch out for the creeps, they are still trying to get into our churches, homes, hearts, and lives.

DAILY SCRIPTURE READING: 1 Kings 18-20

APRIL 20

MORE THAN A FEELING

"To love God is the greatest of virtues; to be loved by God is the greatest of blessings." –Unknown

Pop culture, romance novels, Hollywood flair, and story-book endings have greatly skewed the meaning of love. We have reduced it to an emotional feeling, a shallow appeal of the senses. Do not get me wrong, love certainly is emotional, and it does appeal to our senses, but when it is only that, it becomes nothing more than a fleeting mood, a fluctuating state of mind.

God places a high premium on love, and has a different definition from that of the world. God is love; therefore, it is of the highest and holiest pursuit. As a matter of fact, in the company of faith and hope, it holds the greatest title. True love is more than a sappy feeling you experience at the end of a tear-jerking movie. Love is sacrifice in action, a verb; it is pure, unadulterated giving. It courageously and convincingly lends itself without any need of reciprocation. And I believe we use and abuse its meaning inappropriately.

We cannot say we love curtains, cars, or cats and mean the same thing to describe our relationship with God or others. In doing so, we devalue its meaning and reduce its significance. As Mel Lawrenz contends, "Don't think of love as frilly sentiment or adolescent infatuation. Love is the gutsiest and boldest of human initiatives." It is the fulfillment of the law.

DAILY SCRIPTURE READING: 1 Kings 21-22

APRIL 21

FOLLOWING CHRIST

"Sadly, many Christians while safely in the arms of God, are relationally distant from Him." –Bill Hull

In the ninth chapter of Luke, Jesus encountered three different men who sought to be a follower of Christ. In response to their pursuit, Jesus gave them a description of the life of a true disciple. In essence, He told these men they would have to be willing to follow the Lord **wherever**, **whenever**, and **whatever**.

These three encounters remind us that being a disciple of Jesus Christ is not easy. As a matter of fact, it is anything but easy. Taking the cross, denying the flesh, and dying to self is a continual and constant challenge for the believer, yet it is our obligation and duty in being a genuine disciple of Christ. Dallas Willard said of the subject, "There is nothing in what Jesus himself or his early followers taught that suggests you can decide just to enjoy forgiveness at Jesus' expense and have nothing more to do with him."

What is taught in most religious circles is contrary to the teachings of Christ and His requirements for discipleship. Finding our life is in direct relation to losing it. According to Christ, there are certain mandates given to follow Him. For the next three days, we will consider these various men and their encounter with the Lord. We will discover what it means to follow Jesus wherever, whenever, and whatever.

DAILY SCRIPTURE READING: 2 Kings 1-3

APRIL 22

FOLLOWING CHRIST WHEREVER

"Foxes have holes, and birds of the air have nests; but the Son of man hath not where to lay his head." –Jesus Christ

It was a pretty bold statement, "Lord, I will follow thee, **whithersoever** thou goest" (Luke 9:57). It almost sounded poetic in nature. Reminiscent of Ruth's declaration to Naomi (I will go wherever you go, I will stay wherever you stay, etc.), this man was seemingly pledging his allegiance to Christ. This all sounds great until Jesus sheds some light about His poverty. The Lord replied, "Foxes have holes, and birds of the air have nests; but the Son of man hath not where to lay his head."

"Whithersoever? Wherever? Well, I have to tell you that I do not have a home." Those were pretty much the words of Christ. Jesus wanted this fellow to know that in order to be a genuine disciple, he would have to leave the luxuries and comforts of this life and be willing to live as a pilgrim in this world.

Do you follow Christ "whithersoever?" Does your cross show up in every venue of your life, or do you leave it behind in certain places? Sure, it is assumed we take the cross with us to church and perhaps religious gatherings, but what about our jobs, our social outings, our homes? The Lord is not looking for part-time cross-bearers who will only go to certain places. He is looking for those who are willing to depart from this world and follow Him-**wherever** that may be.

DAILY SCRIPTURE READING: 2 Kings 4-5

APRIL 23
FOLLOWING CHRIST WHENEVER

"Let the dead bury their dead: but go thou and preach the kingdom of God." –Jesus Christ

It seemed like a reasonable request, "Lord, suffer me **first** to go and bury my father." One may assume that Jesus, in His gentle and loving fashion, would have sympathized with this fellow and permitted him to take care of his situation at home; but not so. On the contrary, the reply seemed rather harsh, "Let the dead bury the dead." Those were the words spoken by Christ to the second man in the ninth chapter of Luke. Why does it seem like Jesus was being inconsiderate to this man's plea?

Notice the word "first." This man was not saying "no" in following Jesus; he was saying "not now." There were more important things at home-let me **first** go and bury my father.

The text never says the man's father was dead; it just implies that at some point his father needed to be buried. More than likely, he was waiting on his father to pass. In Hebrew culture, when someone passes away, there is a two-week mourning process. In addition to the two weeks, it takes another two to three weeks to divide the estate or the inheritance. In essence, this man decided that following Christ would have to wait until a more convenient, and perhaps more affordable, time. Unfortunately, his good intentions did not equate into reality. Such is the case for many believers. What is "first" in your life? What keeps you from following Christ **whenever**?

DAILY SCRIPTURE READING: 2 Kings 6-8

APRIL 24

FOLLOWING CHRIST WHATEVER

"No man, having put his hand to the plow, and looking back, is fit for the kingdom of God." –Jesus Christ

The third man in Luke 9 was just about ready to become a full-throttle follower of Christ. His statement "I will follow thee" was followed with a seemingly rational contingency, "but let me first go bid them farewell, which are at home at my house." But such a contingency didn't fly with Jesus. The Lord replied, "No man, having put his hand to the plow, and looking back, is fit for the kingdom of God."

It seems somewhat unfair that Christ would not permit this man to go home and say good-bye to his family, but consider the ramifications of such a request. Imagine the conversation as the young man enters his home and bids farewell. He would be barraged with a line of questions. Where are you going? Who are you going with? When will you return? What about the family business? What about our plans for your life? Parting ways with the homestead to follow the blue-collar carpenter from Nazareth would not have been a popular sentiment with mom and dad.

That is why Jesus said, "Don't look back. In order to follow me, you will have to leave whatever it may be that binds you." Our relationship with Christ must trump any and everything else in this life, including family and friends. Christ is still calling men to follow Him, but that calling requires the attitude of wherever, whenever, and even **whatever.**

DAILY SCRIPTURE READING: 2 Kings 9-11

APRIL 25

THE OTHER GIANTS

"Where the battle rages, the loyalty of the soldier is proven." –Martin Luther

Everyone knows the iconic story of David's triumph over the giant Goliath. But before David slung his sling in victory, he had to overcome some other giants lurking around on the battlefield that day.

1. The Giant of Cause. Not only did David face the adversary of the Philistines, he had to overcome the apathy of Israel. When he arrived on the scene, no one in the camp of Israel wanted to fight; they were ready to succumb to the hand of the enemy. David's spirit was stirred when he saw their lethargy and asked the question "Is there not a cause?"

2. The Giant of Criticism. David's intent was challenged. His brothers accused him of being mischievous and irresponsible. His motives and his methods were criticized by his own family. He had to get past the hurtful feelings and slay the words from those closest to him.

3. The Giant of Conformity. Once David convinced Saul to let him fight, he was forced to try on the armor of the king. This artillery was not proven nor did it fit.

These giants were slain before David ever faced Goliath. He rose to his feet with purpose, he moved beyond the hurtful words of his allies, and he sought not the approval of man. By faith, he overcame the other giants.

DAILY SCRIPTURE READING: 2 Kings 12-14

APRIL 26

DELIVERED FROM DEBT

"There is no slavery that can compare to the ingrained habits of sin." –Bill Hull

The financial crisis over the past few years has increased the amount of personal debt for the average household. When you consider credit card, mortgage, and student loan debt, American families are drowning in approximately $200,000 of financial liability. When you factor in that most families pay only the minimal monthly payments, the scenario gets worse. Most individuals who are in debt actually stay in debt a majority of their lives.

Suppose a generous individual graciously volunteered to pay off all your debt with no strings attached. Free and clear you own your home, your bills are paid, and the monthly payments cease. Within moments your obligation is relieved; you are free from your financial burden. It is safe to assume you would be ecstatic, thankful, and hopeful about your newfound freedom. You would have no problem sharing with others how this individual's kindness and charity changed your life.

Christ has done more than liberate us from the bondage of financial woes; He has, once and for all, paid the sin debt of every person in the world. He has settled the accounts and guaranteed our freedom from the penalty of sin, which is death. If that be the case, tell someone today of the forgiveness and freedom you have discovered in Christ.

DAILY SCRIPTURE READING: 2 Kings 15-17

APRIL 27

VANDALISM AT GOD'S HOUSE

"If I knew I was going to live this long I would have taken better care of myself." –Mickey Mantle

In September of 2012, a string of churches was vandalized in Buffalo, Minnesota. Six local congregations in Wright County were targeted. They each had broken windows, obscene graffiti, and damage to property. The assailant confessed he was "angry with God" over personal issues and was looking for a way to vent.

It always appalls me whenever I hear of church vandalism. It is hard to image the audacity and disrespect of someone who commits such a crime. It is safe to assume that any believer who fears God is repulsed by someone who would treat His House with such contempt.

We are disgusted with such acts. We would dare not spray-paint a steeple or throw a rock intentionally at a stained-glass window. But what we often fail to realize is that our bodies are the true temples of God. The apostle Paul said, "What? know ye not that your body is the temple of the Holy Ghost *which is* in you, which ye have of God, and ye are not your own? For ye are bought with a price: therefore glorify God in your body, and in your spirit, which are God's" (1 Corinthians 6:19-20). If your body is the House of God, wouldn't you serve yourself well to examine how you treat it? When we realize that the God of all glory abides in our bodies, we will attempt to live in holiness and consecration.

DAILY SCRIPTURE READING: 2 Kings 18-19

APRIL 28

LOVING GOD WITH YOUR MIND

"We allow in our thoughts what we wouldn't allow in our actions because people cannot see our thoughts. But God does." –Jerry Bridges

Christ instructed His followers to love the Lord God with all their heart, soul, and mind. Literally, every part of our consciousness should be committed to loving God. But how do we love God with our minds? How does one love God mentally?

We love God with our minds by thinking about God. I realize that sounds elementary, but one cannot affectionately engage God without awakening our minds toward Him. Set aside time each day to think about His goodness.

We love God with our minds by meditating upon His Word. You cannot fully engage the Author without pondering what He has said. When we meditate upon His Word we fill our minds with His promises. Furthermore, we are better suited to make biblical decisions.

We love God with our minds by filtering what comes into our senses. Like a computer, our minds store whatever stimuli we permit to enter our thoughts. By guarding our ears and eyes we keep out worldly debris.

We love God with our minds by engaging in good works. When we witness, study, testify, help the poor, and intentionally give we are forced to think about what we are doing. To love God wholly is to love God mentally.

DAILY SCRIPTURE READING: 2 Kings 20-22

APRIL 29

FEAR IS NOT A FACTOR

"Death is no more than passing from one room to another. But for me, I will be able to see in the other room." –Helen Keller

From 2001 to 2006, NBC aired a show playing on the fears of people aptly called *Fear Factor*. This show placed contestants in ridiculous circumstances to see whether or not they could overcome a particular fear. Challengers experienced everything from drowning in a car to being attacked by a dog to eating a pig's snout. Did I mention it was ridiculous? At the end of the show, the last one standing won the grand prize.

The show's premise struck a chord with its audience, and really with all of humanity: the fear of facing death. Where *Fear Factor* had built-in safety features around their stunts, real life does not. However, God has given us comfort in our fear of death: His presence.

Long before a reality show dealt with this fear, David wrote about it in the 23rd Psalm. He said, "Yea, though I walk through the valley of the shadow of death, I will fear no evil: for thou *art* with me; thy rod and thy staff they comfort me" (Psalm 23:4). No one likes the thought of passing away. But when death's shadow stands across the valley of our life we do not have to fear. Our Great Shepherd will be with us, and He has already defeated death and the grave. For the believer, death is simply the entrance into the reality of God. Therefore, fear is not a factor for us.

DAILY SCRIPTURE READING: 2 Kings 23-25

APRIL 30

LIVING WITH ACCOUNTABILITY

"Wherefore let him that thinketh he standeth take heed lest he fall." –The Apostle Paul

Hundreds of ministries fail each year because of the blurred lines of accountability. Thousands of marriages are destroyed routinely because lines in the proverbial sand are not drawn. We all need accountability systems in place to protect and safeguard our lives. "If we don't have proper and reasonable lines of accountability, then our only guide will be the expectations we put on ourselves," said Mel Lawrenz, "and we should not trust ourselves that much."

"We should not trust ourselves that much" is an understatement. I believe the reason many men of God experience moral failure is because they wrongly assess their strength. They measure their spiritual grit by personality, success, degree, influence, and popularity. As a result, pride permeates the heart and the seeds of temptation germinate in the soul. Delusion sets in and convinces us that we can trust our flesh. Joseph, when tempted in the Old Testament, ran out of Potiphar's house, not because he was spiritual, but because he recognized his own carnality-we all should do the same.

When we think we are above reproach that is typically when it finds us. Paul told the church at Corinth, "Wherefore let him that thinketh he standeth take heed lest he fall." Avoid falling by staying accountable.

DAILY SCRIPTURE READING: 1 Chronicles 1-2

MAY

MAY 1

THE FILLING OF THE SPIRIT

"And be not drunk with wine, wherein is excess; but be filled with the Spirit." –Ephesians 5:18

Many people get confused when it comes to the baptism and the filling of the Holy Spirit. The baptism of the Holy Spirit occurs at salvation and only happens once. When we are born from above, we are baptized with fire, as promised by John the Baptist. We are placed into the family of God and forever secured by the power of the Holy Ghost. The filling of the Holy Spirit occurs frequently; it is not a "second work" of grace, it is a continual occurrence as we yield our life to the Lord.

To be filled with the Spirit means to be controlled by the Spirit. We make a mistake in thinking that "filled" somehow means "getting more." We have all of the Spirit of God we ever need the moment we are saved. However, as we grow in grace, the Spirit of God begins to have more of us: more of our thoughts, more of our heart, more of our time, more of our attitude, more of our behavior.

Much of the frustration we endure as believers come from our unwillingness to succumb to His control. This is "grieving" the Spirit. This occurs when we refuse to yield entirely to His leadership. Being controlled by the Spirit is an ongoing experience in which we minimize the flesh's power in our decision-making process. Being baptized means you have all of Him, being filled means He has all of you.

DAILY SCRIPTURE READING: 1 Chronicles 3-5

MAY 2

THE ANDREW EFFECT

"You don't have to have your name on the marquee to change the marquee." –Kenneth Kuykendall

Andrew was originally a follower of John the Baptist. He was introduced to Jesus the day after the Lord's baptism. When he perceived that Jesus was the Christ, the Messiah of Israel, he immediately left John and began following the Lord.

Andrew was so overwhelmed with his discovery in Christ that he went and found his brother, Simon, and brought him to Jesus. This seems to be the pattern of Andrew's life: he was always bringing others to the Lord. In John 6:1-14, Andrew brought the young lad with the fish and bread to Christ. In John 12:20-22, Andrew brought the inquisitive Greeks to Christ to hear the gospel. He was a connector of people, a conduit of grace.

Andrew's name never topped the list of the disciples-but his brother's did. As a matter of fact, Andrew is introduced in Scripture as Peter's brother, the very one he brought to Christ. Recognition and position were not the pursuits of this meek man of God. His desire was simply to point others to the Lord. Through his ministry thousands were fed in the desert, the Greeks had the privilege of hearing the gospel, and 3000 souls came to faith in Christ on the day of Pentecost. We may never know the effect Andrew had on countless lives, but God does, and to Andrew, that is all that matters.

DAILY SCRIPTURE READING: 1 Chronicles 6

MAY 3

LIVING BY FAITH

"The only reason we can seek Christ in our sinfulness is because Christ has sought us as our Savior." –David Platt

Paul adamantly pronounced and lived his life by this statement, "For by grace are ye saved through faith." All of Scripture validates this truth, but have you ever wondered why it is by *faith*? Why not love, compassion, righteousness, or deeds? God saves us by faith because it is the complete anti-work. Faith requires nothing of our hands. It is only through faith that God justifies His own holiness. Had we been able to do something to merit our righteousness, God would be excluded from the equation of salvation.

Faith leaves everything to God. Faith allows us to rest from our unrelenting and unsuccessful pursuit of eternal life, and causes us to look to Christ. Only by faith can we see Jesus, Who is the Author and Finisher of the very subject. As Andrew Murray said, "Faith expects from God what is beyond all expectation." Trying to approach God with anything other than faith is sin. The essence of sin is us trying to substitute good works for salvation, while the essence of salvation is God substituting Himself for us.

Therefore, we do good works not to be accepted of Christ but rather to be pleasing unto Christ. The just shall live by faith, and what makes us "just" is the very faith by which we live.

DAILY SCRIPTURE READING: 1 Chronicles 7-8

MAY 4

FORGIVING YOURSELF

"It's never too late to be what you might have become." –George Eliot

It has been said that Rembrandt painted himself into many of his portraits. Early in his life he dealt with pride, arrogance, and the pursuit of carnal passions. After reading the parable of the prodigal son from Luke 15, he painted himself into one of his pieces as the son who wandered into the far country and lost his fortune. Like most of his paintings, it was dark and dreary.

Later in life as his health began to slip, he returned to the subject. This time he portrayed himself as the father who forgave his long-lost son. The typical darkness that is found in Rembrandt's painting was replaced with a shining light that emanates from the father's face as he embraces his prodigal. Some art critics believe it was Rembrandt's way of forgiving himself.

Oftentimes we have trouble doing that: forgiving ourselves. We accept the grace of God and claim the promises of redemption; but while we receive forgiveness from God, we oftentimes have difficulty forgiving ourselves. Satan reminds us of our past; he points out our previous failures of yesterday and tries to keep us chained to regret. Forgiveness has two parties: the one who forgives and the one being forgiven. Sometimes those two people need to be the same person.

DAILY SCRIPTURE READING: 1 Chronicles 9-11

MAY 5

AN ETERNAL EMBRACE

"The heartbeat of a godly person is never satisfied with his present experience with God." –Jerry Bridges

Charlie Frank worked in the circus as an elephant trainer for years. He was the personal trainer of an elephant named Neeta. After years of performing, they both retired. Neeta went to the San Diego Zoo and Charlie to his mobile home. Fifteen years passed until Huell Howeser, host of PBS program *California Gold,* wanted to reunite them on film.

With cameras rolling, Charlie approached a group of ten elephants and was able to immediately recognize Neeta. Standing at a distance he gently spoke, "Neeta, come here girl." She immediately recognized his voice, and started trotting toward Charlie. In an emotional scene, both Charlie and Neeta "embraced" one another and then amazingly, Charlie led Neeta through their old circus routine from fifteen years ago.

In John 10:14, the Lord described His relationship with His followers as such, "I am the good shepherd, and know my sheep, and am known of mine." Today we hear His voice, we are led by His Spirit, and we follow His Word. But there is coming a day when we will see Him as He is. The true reward of running our race will not be the prize we receive at the end, but finally meeting, face to face, the Person who walked with us along the way. With no separation, no division, and no retirement we shall embrace Him, and He will embrace us for eternity.

DAILY SCRIPTURE READING: 1 Chronicles 12-14

MAY 6

THE SHOES OF ASHER

"If God sends us on stony paths, He provides strong shoes." –Corrie Ten Boom

Just before Moses died, he gathered the tribes of Israel together and pronounced prophetical blessings upon them. When he came to the tribe of Asher he said something quite unusual. He declared, "Let him dip his foot in oil. Thy shoes shall be iron and brass; and as thy days, so shall thy strength be" (Deuteronomy 33:24-25).

Doesn't it sound strange that Asher would be required to wear shoes of iron and brass? Imagine such a thing. This doesn't seem like a blessing at all. I would think shoes of iron and brass would be weird and weighty. Can you see this tribe as they cross the Jordan or when they walk around the gated city of Jericho? They traveled miles in the desert and over rugged terrain all in shoes that were heavy and burdensome. But what seemed like a burden was actually God's provision.

The elements of the world could never penetrate iron and brass; and though it seemed like a burden to walk in such weighty shoes, it was actually a blessing in disguise. That's the way God works. His blessings are not always wrapped in the prettiest packages. Sometimes what appears to be hurtful and heavy is actually helpful and heavenly. You may be walking in some heavy shoes right bow, but as Corrie Ten Boom said, "If God sends us on stony paths, He provides strong shoes."

DAILY SCRIPTURE READING: 1 Chronicles 15-17

MAY 7

HISTORY-MAKER

"For God no cost is too high. Anything can be sacrificed if only we may please Him." –Watchman Nee

In his book, *Crazy Love,* Francis Chan shares a story about a young girl who had a desire to give Bibles to her unsaved friends. Brooke Bronkowski, a fourteen-year old freshman in high school, would earn money by babysitting so she could purchase the Bibles. When youth leaders heard of her ministry, they would bring boxes of Bibles to Brooke so she could give them away. Brooke literally had hundreds of Bibles in her garage to give her friends.

During her freshman year she was in a tragic auto accident that took her life. More than 1500 people attended her funeral. Francis Chan shared the gospel with the large crowd and over 200 students and friends came to the altar and trusted Christ as their Savior. Each person who trusted Christ received a Bible, courtesy of Brooke Bronkowski. An essay she wrote was included in the book. In her own words she prophetically said, "You see, I'll be one of those people who live to be a history-maker at a young age."

No matter if you live to be 14 or 114, life is short. Brooke led more people to the Lord through her death than most people will ever do in their life. Today you have been given an opportunity to make change, to make a difference, to make history. In this 24-hour period, determine to impact eternity for someone else.

DAILY SCRIPTURE READING: 1 Chronicles 18-21

MAY 8

SPIRITUAL LEADERSHIP 101

"Influence is about the hidden forces that makes visible results that have an enduring effect." –Mel Lawrenz

What is spiritual leadership? Such a vague question warrants caution. Spiritual leadership cannot be defined by the same ethical evaluations found in corporate America, sports teams, or political platforms. Certainly spiritual leadership has elements of integrity, passion, honesty, courage and the like, but it is much more than that, much more.

In short, spiritual leadership is simply the ability to lead others to a better understanding of God's will for their lives. It is influence from within. It is the unseen quality of someone trying to guide someone else to the divine, and succeeding. It is helping others shape their values, principles, and convictions from a biblical perspective.

Too often we think that only pastors, presidents, and prophets can be spiritual leaders, when in reality, a majority of spiritual leaders rarely hold titles or positions of prominence. They can be seen taking their children to school, helping someone find a seat at church, or simply bringing water to the pastor. Quite literally, spiritual leaders are everywhere, doing many things to bring others to the will of God. As a spiritual leader, ask yourself a question, "What is the one defining characteristic that makes for the most effective spiritual leadership?" Tomorrow we will try to answer this question.

DAILY SCRIPTURE READING: 1 Chronicles 22-24

MAY 9

SPIRITUAL LEADERSHIP 201

"The closer we walk to the Shepherd, the further away we are from the wolf." –Anonymous

I recently took a survey about the subject of spiritual leadership. I asked the question, "What is the one defining word that best describes spiritual leadership?" I sought my answer through three avenues. First, I conducted brief "interviews" with many friends and colleagues in the ministry. Then, I took an impromptu poll on Facebook putting the question public. I received over 70 different words describing spiritual leadership. Finally, I studied the people who have had the greatest spiritual influence in my own life.

The top ten words were: servant, integrity, influence, faithful, consistent, compassionate, example, godly, humble, and powerful.

These are all wonderful descriptions of spiritual leadership. I would venture to say that any effective leader should strive to embody all these characteristics. But as I studied the list I noticed a parallel in all of these descriptions: Christ embodied them all. He was a **servant** of men, a man of **integrity**, an **influential** revolutionary, a **faithful** Son, **consistent** in word and deed, a **compassionate** Shepherd, the greatest **example**, the embodiment of **godliness**, a **humble** individual, and yet the most **powerful** human to ever grace our planet. My conclusion is simply this: **the greatest characteristic we can have as spiritual leaders is to be Christ-like.**

DAILY SCRIPTURE READING: 1 Chronicles 25-27

MAY 10

SPIRITUAL LEADERSHIP 301

"Anything less than Christ is a letdown; anything more than Christ is an impossibility." –Kenneth Kuykendall

To reiterate the thought from the past two days: the greatest characteristic we can have as spiritual leaders is to be Christ-like; for in being like Christ all the other qualities freely flow. This is the only characteristic that gives authentic and genuine direction to those you are leading; it takes the attention off of you and places it upon the Lord. This is why John the Baptist was the greatest born among women. John said, "He must increase, I must decrease."

Consider for just a moment those people who have the most influence in your life. More than likely, they have characteristics of Christ. Consider great leaders today in our churches and ministries; the most effective ones are those who have characteristics of Christ. You see anything less than Christ is a letdown, and anything more than Christ is an impossibility. Therefore, as spiritual leaders we must strive to walk with the feet of Jesus, speak with the mouth of Jesus, love with the heart of Jesus, and live with the life of Jesus.

I conclude with a great thought from Mel Lawrenz, "The only enduring influence we have to offer others is the influence God has in our own lives." Christ-like, that's a word worth living up to.

DAILY SCRIPTURE READING: 1 Chronicles 28 and 2 Chronicles 1

MAY 11

HIS PRESENCE OR HIS PRESENTS?

"Not what we say about our blessings, but how we use them is the true measure of our thanksgiving." –W.T. Purkiser

As a father I love giving my children gifts. It is my responsibility to provide things they need; however, it is my delight to give them things they desire. I recently bought a video game they had been asking for. They received the game gladly, and I too enjoyed watching them play. However, after several days passed, I came in from a long day and wanted to spend some time with them. They were so preoccupied with the game that they disregarded my presence in the room. They are children, this is to be expected, but after getting their attention, the Lord got mine.

He is the Giver of all good things. He not only provides for us, I honestly believe He wants to give us our heart's desire. However, something is wrong when those gifts supersede our time with the Giver.

George Hebert said, "Thou who hast given so much to me, give me one more thing- a grateful heart." It is a sad testimony when the gifts of God become the very source of our indifference with God. If God gives you a boat, don't use it to lay out of church on Sunday. If God gives you athletic ability, don't allow it to keep you from prayer and Bible-reading. If God gives you a great career, don't let it prevent you from being faithful. Don't allow the presents of God to keep you from the presence of God.

DAILY SCRIPTURE READING: 2 Chronicles 2-5

MAY 12

LINING UP WITH LOVE

"And now abideth faith, hope, and charity, these three; but the greatest of these is charity." —1 Corinthians 13:13

Are you a loving person? I know that sounds a little vague and superficial, but are you? One way to tell is to compare your life with the qualities of love found in 1 Corinthians 13. Look at the list below; every time you see the word "love" replace it with your own name, and see if the sentence is an accurate assessment of your life.

- Love (your name) is long suffering
- Love (your name) is kind
- Love (your name) doesn't envy
- Love (your name) isn't arrogant
- Love (your name) isn't easily provoked

These are just a few of the characteristics from I Corinthians 13. Take a look at the entire passage and determine if you display these qualities of charity as described by the apostle Paul.

More than likely you will discover your name is not a good fit in some of those biblical declarations. If that be the case, write down those particular sentences that you need work on. Underneath the sentence, write down three things you can do to become a more loving person in that area. Remember, out of all the godly virtues, the greatest is love.

DAILY SCRIPTURE READING: 2 Chronicles 6-8

MAY 13

WALKING WITH JESUS

"People forget how fast you did a job, but they will always remember how well you did it." –Howard W. Newton

A young boy received his driving permit. He asked his father, who was a minister, if they could discuss the use of the car. His father took him to his study and said to him, "I'll make a deal with you. You bring your grades up, study your bible and get your hair cut and we'll talk about it."

After a month the boy came back and again asked his father if they could discuss the use of the car. They again went to the father's study where his father said, "Son, I've been really proud of you. You have brought your grades up, you've studied your bible diligently, but you didn't get your hair cut!" The young man waited a minute and replied, "You know Dad, I've been thinking about that. Samson had long hair, Moses had long hair, why even Jesus had long hair..." to which his father replied...."Yes, and they WALKED everywhere they went!"

We can always find legitimate, and even good reasons why we shouldn't do something. But in doing so, we often sacrifice the "best" God has for our lives for the "good." I personally want everything God has for me, my family, and ministry. Finding the very best is a direct result of complete and total obedience to the will of my Father.

DAILY SCRIPTURE READING: 2 Chronicles 9-12

MAY 14

THANKFUL FOR LITTLE THINGS

"Eyes that look are common, eyes that see are rare." –Oswald Sanders

When we consider the blessings of God we often think of the big-ticket items. Our home, our vehicles, our clothes, our food, our friendships...these all seem to merit our praise to the heavenly Father. But consider how difficult life would be without the little things. When was the last time you thanked God for your toothbrush? How about light bulbs? Or toilet paper? That may sound ridiculous at first, but without these "miniature" blessings we would be extremely inconvenienced.

Today I am thankful for running water, cushions on my couch, highlighters and pens, socks without holes, brooms and mops. Today I give Him praise for headphones, Advil, books, magazines, and the ability to read. I glory in the daily benefits of being able to see, able to hear, able to smell, and able to taste food, whether it is good or bad. I offer praise for my lawnmower, my washing machine, my stove, my hairdryer, and my fireplace. What a blessing it is to have a watch, a wallet, and a window to see the sun rise and set.

Every good and perfect gift comes from above. Too often we walk right by all the blessings without recognizing His goodness. Today I am thankful for all the big stuff, but I am equally appreciative for the little things.

DAILY SCRIPTURE READING: 2 Chronicles 13-17

MAY 15

THE SEAT OF HUMILITY

"You can judge your level of humility by the status and rank of those you are willing to serve." –Kenneth Kuykendall

Honor is always preceded by humility, this is a biblical concept. Consider the parable of Luke 14:7-14. Jesus said to choose the lowest seat in the room-literally, assume a position that will not draw attention to yourself. Choose the inconspicuous seat, and you'll discover an invitation to sit in higher places. Christ said, "Then shalt thou have worship in the presence of them that sit at meat with thee. For whosoever exalteth himself shall be abased; and he that humbleth himself shall be exalted."

Our culture has it backwards. We barge in with our self-proclaimed greatness and take the best seat in the house in an effort to be noticed, recognized, and commended. This was not the approach of the Savior. Christ discreetly came into the world, lived for thirty years as a blue-collar carpenter, chose unlearned and ignorant men, and had no place to lay his head. He could have established His kingdom, announced His glory, and demanded humanity to bow in worship. Instead He chose suffering, a cross, mockery, and shame.

As a result, He was elevated to the highest seat in the heavens. He is forever recognized as the potentate King of the Ages. But His seat of glory was cushioned with the fabric of humility. His omniscient title was first carved into a wooden plaque upon a timber of crucifixion. His honor was birthed out of service. Ours should be no different.

DAILY SCRIPTURE READING: 2 Chronicles 18-20

MAY 16

THE PURSUIT OF HAPPINESS

"No man is more cheated than the selfish man." –Henry Ward Beecher

After instructing His disciples to wash one another's feet, the Lord promised them something in return, "If ye know these things, *happy* are ye if ye do them" (John 13:17).

Happiness is an honorable and obtainable virtue, but should not be the ultimate goal of life. Above riches, wealth, position, or fame, most people just want to be happy. However, a lot of what we do never brings happiness into our lives because we are void of selfless acts of service in the pursuit. Jesus told the disciples that their happiness would be contingent upon their willingness to serve other people; again, "happy are ye *if ye do them*."

A.W. Tozer said, "God is more concerned with the state of people's hearts than with the state of their feelings. Undoubtedly the will of God brings final happiness to those who obey, but the most important matter is not how happy we are, but how holy (and humble) we are."

Tozer is in tune with the sentiment of the Savior. The Lord promised happiness as a byproduct of service. The reason many people never *find* happiness is because of their very *pursuit* of happiness. Our pursuit should be in the vein of holiness and humility; then, as promised by Christ, we will discover true joy and contentment which flows from a life of yieldedness and surrender.

DAILY SCRIPTURE READING: 2 Chronicles 21-24

MAY 17

WHO WILL YOU SERVE?

"The towel of a servant is a constant reminder that things are going to get a little dirty." –Kenneth Kuykendall

If we only serve those who are "deserving" of our labor we will not be very busy. Some only want to posture before presidents, pastors, politicians, and the prestigious. But Jesus took filthy feet into His holy hands and washed the feet of soiled men. This is an uncomfortable gesture for most of us. If Christ condescended to such an estate, perhaps He expects the same out of His followers.

Are you willing to touch the brow of the leper? Are you willing to bow before the broken? Will you eat with the homeless or embrace the orphan? These questions leave us in a spiritual quandary. If we say "yes" then we must remember the last time it happened. If we say "no" then we confess that we are unwilling to do for others what Christ was willing to do for us.

The value of our service is measured by the type of people we are willing to touch. When we fail to assume the position of a servant we work from the premise that we are better than Christ. You see, those disciples were sinners, they were soiled, but they were His. The towel was not just a religious garment to wear, it was an instrument of grace used to wash the feet of those who needed pardon. Touch someone with your towel, and you will touch the very heart of God.

DAILY SCRIPTURE READING: 2 Chronicles 25-27

MAY 18
THE LONE RANGER DANGER

"All your strength is in union, all your danger is in solitude." –Henry Wadsworth Longfellow

As a child I loved watching the old reruns of the Lone Ranger. He would always come through and save the day on his horse named Silver. His sidekick Tonto would assist whenever needed, but for the most part, the Lone Ranger liked working all by himself, thus the name. Such a premise makes for a classic television show, but it doesn't work very well in real life, especially the Christian life.

In the twelfth chapter of 1 Corinthians, the apostle Paul likened the church to a physical body. We are joined together through a variety of parts and functions. As Paul contends, "For the body is not one member, but many." Therefore, our strength and ability is maximized only when we work and operate together in unity and harmony. When there is no unity and harmony in the body, those individual parts cannot operate in their greatest potential. God never intended the "body" of Christ to just be one single, solitary part-we are a whole.

The enemy tries his best to isolate and alienate us from other believers, knowing that we lose strength in prolonged solitude. Corrie Ten Boom said, "When a believer shuns fellowship with other Christians the devil smiles." More than likely you do not have a horse named Silver, or a sidekick named Tonto. Stop trying to be the Lone Ranger; you are not the only cowboy.

DAILY SCRIPTURE READING: 2 Chronicles 28-31

MAY 19

CHANGING CLOTHES

"It is not uncommon to feel unholy the more holy you become." –Kenneth Kuyekndall

Imagine being in a dimly-lit room while trying to get dressed for the day. As you assemble your outfit, everything seemingly looks fine, but when you walk into the hallway, the light is more vibrant. You notice that your jacket is mismatched with your pants. As you walk from the hallway to the living room, the light gets even stronger. It is then you realize your pants are mismatched with your shirt. As you walk outside, the sun is shining brightly. In full daylight, what looked good in the dark has been brought to light, and you notice that even your socks are wrongly matched.

This is the very idea of sanctification. Some would contend that the closer you get to the Lord (the Light) the less conviction you experience; on the contrary, the closer you get to the Lord the *more* conviction you experience. As we draw nearer to Christ, we are forced to line up our lives with His. It is not uncommon to feel unholy the holier you become.

One may ask, "Why bother then? Why not stay in the dark and be content with what I am wearing?" The answer: the darkness may conceal our indifference, but it cannot change our indifference. Only when we are exposed to the glorious Light of Jesus Christ can we begin to rely upon the Holy Spirit to transform us into His image. Change rooms and you'll change clothes.

DAILY SCRIPTURE READING: 2 Chronicles 32-34

MAY 20

A MILE WITH THE MASTER

"We never grow closer to God when we just live life; it takes deliberate pursuit and attentiveness." –Francis Chan

Albert Einstein was asked by one of his students, "How many feet are there in one mile?" Strangely enough, Einstein responded by saying, "I don't know." The student thought his legendary professor was just kidding around, but Einstein really didn't know. When the student pressed for an answer his professor told him, "I make it a rule not to clutter my mind with the simple information that I can find in a book in five minutes."

Einstein's passion was rooted in the exploration of the universe, mathematical difficulties, and the truth of physical properties. His genius was not in simple computation, but rather in mind-blowing discoveries.

The believer should desire to know more than facts and information about God; he should long, nay thirst, to drink from the deep wells of God's glory and presence. You may be able to quote Scripture, memorize doctrine, and accompany the masses to a religious facility; but all of that is meaningless without an ever-growing and ever-expanding relationship with God. Knowledge is only beneficial when used to pursue wisdom. Even so, religious activity is only valuable to the believer when its greater goal is to know God. The measurement of a mile is trivial when compared to walking with the Lord within that mile.

DAILY SCRIPTURE READING: 2 Chronicles 35-36

MAY 21

4 CAUSES OF SPIRITUAL GROWTH

"Genuine growth neither develops nor deteriorates overnight." –Kenneth Kuykendall

The Christian life is one of perpetual growth. Our perfection only awaits us in Glory as we are changed into the image and likeness of Jesus Christ. While we live in the flesh, we must continually and consistently die to self and our sinful desires. Consider these four areas in which we move forward in Christ:

1. Personal and Daily Devotions. Francis Chan contends, "We never grow closer to God when we just live life; it takes deliberate pursuit and attentiveness." You'll never grow in grace unless you intentionally seek Him.

2. Adversities. When a muscle is torn and ripped, it grows and becomes stronger. The same is true of our faith. The hardest groaning produces the hardiest growth.

3. Encouragement from Others. I can trace much of my spiritual development to those who encouraged me to keep going for Christ. Never underestimate the power of the right words when they are seasoned with grace.

4. Mistakes. Henry Ford said, "Failure is the opportunity to begin again, more intelligently." You may not sense that you are growing; you may even feel like you are going backwards from time to time, but remember: genuine growth neither develops nor deteriorates overnight.

DAILY SCRIPTURE READING: Ezra 1-3

MAY 22

GENUINE SPIRITUALITY

"What scares most of us is not following Jesus, but being like Jesus." –Bill Hull

Too often we measure our spirituality by isolated worship experiences. I certainly believe that we are to worship the Lord in "spirit and in truth," but when we confine our spirituality to shouting, raising hands, and saying "amen," we, in essence are saying that spirituality is performance-driven. Some people are introverted, quite, shy, and unlikely to be heard in a worship environment. Does that mean they are not spiritual? Of course not. Spirituality is measured by other criteria:

Our Likeness to Christ. Ultimately a person's spiritual bar is measured by their likeness to Jesus. Walking with Christ is the heartbeat of spirituality. I would rather be around someone who exudes the presence of Christ, then someone who exudes themselves.

The Fruit of the Spirit. Anyone can say "amen" but only those who walk in the Spirit will bear the fruit of the Spirit. Spirituality is measured in our attitude, our responses, our decisions, and our treatment of others.

Obedience to the Word. Someone who walks in the Spirit has to comply with the Words of Christ. Jesus said, "If ye love me, keep my commandments." Serious devotion is measured by daily commitment, not just Sunday-morning worship. Don't just "lip" it, live it!

DAILY SCRIPTURE READING: Ezra 4-7

MAY 23

STEWARDING OUR TRIALS

"We are always on the anvil, by trials God is shaping us for better things." –Henry Ward Beecher

The great tragedy about trials is not going through them, but rather going through them and not learning anything from them. God permits, and sometimes even sends, trials our way so that we can steward those trials. 2 Corinthians 1:4 says, "Who comforteth us in all our tribulation, that we may be able to comfort them which are in any trouble, by the comfort wherewith we ourselves are comforted of God." Notice three principles from this verse:

The Principle of Suffering. Paul used the word "tribulation" to describe the affliction we face as believers. This word speaks of pressure, persecution, and pain. The Christian life is not exempt from such sorrow. We should not expect convenient Christianity.

The Principle of Solace. The suffering we endure is met with the very solace of God. We are comforted by the Lord Himself. He is the God of all comfort. Any comfort we may experience originates from the goodness and compassion of God.

The Principle of Stewardship. We experience the comfort from God so that we will be able to comfort others who go through similar suffering. The comfort we are able to extend to others is a direct result of the comfort we have first been given by God. Because of the trial, we are better equipped to administer grace to those who need comfort.

DAILY SCRIPTURE READING: Ezra 8-10

MAY 24

STORING UP GOD'S WORD

"The Word of God hidden in the heart is a stubborn voice to suppress." –Billy Graham

My wife's grandmother loves to store up vegetables. She has always had a garden, and has used it to be a blessing to others. If you go to her house you will find in her pantry all kinds of jars stocked away with the fruit of her labor.

In Psalm 119:11, we have a similar scenario. The verse reads, "Thy word have I hid in my heart, that I might not sin against God." The word "hid" is *tsaphan* in the Hebrew, and it means to hoard, or store up; quite literally it means to "treasure up" only to bring out at a later date. When the psalmist instructed us to "hide" God's Word, he was not implying that we conceal it, but rather to keep it accessible for a time when needed.

Just as we "store up" vegetables to be consumed at a later date, even so should we "store up" the Word of God. We should hide it in our hearts, so that when we face temptations we will have something to chew on.

We should value, honor, meditate, memorize, and pray over God's Word. We ought to store it up, not as vegetables in a can, but as the greatest treasure on earth. As a result, it will be a guardian and a sword against sin and temptation. It is true, if you keep God's Word, God's Word will keep you.

DAILY SCRIPTURE READING: Nehemiah 1-3

MAY 25

THE NEED FOR REPENTANCE

"It is a poor sermon that gives no offense, that neither makes the hearer displeased with himself nor the preacher." –George Whitfield

The word repentance has become misplaced in the modern church. Because of its unpopular tone, many have discharged it from their preaching; and those who do preach it perhaps do so with negativity and uncertainty. We must know that repentance is not only a biblical concept; it is an essential truth for the regenerative life.

John the Baptist preached repentance to the religious crowd of his day. Jesus preached repentance as the means of entrance into the kingdom. Peter preached repentance on the day of Pentecost as the church was birthed. It is the remedy against the judgment of sin; Scripture teaches us that it is not God's will that ANY should perish but that ALL should come to repentance.

Repentance is not just a one-time occurrence that secures our eternal state (it is that); but it is also an on-going, continual part of the believer's walk with Christ. It is the turning away from our sin, our world, our flesh, and turning to Christ by faith. Paul refers to this in the third chapter of Colossians. We are to "put off" the things of the world while at the same time "put on" Christ Jesus. In essence that is the heart of repentance-changing your heart and mind to the point that you allow God to change your ways.

DAILY SCRIPTURE READING: Nehemiah 4-6

MAY 26

THE NATURE OF REPENTANCE

"Recognition of how sin grieves the Father should be the ultimate cause of repentance, not just the guilt it brings." –Kenneth Kuykendall

In his book, *The Disciple of Grace,* Jerry Bridges says this about the nature of repentance, "The solution to staying on the right side of the fine line between using and abusing grace is repentance. The road to repentance is godly sorrow. Godly sorrow is developed when we focus on the true nature of sin as an *offense to God rather than something that makes us feel guilty*."

True repentance is more than feeling bad about what we have done; it is about being repulsed at the way our sin affects God. Recognition of how sin grieves the Father should be the ultimate cause of repentance, not just the guilt it brings. A good example of this is found in Luke 15. The prodigal son initially wanted to return (repent) to his father because of the consequence of sin in his life (guilt). He said, "How many hired servants of my father's house have bread enough and to spare, and I perish with hunger!" But upon his arrival back to the father he confessed, "Father, I have sinned against heaven, and in thy sight." Somewhere along the journey his guilt turned to grieving.

Ultimately the nature of our repentance should be in line with the concession of the prodigal son. It should not derive from our guilt but from our grieving. Guilt is inward, grieving is Godward. Grieving Godward is the very nature of repentance.

DAILY SCRIPTURE READING: Nehemiah 7

MAY 27

THE NOURISHMENT OF REPENTANCE

"It is the greatest and dearest blessing that ever God gave to men- that they may repent." –Jeremy Taylor

Repentance accentuates grace, and causes even the most spiritually-mature believers to be awakened to their indifference. John Owen, the great Puritan writer declared, "Even the choicest of saints who seek to remain free from the condemning power of sin need to make it their business, as long as they live, to mortify the indwelling power of sin."

Repentance ultimately nourishes the soul of the saint. The process may seem uncomfortable and sore to the spirit but its end ultimately brings joy, growth, and faith. True repentance furthermore confirms that we are indeed a child of God. The writer of Hebrews said, "My son, despise not thou the chastening of the Lord, nor faint when thou art rebuked of him; For whom the Lord loveth he chasteneth, and scourgeth every son whom he receiveth" (Hebrews 12:5-6).

When the prodigal son came to terms with how his sin affected his father, it was then his father lavished upon him the graces of his fortune. This of course cannot be our motivation for repentance, but it is the reality of repentance. "It is the greatest and dearest blessing that ever God gave to men, that they may repent," said Jeremy Taylor, "and therefore to deny or to delay it is to refuse health when brought by the skill of the physician – to refuse liberty offered to us by our gracious Lord."

DAILY SCRIPTURE READING: Nehemiah 8-9

MAY 28

WEDDING DAY WOES

"To some, Christianity is an argument. To many, it is a performance. To few, it is an experience." –Vance Havner

Professional singer Ruthanna Metzger was asked to sing at the wedding of one of her wealthy friends. After the wedding was over, she and her husband headed to the reception at Seattle's Columbia Tower, one of the world's tallest skyscrapers. When the elevator reached the top of the executive floor she was met by the maitre d' who was greeting the guests.

When he searched for her name, it was not recorded in his notebook. Metzger replied, "There must be some mistake, I am the singer, I just sang for the wedding." The maitre d' led them to the service elevators and told them he had strict orders not to allow anyone in the reception who was not on the list, regardless of who they were. As they headed back to the garage, Ruthanna realized that in the hectic schedule of trying to perform for the wedding she actually failed to RSVP for the reception.

So many people are just like Ruthanna Metzger. They will miss the Marriage Supper of the Lamb because they failed to make reservations through salvation. When we stand before Christ to give an account for our lives, it will not matter how well we performed, all that will matter is if our name is recorded in His book.

DAILY SCRIPTURE READING: Nehemiah 10-11

MAY 29

TOMBSTONE TESTIMONY

"Words are engraved in hearts before they are engraved in headstones." –Kenneth Kuykendall

In his book, *Heaven*, Randy Alcorn tells of an Indiana cemetery with a tombstone over one hundred years old. It reads:

Pause stranger, when you pass me by: as you are now, so once was I. As I am now, so you will be. So prepare for death and follow me.

Someone later engraved these words on the tombstone:

To follow you I'm not content, until I know which way you went.

Such humor has a sobering reality: we should be careful whom we follow, especially when it relates to our eternal destiny. Follow the wrong driver and you get to the wrong city. Follow the wrong role model and you get to the wrong character. Follow the wrong teacher and you get to the wrong conclusion, but follow the wrong leader, and you may find yourself on the wrong side of eternity.

If you are leader, use your influence to help others understand the importance of preparing not only for this life, but for the one to come. This is especially true for parents. Our children typically follow in our spiritual steps. Will your path lead them to heaven? The words on your tombstone never speak as loudly as the words of your testimony. Take steps toward eternity every day, and be sure to take others with you.

DAILY SCRIPTURE READING: Nehemiah 12-13

MAY 30

LONG LIVE THE KING

"But thanks be to God, which giveth us the victory through our Lord Jesus Christ." –1 Corinthians 15:57

There is an Irish legend about the King of Ulster. It was believed that his dynamic and powerful presence was such a threat to his enemies that his appearance alone would cause his opponents to flee from warfare. After a long arduous battle, this mighty king was struck by the opposing army and died. His forces knew they would be utterly defeated if the enemy thought the King of Ulster was dead.

Therefore, his soldiers tied his body to a rock and positioned a spear in his hand so that the opposition would think he was alive. They believed that even the presence of a dead king would bring victory over the enemy. If the presence of a dead king brought victory to the province of Ulster hundreds of years ago, how much more does the presence of the Living King of kings bring victory into our lives?

Satan will never tremble at our efforts in warfare. It is when we submit ourselves to the Lord and resist the devil that he flees from us. Our strength, our power, and our victory derives from the fact that Jesus Christ overcame death, ascended to a position of honor and glory and forever intercedes on our behalf. He is not a dead king that has to be hoisted up by his soldiers on a rock. He is the Eternal King and the Rock, and the Victor of our spiritual battles. Long live the KING!

DAILY SCRIPTURE READING: Esther 1-5

MAY 31

THE PLATFORM OF GREATNESS

"Great leaders don't think less of themselves; they just think of themselves less." –Ken Blanchard

William Carey is often called the father of modern-day missions. In 1793 he went to India with the gospel of Jesus Christ and forever changed the spiritual landscape of that country. He translated large portions of Scripture into more than forty languages. His life can be summarized by his famous quote, "Expect great things from God; attempt great things for God." But at the age of 70, Carey wrote this letter to his son expressing his displeasure with sin and self:

"I am this day 70 years old, a monument of Divine mercy and goodness, though on a review of my life I find much, very much, for which I ought to be humbled in the dust; my direct and positive sins are innumerable, my negligence in the Lord's work has been great, I have not promoted his cause, nor sought his glory and honor as I ought, notwithstanding all this, I am spared till now, and am still retained in His work, and I trust I am received into the divine favor through Him."

It's amazing that someone who accomplished so much in the work of the Lord still pictured himself as a sinner, and even possibly a failure; yet it was that humble attitude that afforded William Carey the platform to do great things for God. Spurgeon said, "Humility is to make the right estimation of one's self." I would go a little further and say it is also making the right estimation of God. Carey did both.

DAILY SCRIPTURE READING: Esther 6-10

JUNE

JUNE 1

FALSE ADVERTISEMENT

"Let the words of my mouth, and the meditation of my heart, be acceptable in thy sight O LORD." –Psalm 19:14

I recently saw a van going down the road with a considerable amount of advertisement promoting a particular company's cleaning service. It was fully wrapped in the company's logos, numbers, websites, and service details. However, upon closer examination, the van was filthy. The exterior, though heavily wrapped in advertisement looked like it had not been washed in weeks. The windshield was cracked, the sides were dirty, and the wheels were blackened with brake dust. As we stopped together at a red light, I got a peek of the interior; the dash was littered with fast-food bags and old soda cans. My first thought was, "If their vehicle is a testimony to their service, I wouldn't want them to clean anything I own."

The van turned at the next light, and as it faded in my rear-view mirror I thought about the power of testimony. The van advertised a service that failed to meet its own standards. I am sure the particular company operates a fine business (and perhaps my evaluation was unfair), however, in that moment, they lost all credibility with me because the condition of their vehicle did not correspond with the promise of their advertisement. Sadly, the same is true with many Christians. If you advertise, identify, and promote the name of Jesus, make sure your life matches your lips.

DAILY SCRIPTURE READING: Job 1-4

JUNE 2

WE NEED THE WORD OF GOD

"In those days there was no king in Israel: every man did that which was right in his own eyes." –Judges 21:25

Whether it is in politics, business, sports, religion, or the culture at large, people demand character and morality from their leaders. No one wants to be led by someone who morally fails in their personal lives. People are not necessarily looking for perfection in leadership, just principles. But the problem in our society is that we have failed to recognize where those principles derive. We have repealed absolute truth and challenged people to live by standards that only absolute truth can produce. Thus, we are in a moral, dare I say, spiritual quandary.

David Hunter, sociologist at University of Virginia explains, "We want character without unyielding conviction; we want strong morality, but without the emotional burden of guilt or shame; we want virtue but without particular moral justifications that invariably offend; we want good without having to name evil."

In short, we want to discredit the Word of God while placing expectations upon people to live by moral standards that are obtained only from the Word of God. As made evident by our culture, that just doesn't work. Without clear, precise, and unrelenting principles, leadership will continue to fail, and this generation will continue to experience moral frustration. Moral truth can only be exhibited by leaders when the source for moral truth is passionately embraced.

DAILY SCRIPTURE READING: Job 5-7

JUNE 3
PUTTING THE PIECES TOGETHER

"For there is one God, and one mediator between God and men, the man Christ Jesus." −1 Timothy 2:5

A young boy was having trouble sitting still until his father gave him an assignment. The father ripped a picture of the world from a magazine and challenged him to put all the pieces of the world back together. This would surely keep the boy occupied for at least an hour, but the boy quickly returned with the picture of the world taped back together. When the father asked how he put the world together so quickly the boy replied, "There is a picture of a man on the other side, I knew if I got the man right, I would get the world right."

Man has allowed sin, self, and secularism to tear his world apart. Most would agree that the world is twisted, turned, and torn into irreconcilable pieces. We all feel the "global groanings" of these last days; but I propose to get the world right, we need to get ourselves right.

The only way to get ourselves right is to look unto the real man, the man Christ Jesus. 1 Timothy 2:5 says, "For there is one God, and one mediator between God and man, the man Christ Jesus." Paul concluded that Jesus is the Man! He is the only hope we have in this world to be reconciled to Holy God. Instead of trying to fix the world, we need to look unto Jesus, the One who has overcome the world; the one who can put the pieces of our lives back together.

DAILY SCRIPTURE READING: Job 8-10

JUNE 4

OH, I WANT TO SEE HIM

"Oh, I want to see Him, look upon His face.
There to sing forever, of His saving grace." –R. H. Cornelius

In the book, *The Happiness of Heaven*, a story is told of a compassionate king who meets an orphan in the forest. The child is poor, destitute, malnourished, and blind. The king adopts the boy and gives him all the luxuries of his empire.

When the boy turns twenty years old, a local surgeon performs a radical surgery giving the former orphan his sight. For the first time in his life the young man can now see. The boy had been a prince for many years; he had received all the benefits of being the king's son, but when asked what he was most grateful for since the recovery of his sight he said, "Being able to see the face of my father, who graciously took me in."

I suppose such will be the same reaction of all God's children when at last we see Him face to face. The daily benefits He bestows upon us are many. The good gifts from Glory are innumerable. But more than anything else, I want to see Him. I want to know Him. I want to stand in His presence and glorify Him for taking me out of the forest of sin, adopting me as His child, and giving me eternal life. I concur with the hymn writer R.H. Cornelius, "Oh, I want to see Him; look upon His face. There to sing forever, of His saving grace. On the street of Glory, there to lift my voice. Cares all past, home at last, ever to rejoice."

DAILY SCRIPTURE READING: Job 11-13

JUNE 5

UNEXPECTED PACKAGES

"Even the choicest of saints need to make it their business to mortify the indwelling power of sin." –John Owen

Recently, Federal Express hand-delivered a package to our front door. The professionally-wrapped envelope intrigued me as we were not expecting anything special in the mail. As we tore the parcel and opened the sealed envelope I was dismayed when I discovered it only to be junk mail. It was from a mortgage company soliciting special rates on their financing programs. This is a new procedure for businesses to get you to open their correspondence and read their offers.

As I threw the package in the trash, I considered how Satan works on a similar level. He presents sin in a sincere and intriguing fashion. He peaks our interests and causes us to be excited about the potential it offers. But once we open it up, it fails to deliver; on the contrary, it disappoints and deceives.

In his book, *The Pursuit of Holiness*, Jerry Bridges contends, "We must never consider that our fight with sin is at an end. The heart is unsearchable, our evil desires are insatiable, and our reason is constantly in danger of being deceived." Satan always finds a way to get to our front door. He carefully and intentionally packages sin in a modest and reasonable fashion. Regardless of where we live, we are susceptible to sin and its condemning power. Discard sin's contents immediately and think twice about opening unexpected packages.

DAILY SCRIPTURE READING: Job 14-16

JUNE 6

THE SILENT KILLER

"Man thinks if he can keep away from doing wrong, he does not sin; God's thought about sin is failure to do right." –F.E. Marsh

Suppose you went to the dentist and he discovered an abscessed tooth. At the risk of offending you, he refuses to tell you of the problem, and allows the infection to set up.

Suppose you went to the doctor and he found the early development of treatable cancer. Although he knows he could start treatment, he doesn't want to upset you, so he dismisses you from his care without even a hint of your condition.

Suppose your child wants something to drink. He goes for the milk that has been expired for the past two weeks. You know it will make him sick, but because he is thirsty you let him drink it anyway.

In each of these situations there is a demand for one person to tell another person about potential danger. The consequences of not saying anything is greater than the risk of someone getting upset. Of course the dentist fixes the tooth. Absolutely the doctor treats the patient. Obviously the parent warns the child. But when it comes to sin, and its damnable results, society demands that we be quiet. As believers, we have the awesome responsibility of warning people of the consequences of sin. They may not like the way it sounds, but they will love the way it saves.

DAILY SCRIPTURE READING: Job 17-20

JUNE 7

ONE DAY IN GOD'S HOUSE

"The best church-growth method I know is experiencing the manifest power of God." –Bill Hull

The psalmist declared in Psalm 84:10, *"For a day in thy courts is better than a thousand. I had rather be a doorkeeper in the house of my God, than to dwell in the tents of wickedness."* Just for a moment, consider the magnitude of that statement.

One day versus one thousand days. One thousand days almost equates to three years. So in essence, the psalmist implies that one day in the house of God is better than three years somewhere else…anywhere else. Think of the lush beaches of Hawaii. Consider the majestic beauty of the Rocky Mountains. What about the subtle serenity of the Smokies? Think of palaces, castles, mansions, and coliseums. None of these places compare to the incomparable glory of the presence of God!

The psalmist was so mesmerized and infatuated with God's House that he succumbed to the notion, "I had rather be a doorkeeper in the house of God, than to dwell in the tents of wickedness." He would rather be a lowly servant in God's House fulfilling a menial task than to sit among the world's elite in places of luxury. It is certain that we can worship and serve God outside of the walls of His House (and indeed we should). However, there is something gratifying about approaching our designated places of worship. What you find at God's House, you find nowhere else.

DAILY SCRIPTURE READING: Job 21-23

JUNE 8

A TRAIN GOING SOMEWHERE

"He whose heart is in heaven need not fear to put his foot in the grave." –Matthew Henry

While on a train traveling from Princeton, Albert Einstein was met by the conductor. Reaching for the ticket in his pocket to prove his purchase, Einstein mistakenly misplaced it. The conductor replied, "Sir, I know who you are. I'm sure you bought a ticket. No worries." Einstein thanked the young conductor and went about reading his journal.

As the conductor continued down the aisle punching tickets, he turned around and saw the world-renowned physicist on the floor looking under his seat. The conductor went back to Einstein's seat and reaffirmed, "Sir, you don't need a ticket, I know who you are." Einstein responded, "Young man, I too, know who I am. What I don't know is where I am going."

Einstein, who was one of history's greatest minds, proves a point with his misplaced ticket: intelligence, status, and notoriety will never ensure your eternal standing. The greatest assurance one can experience in this life is having the certainty of the life to come. Matthew Henry said, "He whose heart is in heaven need not fear to put his foot in the grave." There is nothing that replaces the peace and assurance of knowing your name is recorded in the Lamb's Book of Life. When you know who you are in Christ, you have confidence of where you are going.

DAILY SCRIPTURE READING: Job 24-28

JUNE 9

LEAVING A LEGACY

"The final test of a leader is that he leaves in others the will and conviction to carry on." –Walter Lippman

In his book, *The Conviction to Lead*, Albert Mohler tells of his visit to the historic First Baptist Church of Dallas, where iconic pastor Dr. W.A. Criswell served. At the end of the worship service, Pastor Criswell stood before the congregation and welcomed some of the new members. Among those new members was a young boy who recently was saved and baptized. Dr. Criswell told the audience that he not only had the privilege to baptize the boy, but years ago he baptized his father. Then he testified of baptizing the grandfather years before he baptized the father.

Criswell had been in the pastorate at that moment for nearly half a century. He had preached, baptized, and served that one particular family for three generations. Such a thing is only accomplished through perseverance, determination, and patience.

A good legacy is confirmed by the impression, influence, and investment one makes in the lives of others. You will have to be willing to stay in your area of service during hard and difficult times to leave a legacy- it is built upon the back of dependability. As Mohler contends, "If you want to make a lasting difference, you had better make the commitment to endure. Otherwise, your influence will disappear about as fast as the stationery with your name on it."

DAILY SCRIPTURE READING: Job 29-31

JUNE 10

NAIL IT DOWN

"The one thing we are most reluctant to give up is the one thing that has the most potential to become a substitute for Him." –Kyle Idleman

There is a story told of a Haitian man who sold his home during a of financial crisis. Because he desperately needed the money, he was willing to let his house go at an incredibly low price with only one stipulation: he was to maintain ownership of one single, solitary nail on the wall in the living room. The fellow who purchased the home agreed to these terms and signed the contract.

Months later the poor Haitian man recovered from his financial collapse and tried to move back into his home. The new owner refused to negotiate with the former tenant. The Haitian fellow proceeded to "occupy" his one nail by placing a dead dog on it. The contract legally confirmed his right to do so. The odor and stench was so bad that the new homeowner sold the property back to the man at a lesser price than he originally paid.

Paul told the church at Ephesus to "Neither give place to the devil." When we leave just one area of our life, just one nail, under the ownership of Satan, we are subject to the vile and wicked contaminants of the world. Giving him "place" always comes at a price. What may seem like a good deal initially will end up costing us much more than we are willing to pay. Sell out to the Lord and give Him all of your life.

DAILY SCRIPTURE READING: Job 32-34

JUNE 11

SLOW GROWTH

"The greatest difference in the world is the difference between what we are and what we could become." –Ben Herbster

During the first four years of growth, a bamboo tree has little results. It doesn't matter how much water or fertilizer you put on the tree, it has a very slow growth rate. But in the fifth year, the tree shoots up in phenomenal fashion. As a matter of fact, in a span of only five weeks the tree can grow ninety feet in height.

The sudden growth is the result of years of committed harvesting. The tree may appear to shoot up overnight, but without the faithful years of watering and fertilizing it would never get to that point.

Many Christians want to grow overnight, and when they fail to see immediate results, they get aggravated, frustrated, and wearing in well-doing. Spiritual growth doesn't work that way. It takes continual, constant, committed discipline to grow spiritually in the Lord. Growth is a day after day matter. Just a little here and a little there. Ben Herbster said, "The greatest waste in the world is the difference between what we are and what we could become."

Don't sell short your spiritual growth. Keep watering, keep fertilizing, inch by inch, day after day, year after year, and you will eventually bear the fruit of a life committed to God.

DAILY SCRIPTURE READING: Job 35-37

JUNE 12

LIFE-STYLE COMPLAINERS

"Giving thanks to God for His blessings is not just a nice thing to do, it is the moral will of God." –Jerry Bridges

There was a construction worker who was notorious for complaining. Day after day he grumbled about his lunch. "Bologna sandwich again?! The next day the same thing. He opened his lunch box and quickly said, "I hate these bologna sandwiches!" The next day at lunch time it was the same response, "I can't stand these bologna sandwiches!" A fed-up co-worker replied, "Why don't you tell your wife to make you something different?" The complainer quickly responded, "Hey buddy, you leave my wife alone, I make my own lunches!"

Some people aren't happy unless they have something to complain about. Not all complaining is bad: if a school bus is driving recklessly with children on board, it's ok to complain. If you find something in your food to the detriment of your health, it's ok to complain. If you are having major chest pain, and the doctor asks about it, it's ok to complain. But there is a difference between circumstantial complaining and constant complaining. Some people are life-style complainers. They complain about everything. Life-style complainers very seldom consider the blessings of God, and they fail to live with an eternal perspective. If you find yourself complaining more often than you should, remember the instruction of Paul, "Rejoice in the Lord **alway**; and again I say, rejoice."

DAILY SCRIPTURE READING: Job 38-39

JUNE 13
THE BATTLE WITH BURN-OUT

"The great secret of success is to go through life as a man who never gets used up." –Albert Schweitzer

The Olympic games always begins with the lighting of the torch. The torch is actually lit several weeks prior to the start of the Olympics. Once lit, the fire of the torch is exchanged from one runner to the next over the course of several cities until it gets to the opening ceremony of the games. This tradition has its roots in Greek culture.

The Greeks had a race in which the participants ran with fire. The prize did not go to those who finished first; it went to those who were able to finish their race with their torches still lit. The race therefore was not to the quickest, but to the most cautious.

The Christian journey is much the same. It's not about who gets to the end first (we all as believers get to the end). It's about getting to the end with our light still shining, and our fire still burning.

Let's face it; burn-out is a real issue in these last days. The elements of this world continually work against our fire. Schedules, responsibilities, overtime, meetings, traffic, and a plethora of other events will blow out our passion for God. Instead of trying to be the first one to cross the line, try to simply maintain your fire. Be cautious of burn-out; keep your light carefully guarded as you continue your course.

DAILY SCRIPTURE READING: Job 40-42

JUNE 14

FIG LEAVES AND FUR COATS

"Grace is not opposed to effort, it is opposed to earning." –Dallas Willard

When Adam and Eve sinned in the garden their eyes were opened to a new, fallen world. They realized they were naked, but instead of crying out for mercy, they did what all of humanity does when overwhelmed by guilt and shame: they tried to help themselves. They began sewing fig leaves together in an attempt to cover their depravity. Once covered by the glory of God, Adam and Eve now wore the self-righteous cloaks of their own works.

They thought the fig leaves would suffice, and by their own standards, perhaps they did. However, when the presence of God came upon Adam and his wife, they trembled and hid themselves amongst the trees. Their works satisfied the requirements of one another, but the fig leaves would never satisfy God.

God, in His mercy and grace, changed their wardrobe, fur coats if you will. A sacrifice was made to cover the sinfulness of the first man and woman, and such a sacrifice is still required today.

Christ, the perfect Lamb of God was slain in our place because our works of self-righteousness can never satisfy the holiness of God. By grace we can take off the failed fig leaves and put on the Lord Jesus Christ.

DAILY SCRIPTURE READING: Psalm 1-8

JUNE 15

WHERE ARE THE NINE?

"By him therefore let us offer the sacrifice of praise to God continually." –Hebrews 13:15

In the Gospel of Luke, Christ came through Samaria and healed ten lepers (Luke 17). These ten men stood on the outskirts of the city and cried out for mercy when the Lord passed by. Leprosy affected every aspect of their lives: religiously, socially, mentally, physically, and spiritually they were isolated and indifferent. Yet Christ gave them instruction to go to the priest. As they went their way they were made whole of the terrible disease. What a glorious moment that must have been for this band of misfits; but out of the ten, only one turned back to give God the glory.

When this one fellow approached the Lord in praise, Christ asked him, "Where are the nine?" Christ healed all ten lepers of leprosy, but only one from ingratitude.

How often in our own lives do we fail to return thanks to God? Those who fail to worship God on a consistent basis fail to remember what their lives were like before he intervened. They have very little appreciation for His work of grace. If not for the mercy of God, those ten lepers would have died in their depravity; but Christ extended favor upon them and forever changed their circumstance. Today, Christ is still asking, "Where are the nine?" Be the minority and offer unto Him the sacrifice of praise.

DAILY SCRIPTURE READING: Psalm 9-16

JUNE 16
THE REAL THING

"They only people who do not like old-time religion, are those who don't have it." –Maze Jackson

In the mid 1980's, Coca-Cola released a product called the New Coke. This was a reformulation of their iconic drink. Coca-Cola didn't expect such a strong backlash from the public. Most people disliked the new product, and sales drastically dropped. It was deemed as one of the worst marketing events in history.

Coca-Cola took notice of the public's response and brought back the original formula under the new name Coca-Cola Classic. Sales instantly increased and the company seemed to gain favor once again with their customers. The failed campaign proved one thing: there is no replacement for the real thing. As a matter of fact, the recalled product embraced an old song from the 1970's, "Ain't nothing like the real thing, baby."

Too often we try to substitute the power and the presence of God with superficial things. Religion, good works, emotional experiences may all seem similar to God's presence, but they will never sustain or satisfy a true child of God. Once you have experienced His glory, nothing else will do. We should refuse to accept anything less. It is time we rid our lives with the "new" products of spirituality and get back to the "classic" formula – we need the real thing!

DAILY SCRIPTURE READING: Psalm 17-20

JUNE 17

EARLY-MORNING DEVOTION

"Devotion is knowing you will never be able to repay Christ for Calvary, but giving it a daily attempt." –Kenneth Kuykendall

Over the past few years I have tried to live by a daily philosophy...to live every day as though it is the only day to be examined at the Judgment Seat of Christ. Stop just for a moment and reread that sentence.

In case you didn't go back; let me repeat it, "Live every day as though it is the only that will be examined at the Judgment Seat of Christ."

Once the magnitude of that statement settled into my heart, I realized the significance and responsibility of serving God every day. Every day will be examined. Every decision, motive, intent, word, expression, and attitude will fall under the righteous assessment of God. So to set each day into its proper motion, we must intend to start the day with God.

As George Lorimar said, "You've got to get up every morning with determination if you are going to go to bed with satisfaction."

Nothing substitutes our devotion. Nothing. It is from our personal time with God that life flows. Ministry, service, worship, and power are all nurtured through those early morning hours of solitude, study and supplication. Give the first hours of your day to the Lord and it is certain He will guide and govern your steps throughout the rest of the day.

DAILY SCRIPTURE READING: Psalm 21-25

JUNE 18

LIFE'S PRECIOUS COMMODITY

"Time is what we want most, but what we use worst." –William Penn

Every November my staff helps me finalize the annual calendar for the upcoming year. This is one of the most important things we do together as a team. Within the framework of an annual calendar we introduce our new church theme, set meetings and dates, prepare special campaigns, and establish specific ministerial and personal goals. Such a plan helps us to stay organized and focused as we facilitate our vision. But above and beyond that, it helps us to daily embrace one of the most precious commodities of life: time.

"Time is the scarcest resource, and unless it is managed, nothing else can be managed" said Peter Drucker, "Within limits we can substitute one resource for another, copper for aluminum, for instance. We can substitute capital for human labor. We can use more knowledge or more brawn. But there is no substitute for time." This is what the apostle Paul meant when he challenged us to "Redeem the Time." Quite literally, we are to make the proper investments with the time we have been given. If not properly managed, time can get away from us, and before we realize it we have wasted precious, God-given moments on trivial and inconsequential things. At the risk of sounding cliché: we are not only instructed to count our time, we are to make our time count.

DAILY SCRIPTURE READING: Psalm 26-31

JUNE 19

TIME WITH FAMILY

"A happy family is but an earlier heaven." –John Bowring

Thomas Jefferson said, "The happiest moments of my life have been the ones I have spent at home in the bosom of my family." I concur; I am the most content when I am with my wife and children. Therefore, to ensure I invest my time wisely, I have to prioritize my calendar with their best interests in mind.

- Have family devotions each morning or evening. Spend time reading God's Word and praying together as a family.
- Have a special "family day" each week. For my family that day is Friday. We do not always do something big or outlandish; we simply commit our time together in some capacity on that day.
- Plan special date nights with your spouse.
- Make the most of vacation time. Those moments spent together will be cherished for a lifetime.
- Create intentional memories with your family. You don't have to spend a lot of money, or visit exotic locations to make lasting memories. Just involve your attention and invest your affection.

To make these family functions a priority, you may have to scale down other activities from your life. Do not hesitate to make the cuts. The Lord requires it and your family deserves it.

DAILY SCRIPTURE READING: Psalm 32-35

JUNE 20

THE VALUE OF CRITICISM

"There is a kernel of truth in every criticism, look for it and when you find it rejoice in its value." –Dawson Trotman

To think we are above improvement is a dangerous and deceptive notion. We may not like to admit it, but one of the reasons criticism hurts so badly is because it touches one of the most sensitive areas of our heart- the part composed of pride. Norman Vincent Peale accurately contends, "The trouble with most of us is that we would rather be ruined by praise than saved by criticism."

Sometimes pride is only exposed through the loud, irritating, and obnoxious voice of the critic. The one thing we must avoid is trying to avoid criticism altogether. Not all criticism is bad. As a matter of fact, there are some times when it is necessary. When given in the right spirit, with the right motive, under the right circumstances, criticism can be your greatest companion. The Bible says, "Faithful are the wounds of a friend" It is better to fall under the scrutiny of man and adjust accordingly, than to resist God's development and fall under His wrath.

The greater context of our criticism is that God is the Master Potter who is working, shaping, molding us to be the kind of person we need to be. "There is a kernel of truth in every criticism" said Dawson Trotman, "look for it, and when you find it, rejoice in its value."

DAILY SCRIPTURE READING: Psalm 36-39

JUNE 21

THE GRACE OF SELF-CONTROL

"Self-control is the trumping of inner strength over outer weakness." –Kenneth Kuykendall

The epitome of self-control is found in the Garden of Gethsemane. Christ was surrounded by a multitude of burley soldiers, sleepy friends who distanced themselves from Him during His agony, and a back-stabbing, devil-possessed companion who betrayed the Lord for filthy lucre. At any given moment, Christ could have called ten thousand angels to come and wreak havoc upon the entire scene, but Christ opted out. With divine resolve, He restrained Himself and submitted His life to the Father's will.

Such is the characteristic of self-control. Jerry Bridges defines it this way, "Self-control is the exercise of inner strength under the direction of sound judgment that enables us to do, think, and say the things that are pleasing to God." Self-control is the evidence of a Spirit-filled life, the essence of inner strength. It is a virtue of grace.

Had Christ not demonstrated self-control in the Garden of Gethsemane, the entire world would have been convicted, judged, and sentenced by the wrath of God; but instead He willingly gave Himself over to the guards, and ultimately to the cross. As a result, He afforded the opportunity for everyone to receive forgiveness. Self-control therefore derives from love, compassion, and the ability to restrain oneself for the benefit of others.

DAILY SCRIPTURE READING: Psalm 40-45

JUNE 22

THE ACCOUNTABLE LIFE

"The twin sister to autonomy and freedom is responsibility and accountability." –Henry Cloud

The word "accountable' is an old French word that derives from the subject of mathematics. Webster contends that it means to "provide a report from money received." To be "accountable" therefore, means for a person to be held responsible for his responsibilities. It means to give an answer, or quite literally, write a report to be examined or evaluated by someone else. It means to live within prescribed boundaries with integrity and character.

It is only in the framework of accountability that we have the liberty to declare, and to be trusted with the truth. Henry Cloud contends, "The twin sister to autonomy and freedom is responsibility and accountability. You cannot have one without the other. If someone is given an area of responsibility, not only must they be set free to do it, they must also be held accountable for what they do. Accountability clarifies freedom."

The freedom we have in Christ, and the liberty we have in the service of the Lord is not without evaluation or examination. The follower of the Lord Jesus Christ is held to the highest standards of integrity, honesty, character, and morality. We must all give an "account" at the Judgment Seat of Christ. On that day, this day will be examined; therefore live right, do right, and be right, and you will be alright.

DAILY SCRIPTURE READING: Psalm 46-50

JUNE 23

YBH

"No one can produce great things who is not thoroughly sincere in dealing with himself." –James Russell Lowell

There was a man who often read books, magazines, and articles about the Christian life and the pursuit of godliness. One day a friend happened to browse through some of the man's books only to find the letters *YBH* next to many of the statements made by the authors. When the friend asked the man what the letters meant, the fellow replied, "Those letters stand for *Yes, But How?*" He continued, "I agree with what the author is saying, but I need to know how to apply it."

The key to successful Christian living is not just the knowledge of truth; it is the application of truth. Christ instructed us to be like the fellow who built his life upon the foundation of stone. This fellow, according to Jesus, represented someone who not only knew the truth, but lived the truth. "Therefore whosoever heareth these sayings of mine, and *doeth them*, I will liken him unto a wise man, which built his house upon a rock" (Matthew 7:24).

Truth is only applicable in our lives when we learn how to implement it. Find ways to appropriate the Word of God in every-day living. Devotions, studies, and lessons are of no value unless we demonstrate what God has revealed to us in them through the exercise of good works. When we sincerely ask YBH, it is certain God will provide an answer.

DAILY SCRIPTURE READING: Psalm 51-57

JUNE 24

SECURITY IN CHRIST

"Our entire confidence in our acceptance before God is that Jesus is our legal representative." –Jerry Bridges

Humility is a key virtue to a successful life, insecurity is not. Though often packaged in the same wrapping, insecurity and humility are two very different mindsets. The difference is this: humility is the loss of pride, the denial of self; while insecurity is the loss of confidence, the obsession of self. Insecurity comes from several sources:

- Repeated Failures
- Personality Types
- Aggressive Competition
- Family History
- Poor Decisions

I have noticed over the course of my ministry that some people are never satisfied with their "successes." No matter how large their home, no matter how big their accounts, no matter how many degrees they obtain, they always feel like they have something else to prove. Insecurity will rob us of our contentment, and deplete us of our joy. Until we realize that our ability and worth are in Christ, we will always try to outdo others and ourselves, feeling less than adequate in the process. Insecurity is the result of trusting in ourselves, security is the result of trusting in Jesus Christ.

DAILY SCRIPTURE READING: Psalm 58-65

JUNE 25
DIVINE COMPANIONSHIP

"There's a difference between feeling lonely and being alone. Saints have the promise of perpetual companionship." –Kenneth Kuykendall

In 1956, Jim Elliot, missionary to Ecuador, was murdered by the very people he was sent to reach. Left to serve God without a husband by her side, Elisabeth Elliot wrote, "Loneliness comes over us sometimes as a sudden tide. It is one of the terms of our humanness, and, in a sense, therefore, incurable. Yet I have found peace in my loneliest times not only through acceptance of the situation, but through making it an offering to God, who can transfigure it into something for the good of others."

Loneliness is indeed "one of the terms of our humanness." Loneliness is more than seclusion or isolation, it is inner emptiness. It is the inability to connect or commune with others regardless of their proximity. You can be in a kitchen, cathedral, or coliseum full of people and still feel alone.

But the truth is believers are never alone. There may be times when we feel lonely, but we have the promise of His presence. The Lord said, "I will never leave thee, nor forsake thee" (Hebrews 13:5). What great consolation and assurance there is in knowing that the great God of all creation promises His perpetual and continual companionship throughout all the days of our lives. He is with you now, and there will never be a moment when that truth is not a reality in your life.

DAILY SCRIPTURE READING: Psalm 66-69

JUNE 26

THE LOSS OF CHARACTER

"Who you are becoming is more important than what you are doing." –Brad Lomenick

Several years ago my family watched as I put Christmas lights upon the exterior of our home. I worked diligently for six hours in the cold, climbing ladders, and stretching icicle lights across the cornice and facial boards. I hung nearly three hundred feet of lights that year and climbed three different size ladders to do so. After Christmas was over, it was time to box up all the decorations. When I began taking the exterior lights down, I grabbed one end of the string and slightly tugged them away from the roof line. Immediately the entire system of lights began descending, ultimately crashing to the ground.

As I began cleaning up the broken glass it occurred to me that our character is much like the hanging of Christmas lights. It takes time and effort to shine the lights for all to enjoy; but with one slip, the entire show comes crashing to the ground. What takes years to develop can literally be destroyed in a moment's time.

In his book, *The Conviction to Lead*, Albert Mohler states, "Leaders, like all sinners can be forgiven. But forgiveness does not restore credibility, and character must be seen as something that can be lost far easier than gained, much less restored." In other words, lose your character and it is certain, you will lose your testimony.

DAILY SCRIPTURE READING: Psalm 70-73

JUNE 27

HOW TO PRAY FOR OTHERS

"The greatest tragedy in life is not unanswered prayer, but unoffered prayer." –E.M. Bounds

The most important thing you can do for another person is call their name before the throne of grace. Nothing says "I love you, and care for you" more than prayer. But *how* do we pray for others? In the first chapter of Colossians, the apostle Paul gives us instruction on how to specifically pray for those we love:

1. Pray for their Wisdom. "For this cause we also, since the day we heard *it*, do not cease to pray for you, and to desire that ye might be filled with the knowledge of his will in all wisdom and spiritual understanding;" Colossians 1:9

2. Pray for their Walk. "That ye might walk worthy of the Lord unto all pleasing, being fruitful in every good work, and increasing in the knowledge of God;" Colossians 1:10

3. Pray for their Weaknesses. "Strengthened with all might, according to his glorious power, unto all patience and longsuffering with joyfulness;" Colossians 1:11

4. Pray for their Worship. Giving thanks unto the Father, which hath made us meet to be partakers of the inheritance of the saints in light:" Colossians 1:12

DAILY SCRIPTURE READING: Psalm 74-77

JUNE 28

MID-YEAR RESOLUTIONS

"He doesn't give us more to do than we can get done in the time provided." –Paul Chappell

Most people make resolutions at the beginning of the year only to have those aspirations squashed within a few weeks of making them. We aim to lose weight, start Bible-reading programs, exercise, eat healthier, become more positive, and a hundred other decrees which can better our lives. Usually by the end of January, those resolutions have dissipated and we return to our "regularly-scheduled" program.

I propose mid-year resolutions. As a matter of fact, I propose resolutions throughout the year.

It is never too late, or too early to make your life better. If you have failed to persevere, and those New-Year resolutions are just a failed attempt of change, then why not start today, and make a new list?

Benjamin Franklin said, "Doest thou love life? Then do not squander time, for it is the stuff life is made of." You don't have to wait until January to drop ten pounds or pick up your Bible. This is the day the Lord has made, let us rejoice and be glad therein. Plug-in the treadmill, read that book you purchased, start your devotions again, save a few more dollars, spend more time with family…whatever you do, do it as unto the Lord. Stop making excuses, and start making changes.

DAILY SCRIPTURE READING: Psalm 78-79

JUNE 29

WHEN LIFE IS THE PITS

"If we desire our faith to be strengthened, we should not shrink from opportunities where our faith may be tried." –George Mueller

Sometimes life is the pits...literally. In the book of Genesis, Joseph dreamed he would be the rising star of his family. His dream suddenly turned into a nightmare when his older brothers cast him into an empty pit. Ironically, he was now looking up to his brothers in a less-than-hospitable place. But the pit was not without some life-lessons. Joseph learned some things in his pit that changed his life:

1. Not everyone appreciates your dreams. Just because God has given you a dream or vision does not mean that everyone else understands it, or appreciates it. Be careful who you share your dreams with; they may be the very ones who try to throw you in the pit.

2. Your Father still loves you. In spite of being hated by his brothers, Joseph's father loved him dearly, and remained the favored son. When life throws you in the pit, remember that your Heavenly Father still cares.

3. You've got to go down before you rise up. Setbacks are a part of life. Remember, when you get down, God can bring you up. Heartache is part of the journey. Learn to embrace it, and learn from it.

4. God's plan takes time. Almost twenty years passed before Joseph's dream became a reality. God doesn't work on our time-table. Dreams may happen over-night, but the reality of the dream may years to unfold.

DAILY SCRIPTURE READING: Psalm 80-85

JUNE 30

GLORY IN THE CROSS

"At the cross, at the cross, where I first saw the light; and the burden of my heart rolled away." –Isaac Watts

If anyone had cause to glory in themselves it was the apostle Paul. His resume was akin to a Rhodes Scholar. His influence and zeal was incomparable among his colleagues. He was the rising star among the Pharisees, a militant adversary against the church who tried to single-handedly stop the cause of Christ. But those things were counted as "dung" to Paul when he was converted. Paul wrote to the churches of Galatia and said, "But God forbid that I should glory, save in the cross of our Lord Jesus Christ" (Galatians 6:14).

Paul was stripped of those self-righteous, self-promoting, self-centered acts of the flesh when he encountered the resurrected Savior. His view of the cross changed, and it became the central theme of his life and ministry. Paul, the chief adversary of the church became the chief advocate of the church. The great persecutor of Christ became the great preacher for Christ. And his message, his boast, and his glory were all in the cross of Jesus Christ.

Paul carried a cross, he preached the cross, and he loved that old cross. At the cross, man is stripped of his self-righteousness and forced to see the wrath of God upon His own Son. At the cross, our works, our deeds, our religion are made void. If we glory, let us glory in the cross.

DAILY SCRIPTURE READING: Psalm 86-89

JULY

JULY 1

WOULD YOU BE FIRED?

"Let the words of my mouth, and the meditation of my heart, be acceptable in thy sight O LORD." –Psalm 19:14

Suppose you treated your job the same way you treated your church membership; what kind of employee would you be? Would you be highly-valued, or would you be fired within a week's time? Let me ask you a few probing questions:

- Do you go to work when you are supposed to?
- Do you give your all to the responsibilities of your job?
- Do you submit to the authority of your boss, employee?
- Do you show up on time, ready to work, and willing to fulfill the obligations you were assigned?
- Do you have a good attitude and disposition while doing it?

If you answered "no" to any one of these questions, odds are, you would not last very long on the job. Why should we be any less faithful to the membership where we commit our service to the Lord?

When we join our lives to a local church, we are in essence, vowing to support, love, serve, and give to that particular body. Too often, believers flippantly join a congregation and give little thought to their responsibilities. Don't lay down on the job; don't make it harder on others by failing in your commitment. If you've been slacking off, ask God to forgive you, and get back to work.

DAILY SCRIPTURE READING: Psalm 90-95

JULY 2

END WELL

"The hallmark of excellence, the test of greatness is consistency." –Jim Tressel

The Apostle Paul did not have a great start in Scripture. He came upon the biblical scene as a zealot whose ministerial ambition was to destroy the church of Jesus Christ. However, upon his conversion, he became the chief advocate of the very church he once sought to destroy. In the closing chapter of his life, he wrote, "For I am now ready to be offered and the time of my departure is at hand. I have fought a good fight, I have finished my course, I have kept the faith" (2 Timothy 4:6-7). Paul had a lousy start, but a great finish.

In those closing remarks, Paul mentioned a man by the name of Demas. Demas was a co-laborer in the work of the Lord. Demas started out strong in the Lord but failed to stay on course. Paul wrote of this man, "For Demas hath forsaken me, having loved this present world, and is departed unto Thessalonica" (2 Timothy 4:10). Demas had a great start, but a lousy finish.

Somewhere in the journey, Demas became mesmerized and distracted by the world around him. He took his eyes off the eternal, and placed them on the temporal. As a result, he will forever be remembered as a man who finished poorly. Consistency is the key to crossing the finish line in good standing with God.

DAILY SCRIPTURE READING: Psalm 96-102

JULY 3

INFLUENCING OUR CHILDREN

"We teach what we know. We reproduce what we are." –John Maxwell

Our influence is felt most significantly by those closest to us. This is especially true as it relates to parents and children. Henry Ward Beecher said, "The humblest of individual exerts some influence; either for good or evil upon others." Regardless of *how* you influence your children, be certain, they are being influenced. Here are three essential elements of influence:

1. Time. Hanz Finzel said, "Only through association is there transformation- we cannot change people if we do not spend time with them." This is especially true as it comes to our kids. Years from now they will not remember the gifts or presents you bought them as much as they remember the moments you shared with them.

2. Training. We are instructed in Scripture to "train up a child" in the way he should go. Training involves trial and error, correction and discipline, love and grace. Effective training is ultimately rooted in the relationship you have with your child.

3. Trust. John Maxwell said, "The length and breadth of our influence on others are directly related to the depth of concern we have for them." Trust is built through consistent love and affection. It is the hinge upon which our influence turns.

DAILY SCRIPTURE READING: Psalm 103-105

JULY 4

FAITH IN THE FOG

"Christ will always accept the faith that puts its trust in Him." –Andrew Murray

We had promised our children how beautiful the scenery would be when we reached the top of the mountain. But on our way to Pigeon Forge, Tennessee the Smokies lived up to their name. The fog that filled the atmosphere was deeply dense. It felt like we were traveling in the clouds. Instead of gazing across the Appalachian canyons, my children played with IPods and watched a movie. No one wants to take pictures of smoke.

After a few days of rest and relaxation we began our journey back home; this time the fog had lifted. We stopped for pictures, spent time at rest-stops, and stood amazed at God's creation. My children were mesmerized at the views. One of them said to me, "Dad, it was just like you said."

Sometimes the promises that are made by our Heavenly Father are difficult to see. The fog skews the view, and leaves us wondering if the mountain-top experience will ever come to pass. We travel in doubt, we wait in frustration, and we become pre-occupied with worldly devices. But when the fog finally lifts, we see the reality of His promise, and the view is breath-taking! Keep your faith in the fog, it will soon be lifted.

DAILY SCRIPTURE READING: Psalm 106-107

JULY 5

LEECHES AND WORMS

"For where a testament is, there must also of necessity be the death of a testator." –Hebrews 9:16

A story is told of a wealthy French industrialist who bestowed his inheritance to a leech. Capitaine Furrer was so appalled at the insatiable greed of his family that he refused to leave his inheritance to such a selfish clan. Instead, he appointed his fortune of coal mines and textile mills to a blood-sucking leech as a testimony against his self-seeking heirs.

This may sound ridiculous, but it is similar to what God has done for us. Isaac Watts penned down these iconic words in 1885:

Alas and did my Savior bleed?
And did my Savior die?
Would He devote that sacred head
For such a worm as I?

We were undeserving of His grace and mercy; we were as the lowly worm and the blood-sucking leech. But through the death of Jesus Christ we received an eternal inheritance. As Peter said, "To an inheritance, incorruptible, and undefiled, and that fadeth not away, reserved in heaven for you" (1 Peter 1:4). The estate of Furrer's leech is no more astounding than the inheritance you and I receive as lowly worms.

DAILY SCRIPTURE READING: Psalm 108-114

JULY 6

BEYOND THE GRAVE

"Death may be the king of terrors...
but Jesus is the King of kings!" –D.L. Moody

There was a Chinese man who kept his family tradition by placing meals on the graves of his loved ones. An American in the same graveyard witnessed this unusual sight and wondered about the odd practice. He approached the Chinese fellow and said, "Sir, let me ask you a question. When will your loved one eat that meal?" Pointing to the fresh flowers in the hands of the American, the man replied, "As soon as your loved one will be able to smell those roses!"

Death is an appointment that every man is required to keep. It cannot be postponed or rescheduled. What we do with Christ determines how we die. In Luke 16, two men died simultaneously; one man was buried and lifted his eyes in hell, while the other was carried into the presence of the saints of God in heaven. Two very different destinations, yet both of their fates were final.

In death there are no more roses to smell or meals to consume. There are no second chances. This issue of death is an urgent matter. Today is the day of salvation, now is the appointed time to believe in Christ and place your faith in Him for eternal life. Roses will fade, meals will perish, but the souls of men live forever.

DAILY SCRIPTURE READING: Psalm 115-118

JULY 7
FAITH AND FLEAS

"Comfort and prosperity have never enriched the world as much as adversity has." –Billy Graham

In 1944, the Nazis discovered that Corrie ten Boom had been hiding various Jewish families in her home. As a result, she and her sister Betsie were taken captive and held as prisoners in one of the concentration camps in the Netherlands. In addition to the evil that filled the facility, this particular camp was infested with a severe plague of fleas.

Betsie, known for her piety and devout commitment to God, began thanking the Lord for the infestation. Corrie, annoyed by the influx of fleas thought it was ridiculous to be thankful for such an aggravation. Little did she know however, that the guards were equally aggravated by the fleas. As a result, they refused to check the barracks which Corrie and Betsie occupied. This meant that the sisters could keep their Bibles hidden without fear of the Nazis. The fleas actually fueled their faith.

Sometimes those little aggravations are used by God to help grow and mature our lives. Though irritating and annoying, they are part of a bigger picture and plan. A plan designed for our ultimate good, and God's ultimate glory. Someone has anonymously said, "The soul would have no rainbow if the eye had tears." Corrie and Betsie would say, "The camp would have no Bible if the barracks had no fleas."

DAILY SCRIPTURE READING: Psalm 119:1-Psalm 119:88

JULY 8

GIVING SILVER, GETTING GOLD

"The more I gave away, the fuller of happiness and blessing my soul did become." –Hudson Taylor

Before Hudson Taylor became the world-renowned missionary to China, he worked with a field doctor in preparation of his ministry. One night he was asked to visit a poor widow woman who had become very ill. He began praying for the lady in her desperate situation but was convicted by the fact that he possessed the exact amount of money this sick, starving mother needed. Although this was his last piece of silver, Taylor thought to himself, "How can I ask this woman to trust God's provision when I will not trust God for my own?" Taylor gave her the coin.

The next day, an unmarked, anonymous package arrived for the soon-to-be-missionary containing gold that was worth ten times the amount of that silver coin. Taylor never discovered who sent the package, but attributed the gift to the provision and providence of God.

Taylor would later write about God's goodness, "I soon found that I could live upon very much less than I had previously thought possible. My experience was that the less I spent on myself and the more I gave away, the fuller of happiness and blessing did my soul become." China and the world at large have since felt the impact of such generous faith.

DAILY SCRIPTURE READING: Psalm 119:89-119:176

JULY 9

ON TOP OF THE MOUNTAIN

---

*"When God changes your heart,
He will also change your face."* – Kenneth Kuykendall

When Moses received the Law of God on Mt. Sinai he was with the Lord for forty days and nights. The Bible says that God came down in a cloud and stood beside Moses and proclaimed His name to the man of God. Though Moses did not eat bread and drink water, He did sit at the table of the Divine and received the Word which nourished and strengthened his soul.

When he came down from the mountain he had the Word of God in his Hand, the Worship of God in his Heart, and the Witness of God on his Head. The face of Moses shined with the glory of Almighty God. It was evident to those in the camp by the radiance and brilliance on his face that he had been with the Lord.

Today, will those you come into contact with see the glow of God on your face? Will it be evident to them that you have been with God? We need to get on the mountain with God, hear His word, honor and bless His wonderful name so that when we come down from the mountain we can make Him known to those in our life.

The only way to face the groaning of the valley is to find the glow on the mountain. May God's presence shine on our faces!

DAILY SCRIPTURE READING: Psalm 120-132

JULY 10

UNUSED CARDS

"The greatest waste in the world is the difference between what we are and what we could become." – Ben Herbster

Every year millions of dollars are unclaimed through unused gift cards. It is said even if the card is used there is oftentimes a small percentage that is left on the balance. This proves to be a gain for department stores and businesses, but a loss for consumers. Recently I came across a few gifts cards people have given me over the past year. Several of them had a few dollars or a few cents left on them. Even though this seems like an insignificant amount- it does add up if given enough cards.

These unused gift cards resemble our potential. Someone has accurately stated, "Many people often reach their goals, but few people rarely reach their potential." Too many people are like these cards- they never give all they have- they always leave a little leftover.

It is easy to set goals and reach those goals; but just because you reach a goal doesn't necessary mean you have reached your potential. Calvin Coolidge said, "The most common commodity of this country is unrealized potential." I certainly do not want to get to the end of my life and realize I did not give everything I could have given. Give all your love, all your time, and all your effort. Our gifts, talents, and abilities benefit no one if left unused.

DAILY SCRIPTURE READING: Psalm 133-139

JULY 11
THE GIFT OF GIVING

"Giving is one of the great experiences of the Christian life. Embrace it, enjoy it; and God will enlarge it." –Kenneth Kuykendall

It was John Bunyon who said, "You have not lived today unless you have done something for someone who cannot repay you." Giving is not just an act; it is an attitude, a mindset. Giving may manifest itself in the form of an offering, pledge, or neatly wrapped present, but it is birthed in the heart and nurtured in the soul. The person who constantly pours out the goodness of God from his life will never go wanting.

It has been frequently said that "God will give you to give more than He will give you to keep." If this is true, we are forced to frequently evaluate our stewardship over God's daily benefits. To the self-made man, "keeping" is a natural inclination. We hoard up our possessions, invest our savings, collect our treasures and stock-pile our belongings, all in the name of security. We make a living, but we miss out on building a life.

When we selflessly give our last portion of meal to kingdom advancement, God ensures and maximizes scoops from the barrel. He enables us to stand amazed in the kitchen as we prepare each meal of provision with the widow. You may argue, "But I worked for this house, or I paid for this car." And it is probable you did. But it is improbable that you did without the strength, ability, intellect, and breath of God.

DAILY SCRIPTURE READING: Psalm 140-145

JULY 12

CLUTTER

"Self-discipline is when your conscience tells you to do something and you do not talk back." –W.K. Hope

It happens every year. We go through our closets, clean out our basement, and straighten up our cupboards. It is amazing how many things we accumulate over a short-period of time. And most of the items we gather have little or no value. It is called clutter, and it takes up a lot of space in our lives.

The dictionary defines clutter as: a collection of things lying in an untidy or unorganized manner. If you are like most people, you have clutter somewhere in your home. Old, useless receipts in a drawer. Stacks of magazines piled in the bottom of a closet. Clothes that need to be given to charity. Expired cans of food that just sit on the shelves. Yes, clutter is all around us, and it prevents us from utilizing our space properly and efficiently.

The same holds true when it comes to our spirituality. Our relationship with the Lord can become crowded with clutter. Before we know it, we have been overtaken by "things" and "stuff." Most of the time, these "things" have little meaning or value, but they do exist. They pile up, get in the way, and occupy valuable space. Occasionally, we should go through the closets of our life and rid the clutter from our hearts.

DAILY SCRIPTURE READING: Psalms 146-150

JULY 13
KITCHEN PROVISION

"Therefore take no thought saying, What shall we eat? Or what shall we drink? Or wherewithal shall we be clothed." –Jesus Christ

An elderly grandmother was visiting her newly-married granddaughter. As they prepared a meal together in the kitchen, the grandmother was amazed at all the technology imbedded in the appliances. She stopped for a moment and asked the granddaughter, "What's the most valuable thing to you in this kitchen? What's the one thing you couldn't live without?" The young girl paused for a moment and said, "I don't know, I guess the microwave; what about you?" Without hesitation the grandmother replied, "The running water."

Most of us are like the young girl, we take for granted those basic, every-day provisions of God. Running water, central heat and air, electricity, indoor plumbing, the comfort of a bed: these are things we expect to have in our lives. But the truth is, many people in the world live without some of those luxuries we take for granted. If they were taken away, we would immediately become inconvenienced, and disgruntled.

George Herbert said, "Thou who has given so much to me, give me one more thing: a grateful heart." If you are blessed to have a microwave, odds are, you have running water as well. Don't forget to thank God for both!

DAILY SCRIPTURE READING: Proverbs 1-3

JULY 14

DYING TO LIVE

"I am resolved to never do anything which I should be afraid to do if it were the last hour of my life." –Jonathan Edwards

There was a young man who was dying to graduate and get out of high school. After high school he went to college and was dying to get out of college. After college he was dying to get married. After he got married he was dying to have children. After he had children he was dying to get them through high school and out of the house. After his children got out of the house he was dying to have grandkids. Once he had grandkids he was dying to retire from his job. Once he retired he was dying to travel. After he traveled a few years he was just dying. On his death bed dying he looked back and realized he had never lived.

Many people live in the past. They can't get beyond the failures or successes of yesteryear. Who they are is defined by moments that have come and gone. The good ole days are their moments of glory.

Many people live in the future. They anticipate some huge, fanciful event to come and change their life. Like the fellow who was dying- he was always looking forward to something else. Those who live in the future are always planning and preparing for something else. Certainly we should remember our past; and indeed we should prepare for our future. However, living in the past and the future robs us of enjoying where we are, and who we are in the present. Don't live to die- die to live!

DAILY SCRIPTURE READING: Proverbs 4-6

JULY 15

SPECTATOR SPIRITUALITY

"Creedal Christianity has created a church of people who profess their faith but whose lives are disconnected from their words" –Bill Hull

They crowd the stadiums in droves. They bring their signs, paint their faces, buy their tickets, and lift their voices. They cheer for their team in semi-psychotic fashion. They spend hundreds, if not thousands for the experience; and seem to be enthralled with rapture from start to finish. In religious fashion, they bow down to the "gods" on the field. They breathe in every moment until the final play is complete.

After the game is over they depart with hoarse voices, and empty wallets. They wash off the war-paint, discard the empty pop-corn boxes, and return to their cars, looking for their sanity on the way. The last few hours were "spirit-filled" to say the least, but reality is calling, it is time to go home. It will be days before they return; for some, longer than that. Although they enjoy the weekend adventure, they are just fans, they are not players.

This could be a scenario at any sporting event in America…it could also describe the spiritual reality of many Christians. The modern church is full of spectators; militant perhaps, but spectators nonetheless. Although they involve their lives and invest their time, they are not actually part of the team. The difference between a player and a fan is what you do after the game is over. Live for God daily, not just when the crowd gathers.

DAILY SCRIPTURE READING: Proverbs 7-9

JULY 16

INTENTIONAL DEVOTION

"It's hard to meet the complications of the day if we fail to meet the Creator of the day." –Kenneth Kuykendall

I never use an alarm clock. My wife has always been amazed at my ability to get up without any assistance from obnoxious sounds. To be honest, I am pretty good at it. It is though I have an internal timer that arouses my senses at whatever hour I need to rise. The reason I can get up at whatever time I need to without an alarm is because I intend to do so; I have purposed in my mind to get up. I go to bed with that intention; I rise up to that reality.

The same is true with the devotional life. The reason why many Christians will never know the joy of daily devotion is because they have failed to make it their goal. They intend to do other things: work, play, rest, read, sleep, exercise, go to the ball game, and whatever else. Their schedules are kept and maintained through the forces of priority and intention. In the face of busy lives, they find themselves in an unsuccessful search for meaning, fulfillment, and contentment.

Like any other discipline, daily devotions must be regimented and regularly maintained until it becomes a natural inclination. Devotions should not be robotic or mechanical, but they should be integrated in such a way that we grieve if they are forfeited. It's hard to face the complications of the day if we fail to meet with the Creator of the day.

DAILY SCRIPTURE READING: Proverbs 10-12

JULY 17

GODLINESS AND CONTENTMENT

"The virtue of contentment is the acquiescence of the mind in the lot God has given." –William Ames

In his first epistle to Timothy, the apostle Paul gave us a formula for success. He said, "But godliness with contentment is great gain" (1 Timothy 6:6). When joined together, godliness and contentment produce something very special in the life of a believer. Though this formula sounds simple, many people have it confused.

1. Some Have Neither Godliness nor Contentment. These people live in a state of rebellion to the things of God. They refuse to acknowledge His ways in their life, and are miserable in the process.

2. Some Have Contentment but Lack Godliness. These people enjoy the world and their sin. On the surface they may seem happy, but their joy is superficial and shallow. They accumulate earthly wealth, degree, and position, but give little or no thought to eternal things.

3. Some Have Godliness but Lack Contentment. These people have rules, regulations, and standards by which they live, but lack joy and peace. They may be saved, but they don't enjoy it the way God intends.

4. Some Have Both Godliness and Contentment. These are people who have learned the simple formula of the good life. They live for God and pursue those things that advance the kingdom. They are saved, separated, and satisfied with the Lord. They have great gain.

DAILY SCRIPTURE READING: Proverbs 13-15

JULY 18

MORE THAN RULES

"If God allows you to be stripped of the exterior portions of your life, He means for you to cultivate the interior." –Oswald Chambers

Rules, regulations, requirements, and restrictions. They are all part of life. Every entity, whether business, family, sports, or religion, has expectations, limitations, and consequences to the prescribed order of their operation. Without rules there is utter chaos and I for one need guidelines and boundaries to help clarify my responsibilities. If this is true for the secular, it is certainly true for the development of the spiritual.

All of Scripture, and all of life, follow this pattern. It is certain, we need rules. They keep us safe, they protect us; they are given for the well-being and security of life. However, there has to be more in the spiritual journey than a long, laundry list of do's and don'ts. If we are keeping rules for rule's sake, we have missed the joy of devotion.

Many believers will live and die within the confines of rules and somehow equate those rules as a relationship with Jesus Christ. Shouldn't there be more to the Christian faith than just learning how to dress, how to talk, and how to go to church? Devotion certainly includes those things, but it only includes those things as a byproduct of something deeper: a hunger and thirst to live, know, and experience the presence of God in our daily lives. Embrace rules, adhere to restrictions, but do so out of a relationship with Christ.

DAILY SCRIPTURE READING: Proverbs 16-18

JULY 19

STIRRED, NOT SHAKEN

"Our chief want is someone who will inspire us to be what we know we could be." –Ralph Waldo Emerson

In 2 Timothy, the apostle Paul reminded his young protégé to "stir up the gift of God that is in you." Timothy had been facing some very difficult situations as a young pastor. He grew discouraged and disheartened by the false doctrine and worldly tendencies of his congregation. By all implications, it seemed as though Timothy was tempted to leave his pastorate and pursue other options.

To say the least, Timothy was shaken. He was shaken by the failures of others and the fear of his own inabilities. You and I can certainly relate to Timothy's plight. When you look at the condition of the world, the apathy of the modern church, and the prevailing wickedness of society, it is easy to get shaken. But the words of Paul serve as a reminder to us all: we are not to be shaken, we are to be stirred!

The catalyst for our stirring is none other than the gift of God. This "gift" refers to the calling of God placed upon Timothy's life. His calling was confirmation enough. However, it was up to Timothy to "stir it up." If you are disheartened in this hour, remember, God has called you to a specific purpose. Every now and then you should remind yourself of God's power in your life, and realize the only thing that stands against your fear is the call of God. When it feels like you are being shaken, remind yourself to get stirred!

DAILY SCRIPTURE READING: Proverbs 19-21

JULY 20

WE ARE ONE IN CHRIST

"Our entire confidence and acceptance before God is based solely upon the fact that Jesus is our legal representative." –Jerry Bridges

In the late 1800's, Chile and Argentina were positioned against each other for war. It seemed as though conflict was inevitable; however, during Holy Week, Monsignor Benavente preached a message of peace and hope on Easter Sunday. The sermon influenced the leadership of the church in such a way that a campaign for peace between the countries was underway. Slowly the mindset of the people began to turn against warfare and toward harmony.

With the movement now in full swing, a peace treaty was officially signed by the two governments which promised arbitration for future conflicts. As a result of the agreement, all the guns of the frontier fortress was melted down and used to create a bronze statue of Jesus Christ. Erected 13,000 feet up a mountain in Buenos Aires, the statue stands as a monument of grace. Beneath the statue an inscription reads, "He is our peace who hath made both one" Ephesians 2:14.

Christ Jesus is the end of the conflict. His death on the cross abolished the eternal battle with sin. He united humanity into one body and one faith. Today we stand with Him in victory, claiming His promise of eternal life. We can lay down our guns, and rest in His peace atop the mountain.

DAILY SCRIPTURE READING: Proverbs 22-23

JULY 21

ARE YOU RUSHED?

"Our problem is not too little time, but making better use of the time we have." –Oswald Chambers

It seems like everyone is constantly on the move these days. We go from one stop to the next without blinking an eye. We hurriedly check items off the proverbial list just so we can get to the next thing. Our schedules are full, our responsibilities are many, and our stress level is elevated. What are we to do when we feel RUSHED?

R- Resist the urge to do everything. You are only one person and you cannot do it all. If you juggle too many things, make some cuts.

U- Undertake assignments that glorify God. Abide within your calling and vocation; and whatever you do, do for the glory of God.

S- Schedule your calendar with eternity in view. Don't crowd your datebook with trivial and meaningless events. Keep your affection on things above, and your calendar will appreciate you for it.

H- Hurry up and get some rest. I certainly do not promote laziness or lethargy, but sometimes you need to step away from the hustle and bustle and get some rest and relaxation-Jesus did.

E- Energize your spirit through a devotional life. Nothing revitalizes the soul like a fresh encounter with God. Rise early and rise often to meet the Lord.

D- Delegate some tasks to others. Ask others for help, especially if you are in leadership. Utilize your team for the most efficient results.

DAILY SCRIPTURE READING: Proverbs 24-26

JULY 22

PUT LAUGHTER IN YOUR LIFE

"All the days of the afflicted are evil: but he that is of a merry heart hath a continual feast."—Proverbs 15:15

I certainly agree that we have much to be concerned over during these turbulent, wavering times; but in spite of all the heralded doom and gloom, the church needs to reclaim its joy. Sometimes I wonder if people resist salvation simply because of their fear of becoming like the calloused and miserable Christians they encounter from week to week. Hypocrisy at its greatest height is to tell others of the sufficiency of Christ while wearing a frown on our face.

I wonder, do you laugh very often?

I asked myself that question the other day, and to be honest, I was not pleased with the answer. I laugh, but not as much as I should. I want to laugh more. I am not talking about silliness or dim-witted jesting; I am talking about good, clean, hearty, knee-slapping laughter. If laughter is not a part of your life it should be.

Laughter is biblical, it is free, it provides escape, it produces joy, it is infectious, it is healthy, it feeds the soul, and it strengthens relationships. So go ahead and try it. Laugh out loud right now and see if it doesn't make you feel better. Learn a new joke, share it with friends, smile a little more, and reclaim laughter as a part of your every-day life.

DAILY SCRIPTURE READING: Proverbs 27-29

JULY 23

I'M NOT LUCKY, I'M FREE

"Our biggest problem in life is not getting the victory, it is keeping the victory." –Kenneth Kuykendall

There is a dog in our neighborhood who is notorious for escaping his leash. His name is Lucky, and he has, at times, been on the loose for days just roaming the subdivision. His elusive behavior makes him very difficult to catch.

Recently, we heard a loud scrapping noise outside of our home. When we traced the sound to the street, we saw where Lucky had once again escaped. However, this time he didn't break his leash; he actually pulled the metal plate and pole out of the ground from which his leash was tied. Needless to say, Lucky was on the loose, but moving very slowly. This time, Lucky was not that lucky. His owners quickly responded and easily captured their wayward dog.

Many Christians live the same way. They are "loose" from the bondage of sin, but they are dragging around things that slow them down. Living in such a way makes it a lot easier for the capture to take hold of their lives.

Christ said, "If the Son therefore shall make you free, ye shall be free indeed" (John 8:36). Jesus did not die so that your sins could be tied around your neck. He died to liberate you from a life of bondage and oppression. That doesn't make you lucky, that makes you free!

DAILY SCRIPTURE READING: Proverbs 30-31

JULY 24

BELIEVERS AT THE BUFFET

"Stand fast therefore in the liberty wherewith Christ hath made us free, and be not entangled again…" –Galatians 5:1

As a child, I loved eating at buffets. The buffet not only meant a wide variety of food, but it meant unlimited access to as much of it as you wanted. Skip the salad, go straight to the pizza, chicken-leg, taco and mashed potato combo. Top it off with freshly-baked cookies and sprinkled-covered ice-cream and you have experienced "fine dining" at its best. C'mon, what kid doesn't love that?

The older I get, however, the more I realize something: sometimes you need to say "no" even if you are allowed to say "yes." Sometimes, for the betterment of life and health, we must restrict and refrain ourselves from selfish and sinful desires. The liberty we have in Christ does not give us a free, unlimited pass to frequent the world's buffet.

The apostle Paul spoke of this when he said, "Stand fast therefore in the liberty wherewith Christ hath made us free, and be not entangled again with the yoke of bondage" (Galatians 5:1). The believer is free in Christ and should glory in the liberty of grace. But God never intends liberty to be used as a means of indulgence and worldly pleasure. The price has been paid, and we can make our rounds at the buffet. But just because we can, doesn't mean that we should. Godliness is saying no, even when you have the liberty to say yes.

DAILY SCRIPTURE READING: Ecclesiastes 1-4

JULY 25

WRESTLING AND RESTING

"Surely I have behaved and quieted myself, as a child that is weaned from his mother: my soul is even as a weaned child." –King David

When my children were smaller we would "wrestle" them to sleep. As the evenings grew late, we would cradle them in our arms and go into battle. They wanted their freedom, but we wanted their silence. They wanted to play, but we wanted them to rest. We knew what was best for them; they needed their sleep. In our arms, they would wiggle, twist, squirm, and resist. As the battle raged, the inevitable moment came when they grew still, became relaxed, and fell asleep. The arms in which they fervently protested were now the very arms in which they were faithfully protected.

I must confess: like Jacob of old, I too have wrestled in the arms of God. With an anxious, restless spirit, I have tried to fight for my freedom. With the will of a rebel I have wiggled, twisted, squirmed, and resisted His melodic song and gentle sway. Many times I have tired and exhausted myself in His divine grasp only to fall fast asleep in the very arms I fervently opposed.

But I too have awakened in the sweet presence of His protective grace. Oddly enough, it is the struggle that gives way to peaceful, restful sleep. Because God is our Father, He is willing to endure the squirming. He knows the wrestling makes way for the best rest.

DAILY SCRIPTURE READING: Ecclesiastes 5-8

JULY 26

MORE IS LESS, LESS IS MORE

"Eden is that old-fashioned house that we dwell in every day, without suspecting our abode until we drive away." –Emily Dickinson

There is a four-letter word that destroys, hinders, and greatly restricts our lives. It is the word "more." The culture at large has bought into the notion that we need more; and so we work fervently to have more. Technology gives us more ways to communicate, and more ways to stay connected. Our economy gives us more possessions than any other people group in history. Our entertainment industries give us more options for leisure than ever before. We constantly long and look for more.

However, with the abundance of more things, we also have more deadlines, more meetings, more responsibilities, and more activities. As a result, we have more stress, more headaches, more depression, more physical constraints, and more issues.

Ironically, in the pursuit of more, we actually have less: less time, less joy, less peace, less service, less contentment. In this age of constant progression, we seem to be moving nowhere very quickly. We have more, but we have more of the wrong things; at least things that bring little value to life. In our attempts to live successfully, we have failed to live simply. What we need more of is Christ. More of Him in our hearts. More of Him in our pursuits. More of Him in our relationships. Only then will more be more. Without Him, more is really less.

DAILY SCRIPTURE READING: Ecclesiastes 9-12

JULY 27
YOUR LAST DAY ON EARTH

"He who provides for this life but takes no care for eternity is wise for a moment, but a fool forever." –John Tillotson

Have you ever thought about your last day on earth? There will come a day when you wake up for the last time, or go to sleep for the last time. There will come a day when you eat your last meal, hug your child for the last time, or kiss your spouse for the last time. There is coming a day when you make your last phone call, watch your last movie, or send your last text. There will be a day when sing your last song, pray your last prayer, and speak your last words.

Statistics indicate that 1.8 people die every second which equals 108 people per minute, which equals 6480 per hour, which equals 155,520 per day, which equals 1,088,640 per week, which equals over 56,000,000 per year –every single one of them will have a last day on earth.

The Bible calls death an "appointment." It is appointed unto men once to die. This appointment cannot be postponed, rescheduled, or cancelled. And life does not end after death. As a matter of fact, the writer of Hebrews said that "judgment" occurs after death is realized. We must all stand before our Creator to give an account for our lives. If death is certain and judgment is inevitable, we would do ourselves well to be ready for our last day on earth. The only way to ensure that you will finish right is to be right with God right now! Get ready today for your last day on earth.

DAILY SCRIPTURE READING: Song of Solomon 1-8

JULY 28

LOW-BUDGET WORSHIP

"We are called to an everlasting preoccupation with God." –A.W. Tozer

In his book, *King Me*, Steve Farrar makes an insightful observation concerning worship. He said, "In the Old Testament, they didn't turn down the lights and set a mood. They slit the throat of animals, poured out their blood, gutted their intestines, and burned them in the fire. That sacrificial system is no longer in place because the Lord was the Lamb of God who took away the sins of the world. But there was a reality in that worship and it was centered in the truth that sin is terrible and horrible and that forgiveness of sin is not cheap."

Worship is not a mood or atmosphere that can be set by a digital board. Certainly God has given us lights, sound, and technology to help us in the furtherance of the Gospel; and I believe they can be incorporated in the worship hour. However, when we rely on those things in particular to lead us into the presence of God, we cheapen the act of worship.

The very act of worship suggests a cost on our part.

Let me ask you something: what does it cost you from week to week, nay, day to day to worship your Savior? If you are on a low-budget worship, make the necessary adjustments. The greater your investment, the greater your worship experience.

DAILY SCRIPTURE READING: Isaiah 1-4

JULY 29
BETTER FAITHFUL THAN FAMOUS

"God estimates us not by the position we are in, but by the way we fulfill it."–Tryon Edwards

The Battle of San Juan Hill was the bloodiest and deadliest combat of the Spanish-American War. The fight for this territory gave the Rough Riders (a name given to the United States Calvary by the American Press) their greatest victory. Leading the way was a man who would become the future president of the United States, Theodore Roosevelt.

As a result of this great victory, Roosevelt became one of the most famous men in the land. His leadership skills and capabilities quickly propelled him to a position of recognition. However, in a letter written to one of his sons during that time, Roosevelt penned down these words describing his attitude and approach to the newfound fame. He simply wrote, "Better faithful than famous."

These words should be the motto for the soldier in the army of God. Our great Captain has not called us to fame, fortune, popularity, and name-recognition; He was called us to battle. And in the midst of battle it is better to be faithful than famous. Tryon Edwards said, "God estimates us not by the position we are in, but by the way we fulfill it." Whatever God has called you to do, do it "as unto the Lord." Be faithful to your calling, and be assured, God will be faithful to you.

DAILY SCRIPTURE READING: Isaiah 5-8

JULY 30

DON'T BLAME GOD FOR THE BRUISES

"The most important thought that ever occupied my mind is that of my individual responsibility to God." –Daniel Webster

There is a story told about a man who became so obsessed with the sovereignty of God that he had difficulty functioning in society. His fatalistic approach to life caused him to question everything he did. One day while walking down a flight of steps he carelessly plunged himself headfirst. When he reached the bottom of the staircase he picked himself up, dusted himself off, and said, "Well, I am glad that is over."

The sovereignty of God is a reality of Scripture and life. He is in control. All of creation was made by Him, for Him, and sustained through Him. However, in the midst of His sovereignty, God created mankind with a free will. Such a will gives man the ability to make decisions. Those decisions have consequences which simply unfold in a fallen world. This in no way limits or restricts God's sovereignty; as a matter of fact, it actually promotes it. As one writer put it, "God is so sovereign that He can give us a free will and can still be sovereign."

However, some things take place as a result of natural process. If you willingly toss yourself down a flight of steps, you, by your own volition, endure the consequences thereof. Free will gives choice, but it also holds us accountable to those choices that are made. In other words, you can't blame God for the bruises.

DAILY SCRIPTURE READING: Isaiah 9-12

JULY 31

THE RARITY OF REVIVAL

*"We don't need more methods on file,
we need more men on fire."* –Vance Havner

The modern church has learned how to create a pretty effective religious experience. Lights, visuals, sound, slides, screens, smoke, stage, mood, and atmosphere all play into the state-of-the-art modern worship service. The problem, however, is that in spite of all the wonderful, sensational, and extraordinary experiences we have, very seldom does the church have actual encounters with God.

Nothing, absolutely nothing, can duplicate, replicate, or authenticate the presence of God except for the presence of God. There are no substitutes. But substitutes are what we usually get. Like the moneychangers in the temple, we happily sell people a worship experience that offers no transformation; all the while, the tables in our own hearts are being turned over by the Messiah who simply longs for our affection and attention.

It is evident: we need revival. But have you ever wondered why we rarely see it? I am not contending that it doesn't exist; neither do I promote revival as a lost cause. With fervent heart I believe God can still speak to dead, dry bones. But the key to revival is intention and repentance. If God's people do not intend to seek God, turn from sin, and thirst for His presence, revival will only be read in the catalogues of history.

DAILY SCRIPTURE READING: Isaiah 13-17

AUGUST

AUGUST 1
DON'T BE USELESS

"Do not forget that children learn more by the eye than they do by the ear." –J.C. Ryle

At seventeen years of age, he was aimless and without direction. Although he was from a privileged family, he couldn't find his lot in life. His disinterest and indifference gave way to the nickname "Useless."

Sensing the need for discipline, his father knew he had to do something to help his son; so he sent him to West Point. "Useless" fervently fought his father about the decision, but eventually gave in.

After several months of being away from home, he returned to his family a changed man. He was confident, poised, and resolved about his direction in life. No one called him "Useless" anymore; instead, they called him by his real name –Ulysses. Ulysses S. Grant would go on to win the Civil War and eventually become president of the United States.

Had it not been for his father's resolve, Ulysses might have been "Useless" his entire life. All he needed was some direction and encouragement. As parents, we have a great responsibility to point our children in the right direction. We are to help them find their God-given purpose so they can use their God-given talents. It is only then they can become "Useful" in the work of the Lord.

DAILY SCRIPTURE READING: Isaiah 18-22

AUGUST 2

I KNOW THE WHO

"Strength of my heart, I rest in Thee. Fulfill thy purposes through me." –Amy Carmichael

When adversity strikes our lives the natural response is to ask questions. What is God's purpose? What did I do wrong? For what reason did this occur? Why did God permit this trial? How will I survive? When will it all end? Sickness, loss of job, severed relationships, the death of a loved one, emotional distress. All of these things, and many more, give way to a multitude of questions.

But I have discovered something: when you know the WHO, you don't have to know the why, how, what, or when.

Jerry Bridges contends, "Trusting God is worked out in the arena that has no boundaries. We do not know the extent, the duration, or the frequency of the painful, adverse circumstances in which we must trust God. We are always coping with the unknown." And perhaps this is the most difficult part of adversity –the unknown. But I repeat, when you know the WHO, you don't have to know anything else.

Our adversity should always be endured with the understanding that God is loving and kind and would never allow anything into our lives that does not eventually become valuable. As Spurgeon stated, "I have learned to kiss the wave that throws me against the Rock of Ages."

DAILY SCRIPTURE READING: Isaiah 23-27

AUGUST 3

TOE-LESS TRIUMPH

"If I were to alter any part of God's plan I would only spoil it." –John Newton

The year was 1970. The New Orleans Saints were trailing the Detroit Lions by one point with just seconds remaining in the fourth quarter. Place-kicker Tom Dempsey took the field to attempt the longest field goal in NFL history. The crowd cheered passionately as Dempsey not only set an NFL record, but edged out the Detroit Lions to win the game 19-17. Oh, and by the way, Dempsey had no toes.

You read that correctly. Dempsey was born without any fingers or toes on his right side. When asked if he had an unfair advantage in kicking the game-winning goal, he replied, "Unfair eh? Why don't you try kicking a 63-yard field goal to win it with 2 seconds left while wearing a square shoe; oh, yeah and no toes either."

Some would contend that Dempsey's handicap was actually his greatest strength. I believe God would agree. Dempsey, like all of us, was created uniquely by God. Every imperfection, disability, weakness, and handicap we may have is ultimately designed for the glory of God. Ironically, it is through weakness that the strength of God is made perfect. So whether you are a toeless place-kicker or a short-statured preacher, give God the glory He deserves through your weakness –it just might be your biggest strength.

DAILY SCRIPTURE READING: Isaiah 28-30

AUGUST 4

ASKING FOR HELP

"In prayer we shift the center of living from self-consciousness to self-surrender." –Abraham Joshua Heschel

John Newton, author of *Amazing Grace*, watched his wife die slowly from cancer. Suddenly struck with grief and pain, he asked God to help him endure the emotional despair of seeing his spouse suffer so greatly from her condition. And God did.

During her fight, Newton not only took care of his wife, but he maintained his duties as a minister. His preaching scheduled was not altered at all during her suffering. He actually preached on the day of her death; he also preached three times while she lied in state at their home; and preached her funeral sermon with conviction and power.

When asked how he was able to maintain his strength during such a sorrowful time, Newton replied, "The promises of God are true; surely the Lord will help me, if I am willing to be helped. We are often led to indulge that unprofitable grief which both our duty and our peace require us to resist to the utmost of our power. I am willing to be helped, without reserve"

One of the reasons we struggle during times of sorrow is because we refuse to ask God for help. James said, "Ye have not because ye ask not." God is willing to help when we are willing to ask.

DAILY SCRIPTURE READING: Isaiah 31-35

AUGUST 5

VICTORY OVER SIN

"The way to conquer sin is not working hard to change our deeds, but trusting Jesus to change our desires." –David Platt

Sin corrupts, condemns, and consumes. It leads to dangerous, destructive, and deadly consequences. It is not only a problem for the sinner, but for the saint as well. I say with full persuasion –God wants us to have victory over sin, and has provided the ultimate sacrifice for sin in the death, burial, and resurrection of Jesus Christ. So once we are saved, how do we maintain and keep that victory?

Obviously, Christ does the keeping. Our standing in Him, and Him alone, validates our righteousness before God. But as born-again believers, we are not altogether exempt from the process of sanctification. If you are struggling with sin, there is victory:

1. Repent. The first thing to do is turn from your sin right now, and turn to the living God for help, strength, and forgiveness.

2. Restructure. Set new boundaries in your life. Learn to live within those parameters. Stay away from places and people who bring temptation.

3. Rely. Lean upon the indwelling power of the Holy Spirit of God. You cannot do it by yourself. Seek His counsel every single day.

4. Relate. Work on your relationship with God. Talk to Him, read His Word, involve yourself in His work. He wants you to have victory!

DAILY SCRIPTURE READING: Isaiah 36-41

AUGUST 6

HOW BUSY ARE YOU?

"Let us never forget that what we are is more important than what we do." –Hudson Taylor

We are busy people, traveling on busy streets, with busy calendars, living busy lives. In the name of progress and advancement, we fill our datebooks with multiple appointments, engagements, and meetings. I certainly do not promote laziness or apathy, but I contend we are, at times, overwhelmed with too many conflicting responsibilities. This leads to physical burnout and spiritual fatigue. What are we to do if we find ourselves too busy?

B. Balance Your Life with Order. When we lack balance and order, we set ourselves up for unnecessary activities. A lot of our busyness is the result of not doing the little things properly.

U. Understand Your Mortality. Life is precious, time is fleeting. Those things we worry and stress over are really trivial in light of eternity.

S. Simplify Things. If necessary, cut some things out of your schedule. Get back to the basics. Realize that you do not have to be everything to everyone. Live for God, love your family, and let some things go.

Y. Yield Each Day to the Will of God. Begin each day by asking the Lord to reveal His perfect will for that 24-hour period. Many times we are dealing with things that were never ordered by God.

DAILY SCRIPTURE READING: Isaiah 42-44

AUGUST 7

GOD KEEPS HIS PROMISES

"The Lord is not slack concerning His promise, as some men count slackness; but is longsuffering to usward." –The Apostle Peter

An elderly Christian lay on his death bed and called for the pastor. As the man of God entered into the room, the dying saint said, "Preacher, all of my life I have relied on the promises of God, but now, in the hour of my death, I cannot recall one promise by which I lived." The pastor took the man by the hand and said, "Dear brother, it may very well be that we forget the promises of God. But the One who made the promise has no trouble at all remembering what He said."

It is true. God keeps His promises regardless of our ability to remember or embrace them. The apostle Peter said it this way, "The Lord is not slack concerning His promise, as some men count slackness; but is longsuffering to us-ward" (1 Peter 3:9).

On any given day, my children receive promises I have made them; many to which they did not even ask. I fulfill my promises to them out of love and desire to provide for their needs. As young children they do not know what is best for their lives; they, at times, do not know what to ask for. But regardless, they are recipients of my care and provision. Therefore, don't be dismayed. God knows what is best for your life, and He is weaving His promises through every situation. You may forget to claim them, but He never forgets to keep them.

DAILY SCRIPTURE READING: Isaiah 45-48

AUGUST 8

GIVE SOMETHING GREATER

"You have not fulfilled every duty, unless you have fulfilled that of being pleasant." –Charles Buxtom

Leo Tolstoy, the Russian writer, was walking along a street one day when he passed by a common beggar. The man pleaded with Tolstoy for some money. As the great writer searched his pockets for a coin, he said, "Please do not be angry with me, my brother, but I have nothing with me. If I did I would gladly give it to you."

The beggar seemed stunned by the reply of Tolstoy, and humbly replied, "Dear sir, you have given me more than I could ask, for you have called me brother."

Christian Bovee said, "Kindness is a language the dumb can speak, and the deaf can hear." It is also a language the sinner can understand. Peter and John faced a similar situation in Acts 3. They didn't have a coin to give to the beggar, but what they had was the power of the gospel. They could have easily ignored the poor man's plea, but in kindness and love they extended a hand of mercy. When they touched his hand, they in essence, touched his heart.

Sinners are more apt to hear the gospel through the voice of kindness. We are not only instructed to lead men to Christ, we are called to love men to Christ. When you can't give a coin, give something greater– compassion.

DAILY SCRIPTURE READING: Isaiah 49-53

AUGUST 9
THIS DAY AND THAT DAY

"Knowing we will stand before God on that day should change the way we think about this day." –Kenneth Kuykendall

The Bema Seat was an elevated place of judicial and official business in Greek cities. At the Bema Seat, athletes would be evaluated on how they played the Olympic Games. Paul had this place in mind when he wrote to the Corinthian believers. He said, "For we must all appear before the judgment seat of Christ; that every one may receive the things done in his body, according to that he hath done, whether it be good or bad" (2 Corinthians 5:10).

All believers will stand before God to give an account of their lives. We will not be judged for our sins at the Bema Seat; Christ judged our sins at the cross of Calvary. Rather, our works and service for the Lord will be judged. Our behavior, intentions, words, relationships, responsibilities, and compliance to God's call will come under investigation.

Knowing we will stand before God on that day should change the way we think about this day. In other words, when we face this day with that day in mind, our actions, affection, and attitude should change. We should live every day as though it is the only day to be examined at the Judgment Seat of Christ. Take inventory of this day, because on that day, this day will be examined.

DAILY SCRIPTURE READING: Isaiah 54-58

AUGUST 10

BURIED WITH BITTERNESS

"Unresolved feelings deposit themselves in the strata of our souls, waiting for the other person to die." –Gordon MacDonald

A man by the name of Otis Pratt was bitter over the treatment he received as a sculptor and artist. He carved his bitterness into a tombstone in the Greenwood Cemetery of Lorain County, Ohio. Since his death in 1921, many people have read these words:

"Stranger, I lived in an age when law and respect clung to the rich and shunned the poor; when money and fashion had the brains and talent went over the water for want of free schools of art supported by our government. Such were the conditions which caused my landscape to decay with me as nature shows it. Farewell."

It is obvious that Pratt never got over the mistreatment he received as a struggling artist. His legacy was never captured in a painting or sculpture; unfortunately it was captured in bitter words engraved in marble.

John Courson said, "This is what bitterness does: it is like taking a bottle of poison, swallowing it, and waiting for the other person to die." Otis Pratt apparently took the poison and died with a sour and unforgiving spirit. Perhaps, hiding in the recess of your heart, bitterness lurks. If so, bury your bitterness before you are buried with it.

DAILY SCRIPTURE READING: Isaiah 59-63

AUGUST 11
NOT-SO-BIG, BIG MOMENTS

"Sometimes God dresses the miraculous in the garments of the mundane." –Kenneth Kuykendall

Little, insignificant moments. They fill our lives. I used to call it boredom, but the older I get, I call it "blessings." Taking out the trash. Watching an old movie with my children. Walking the park with my wife. Doing paper work. Reading a good book. Reading a dull book. Cutting the grass. Brushing my teeth.

I have come to believe that monotony is underrated. Sometimes God dresses the miraculous in the garments of the mundane. Think about how much we take for granted. We give little thought to the daily and consistent blessings of God. However, if those "little" things were extracted from our lives we would find ourselves with gaping holes of discontent.

So learn to appreciate the predictable. Be thankful for the "humdrum." Glorify God in the simple, small, and seemingly insignificant moments of life. For in those moments, God is preserving us from tragedy, trials, and tears.

Take a few moments today and be thankful for the little things. The smallest of circumstances shine with the goodness and providence of God.

DAILY SCRIPTURE READING: Isaiah 64-66

AUGUST 12

THE RIGHT THING TO DO

"The pursuit of integrity includes a growing coherence between public and private life." –Mel Lawrenz

In 2001, medical supply manufacturer, Baxter International, experienced some major issues with a few of their products. Statistics and reports showed that a large number of their dialysis patients had passed away. CEO, Harry Kraemer launched an internal investigation and hired outside experts to search for potential flaws in their operation.

Kraemer received immediate criticism from his shareholders over the investigation. They contended that he should have exercised damage control and placed the blame somewhere else. Instead, Kraemer proceeded with the investigation, removed particular products from the market, and shut down the troublesome division of the company. These moves cost Baxter International $189 million. He reported the problems to rival manufacturers so that they would not have to incur the same expenses or liabilities. That year, Baxter suggested to his board that they reduce his performance bonus by forty percent.

When asked why he would go to such lengths, Baxter simply responded, "It is the right thing to do."

Sometimes the right thing to do is the hardest thing to do; but without any doubt, it is always the best thing to do.

DAILY SCRIPTURE READING: Jeremiah 1-3

AUGUST 13

CONVENIENT-STORE FAITH

"Knowledge of the truth comes with the surrender of the will." –R.A. Torrey

Cravings. Sometimes I have them late at night. I call it the chocolate-itch; and it will not go away until I drown a few Reese's cups (chocolate manna) with a tall glass of Mayfield milk. The problem, however, is that I have three growing boys in my household, and they devour any and everything that contains sugar. I cannot tell you how many late-night runs I have made to the convenient store near my home to scratch my itch.

They call it the convenient store for a reason: it is convenient. I can be there in just a few minutes. Everything is easily accessible. No long aisles. No far-away parking spaces. No buggies with noisy wheels. In and out with ease, and my chocolate delight is in hand. But as you know, the convenience of the convenient store is reflected in the inconvenient prices. Yes, you will pay more at the convenient store.

Many believers want convenient-store Christianity. They look for something quick, something easy, something to scratch their short-term itch. But the truth is, living with such convenience is expensive. Be sure to inventory enough faith for those late-night itches. Living without it is sure to be more costly in the long-run.

DAILY SCRIPTURE READING: Jeremiah 4-6

AUGUST 14

DON'T LET THEM FALL

"No one can whistle a symphony. It takes an orchestra to play it." –Alford E. Luccock

In 1793, God placed a burden in the heart of missionary William Carey. That burden was for the lost and dying people of India. Just before his departure into the mission field, someone told Carey, "There is a gold mine in India, but it seems almost as deep as the center of the earth." William Carey replied, "I will venture down, but remember that you must hold the ropes!"

The work of the Lord involves teamwork. It takes each individual fulfilling their particular function as they labor in the vocation of their particular calling. Although William Carey is named the "father of modern missions," it took others holding the ropes for him as he ventured into the "gold mine."

Teamwork in the ministry is not only a powerful force, it is a necessary reality. We are instructed to strive together, pray together, labor together, come together, work together, and gather together. Furthermore, we are called together, knit together, joined together; and will one day be caught up together, raised together, so that we may sit together in heavenly places.

You may never travel to India, preach a sermon, sing a song, or teach a class; but you can hold the ropes for those who do. Don't let them fall.

DAILY SCRIPTURE READING: Jeremiah 7-9

AUGUST 15

DO YOU PRY OR PRAY?

"The greatest tragedy in life is not unanswered prayer; but unoffered prayer." –E.M. Bounds

When text-messaging first came out, I did not really like it. It was difficult to type the words and I felt it was an impersonal way to communicate. However, after getting used to the format, I have learned to love it. It is a quick way to communicate, and it allows me to keep at task while engaging in various conversations with others.

Not long ago I sent a text message to a friend in the ministry. He was dealing with some personal issues, and I wanted to encourage him with a few words of kindness. I intended to say in the message, "I have been praying for you." Well, as you know, many times the words don't type out the way you want them to. Instead of saying "I have been praying for you" it came up, "I have been prying on you." Big difference, huge difference.

Thankfully I was able to correct it before I sent over the message; but as I looked at the words on my phone, I wondered which was more accurate. Do we pry on people as much as we pray for people? We look at their lives, we question their motives, we examine their faults, we discuss their attitudes. Let's admit it, sometimes we pry. The next time you find yourself prying on someone, try praying for them. It could save you from an embarrassing text.

DAILY SCRIPTURE READING: Jeremiah 10-13

AUGUST 16

SNAKES IN THE GARAGE

"Almost every man wastes part of his life in attempts to display qualities which he does not possess." –Samuel Johnson

Recently my parents found a copperhead snake in their garage. Like most people, they were unnerved at its discovery. It was coiled up in the shadows and could have easily struck at them in passing by. My dad quickly "removed" the snake –yes, both halves. Two days later, they were alarmed when, yet again, they found another snake trying to make its way into the same location.

When I heard the news, I jokingly told them, "If you were living right, you wouldn't have to worry about snakes in the garage." One week later I would have to eat those words.

I pulled into the driveway late one evening after a revival service. Waiting for the garage door to open, I noticed a black, squiggly line making its way into the shadows. You guessed it; I too, had a snake in the garage. I immediately remembered my words of rebuke, "If you were living right, you wouldn't have to worry about snakes in the garage."

Satan, the old serpent, is constantly on the prowl; he is trying to find a way into our lives. So we shouldn't assume that someone is living in sin if or when he is attacked. You, too, may have a snake in your garage, and not even know it.

DAILY SCRIPTURE READING: Jeremiah 14-17

AUGUST 17

WHEN YOU'RE NOT THERE

"You may not go to church every day, but you are the church every day." –Kenneth Kuykendall

The Bible is emphatic about church attendance. The writer of Hebrews challenges us with convicting words, "Not forsaking the assembling of ourselves together, as the manner of some is; but exhorting one another: and so much the more, as ye see the day approaching" (Hebrews 10:25). Have you ever thought about the effect your absence has in the House of God? When you are not there:

- The body of the congregation is incomplete
- Your voice is not heard in the worship and singing of the saints
- You cannot actively serve others who may need your gifts
- You cannot contribute in the offering
- You do not receive the Word in a preaching format
- You miss out on corporate prayer
- You forfeit fellowship
- You send a message to the youth that missing church is acceptable

Faithfulness to the House of God is still a required characteristic for believers. From time to time we all need sabbaticals, vacations, and sick days. But when missing church becomes a regular practice, we not only stymie our spiritual growth, we weaken the abilities of the entire congregation.

DAILY SCRIPTURE READING: Jeremiah 18-22

AUGUST 18

PRAYER PARTNER QUALITIES

"When you pray for anyone, you tend to modify your personal attitude toward them." –Norman Vincent Peale

Oswald Chambers said, "Prayer does not fit us for a greater work; it is the greater work." We all know the importance and power of prayer, but for some reason, it is an area of weakness for most believers. Bearing the burden of emotional and spiritual weights can fatigue your soul, discourage your heart, and stymie your growth. That is why the Bible instructs us to pray with, and for, one another. We often struggle in prayer because we go at it all alone.

Rarely does a single soldier obtain victory in his own strength. It is seldom that a farmer yields a fruitful crop without the assistance of many laborers. Churches and families are never constituted without the power of partnership. In short, we need one another. Having a prayer partner will not take away the bumps on the journey of life, but it can make the experience more tolerable. However, before you pick up anyone for the ride, you should make sure you are partnering with the right person.

1. Make sure your prayer partner is someone you can trust
2. Make sure they are themselves committed to spiritual growth
3. Make sure they promote God's will over their own advice
4. Make sure they attempt to live by the standard of God's Word
5. Make sure they will hold you accountable

DAILY SCRIPTURE READING: Jeremiah 23-25

AUGUST 19

SPIRITUAL ANOREXIA

"Man shall not live by bread alone, but by every word that proceedeth from the mouth of God." –Jesus Christ

In the United States of America, nearly 24 million people suffer from anorexia. There are a variety of reasons for the disorder: genetics, stress, depression, abuse, hormones, and low self-esteem. In its simplest and purest definition, anorexia is a loss of appetite for food. Someone who deals with this serious condition typically has a distorted view of their body, and goes to drastic measures to alter their appearance. They often develop a disdain for food and drop to an unhealthy weight.

As serious as this condition is, there is something even more deadly – a loss of appetite for the Word of God. Some believers are suffering from spiritual anorexia.

Imagine going for days or weeks without little or no food. If you maintained such a practice for long periods of time, your body would suffer greatly. The same holds true with the lack of consumption of God's Word. The Lord Himself said, "Man shall not live by bread alone, but by every word that proceedeth from the mouth of God." When we fail to have a daily intake of the Bible, we slowly starve the spiritual man. Don't allow the things of this world to keep you from dining with the King. God has prepared a feast for you in His Word. Take hold of it daily, and throughout the day.

DAILY SCRIPTURE READING: Jeremiah 26-29

AUGUST 20

BE A BLESSING TO THE YOUTH

"Do you not know that your children have precious and immortal souls within them? They are not all flesh." –Cotton Mather

If we are going to make an impact in the lives of young people, we must do it quickly, emphatically, and intentionally –they grow up pretty fast, and if you don't influence their faith, heart, and mind at a tender age, it is certain, someone else will. I know many young people who are growing into fine young Christians. And when you consider the context of their daily lives, such spiritual growth is a praise-worthy accomplishment.

Their world is vastly different than the world of their parents. The culture at large fights for their attention and affection. They are exposed and connected, much sooner, to pervasive and wicked worldviews. They are inundated with relative thinking and humanistic mindsets. They are pressured to adopt a "coexist" philosophy of life, which ironically promotes toleration for all views except Christianity. If the church fails to make investments into the youth department, the church will eventually cease to exist. I, for one, do not believe they are the "church of tomorrow." I believe they are a vital part of today's church.

Make a special effort to encourage a young person this week. Give them a call, send them a card, call out their name in prayer, give them a gift. Make an investment in their lives and enjoy the dividends for generations to come.

DAILY SCRIPTURE READING: Jeremiah 30-31

AUGUST 21
BURN YOUR PLOW

"I realized that, as the leader, I have to be all in, or all gone." –Hans Finzel

The call of Elisha into the prophetic ministry was an unusual event. The nineteenth chapter of 1 Kings records the occasion. Elijah, the seasoned national prophet of Israel walked by Elisha, the young farm boy, and threw his mantle upon him while he was working. Elisha chased after his newfound mentor and began ministering to him. However, just before he followed Elijah, Elisha did something amazing – he burned his plow, and killed his oxen.

Quite literally, Elisha made sure he had nothing to go back to. For Elisha, there was no plan B. He accepted the invitation of God, and sold-out to his call. He realized that in order to latch on to the will of God, he had to first let go of those things that could potentially hold him back.

Most believers want the blessings of God on their lives; however, when it comes to letting go of certain things, we have a tendency to keep hanging on. Those things we hold on to can keep us from fully and completely following after God. We all have our plows. But God calls us to set them aflame. What holds you back? What keeps you from wholly pursuing God? Whatever it is –let it go. Get on fire for God, and with that very fire, burn your plow.

DAILY SCRIPTURE READING: Jeremiah 32-34

AUGUST 22

ONE-WAY TICKETS

"Before we can conquer the world,
we must first conquer the self." –Oswald Sanders

Missionary A.W. Milne felt a strong and intense call from God for the people of the New Hebrides in the South Pacific. Although he knew about the headhunters who killed all the missionaries before him, he could not get away from the fact that God had pointed his life to this specific region of the world. When asked about his fear of dying in the hands of the barbarians, Milne replied, "I have already died."

His ticket was one-way, and so was his heart. When he set sail for the region, he packed all that he had in a coffin. Yes, a coffin. A.W. Milne had died to his own plans, and embraced God's call upon his life. The barbarians could never take his life; he had already given it to God.

Because he had given God his life, God in return, gave him favor. He was able to build relationships with the people in the South Pacific like no other missionary before him. For thirty five years he lived and preached the gospel to those headhunters in that land. When he died, the people buried him in the village with this epitaph upon his tombstone:

When he came there was no light
When he left there was no darkness

Buy your one-way-ticket, pack your coffin, and let God use your life!

DAILY SCRIPTURE READING: Jeremiah 35-37

AUGUST 23

WHAT'LL YA HAVE?

"If Christians spent as much time praying as they do grumbling, they would soon have nothing to grumble about." –Unknown

Since 1928, the Varsity Restaurant has been a fixture in Atlanta culture. It has the world's largest drive-through, accommodating six hundred cars at any given time; and the capacity to serve eight hundred people on the inside. It is known for its world-famous chili, greasy onion rings, and delicious peach-pies. Anyone who has ever visited the Varsity will immediately be faced with the famous question, "WHAT"LL YA HAVE?"

I recently took my family to the restaurant for the first time. As soon as we entered the premise, we could hear that question echoing down the hallway and through the stairwell –WHAT"LL YA HAVE? It is the question every cashier is required to ask every customer. It originated years ago to keep the lines moving on busy game days, and has become an iconic slogan for the restaurant.

If the Lord asked you that question today, what would you ask for? Obviously, God doesn't operate in such greasy fashion; but I do believe He wants to give us good gifts. What is the desire of your heart? What is your request? What problems do you need solved? What questions do you need answered? James said, "Ye have not because ye ask not." Again I ask, if you could ask the Lord for anything, what'll ya have?

DAILY SCRIPTURE READING: Jeremiah 38-41

AUGUST 24

WORRY-FREE LIVING

"Casting all your care upon him; for he careth for you." - Simon Peter

There was a man who constantly worried about everything in his life. He worried about his children, his job, his wife, his health, his church, his neighbors, and everything else. One day a friend of this man noted that he was extremely calm and peaceful so he asked him, "You have always worried about every-thing. What happened?" The former worrier replied, "I just hired a man to do the worrying for me." "Well, how much are you paying him?" His friend inquired. "A thousand dollars a week," the man replied. "A thousand a week? You can't afford a thousand dollars a week." The worrier responded, "That's his problem!"

Worry, doubt, and fear bombard our life on so many levels. As believers we are overwhelmed by so many things, but we must never forget that our problems belong to God. You may be reading this today and you too are worried about something, or perhaps like the fellow in this story you are worried about everything. May I remind you of the words of the apostle Peter, "Casting all your care upon Him for He careth for you" (1 Peter 5:7).

Why worry the day away when you can take it to the Lord in prayer? Remember, your problem is His problem!

DAILY SCRIPTURE READING: Jeremiah 42-45

AUGUST 25

JESUS AT YOUR HOUSE

"The Church is God's, and the Home is God's—they should work together." – Paul Chappell

There was a local church that sponsored a family day for the community. The entire day was committed to the promotion of family time and family values. Many of the couples came down with their children and prayed to be more committed one to another. After the service one couple noticed that their little four-year old boy was sitting on the pew crying. When they asked him what was wrong he said, "The preacher said he wanted me to be raised in a Christian home…but I want to stay with you guys."

Interestingly enough, there are many Christians who do not have Christian homes. Just because believers live in a house together does not necessarily mean that the home has a Christian environment. A Christian home embraces God's design for the family. A Christian home loves and honors one another. A Christian home has the Word of God as its defense. A Christian home has a spirit of harmony and grace. A Christian home prays together and seeks God's will together.

No, a Christian home is not a perfect place; but it does attempt to live by the blueprints given in God's Word. Do you have a Christian home? We understand the great need of having Jesus Christ as the Lord of our hearts; but we also need Him as the Lord of our homes.

DAILY SCRIPTURE READING: Jeremiah 46-48

AUGUST 26

HOW GOD USES PAIN

"Oh what a happy soul am I although I cannot see, I am resolved that in this world contented I shall be." – Fanny Crosby

One of the greatest difficulties of the ministry is seeing people suffer. As a pastor I have watched the sick take their last breath; I have seen parents weep bitterly over their wayward children; I have prayed with people who have lost their jobs, their cars, and their homes. Whenever I visit someone going through great adversity I try my best to offer encouragement and strength in their hour of need.

But through my many years of ministry I have discovered something interesting –oftentimes those people who are enduring affliction are more of an encouragement to me than I am to them.

Amazingly enough, God uses affliction to bring hope and comfort to others. King Nebuchadnezzar would have never seen the "fourth man walking" had not the three Hebrew boys been in the fire. Mary and Martha would have never known resurrection power had not Lazarus died. The world would have never understood the sovereignty of God in such a personal way had not Job lost all that he had. Consider how God used their lives to encourage and equip millions of people down through the years. Sometimes the affliction we endure is ironically for the benefit and blessings of others. Instead of asking God to take away your pain, ask Him to use it for someone else's gain.

DAILY SCRIPTURE READING: Jeremiah 49-50

AUGUST 27

JOGGIN' WITH 'POSSUMS

"Life is either a daring adventure or absolutely nothing." –Helen Keller

It's one of my favorite things to do. There is something about getting up early in the morning and jogging in the neighborhood. All is quiet, all is dark, and all is peaceful around my home. With earphones plugged in, and worship music prepared, I get ready to spend the next half hour walking and talking with the Lord. But on that particular morning I had company.

I was almost finished with my regular route; it was time to start slowing my pace. As my trot turned into a plod, I sensed some movement behind me. Taking my earphones out and turning slowly to see the commotion, I was shocked to see an opossum right behind me. Apparently he (it) had darted out of the patch of woods trying to cross the road. I suddenly felt the urge to speed my run back up to a full-on sprint. I have been chased by dogs before, but never an opossum. I believe I startled it (him), as much as it (he) startled me. Needless to say, we quickly left one another's company without any sad farewells.

That morning I not only finished my route in record time, I learned that the smallest and ugliest things can disrupt your walk with God. As you jog peacefully along the path of life, stay on guard. You never know when the devil will send one of his opossums along to throw you off course.

DAILY SCRIPTURE READING: Jeremiah 51-52

AUGUST 28
HIGHT DON'T MAKE IT RIGHT

"Those who think they are above improvement, typically live below their potential." – Kenneth Kuykendall

John Holliday was the founder and editor of the publication *The Indianapolis News*. One day while reading a particular article, he noticed the world *height* spelled as *hight*. Perturbed about the incident, Holliday demanded to know who was responsible for the misspelling. When the original copy of that edition was discovered, it was indicated that Holliday himself was to blame.

Refusing to acknowledge his wrongdoing, Holliday said, "Well, if that's the way I spelled it, it has to be right." For thirty years, the publication blatantly misspelled the word *height* in every edition of their paper.

When we reject the notion that we may possibly be wrong, we set ourselves up for widespread scrutiny. Just because you spell height *hight*, doesn't mean you are right! Sydney Howard Gay said, "Pride is to character like the attic to the house – the highest part, and generally the most empty." No one lives a mistake-free life, and to believe otherwise is a recipe for failure. Those who think they are above improvement, typically live below their potential. Drop your pride so that you can reach your greatest hights…excuse me, heights.

DAILY SCRIPTURE READING: Lamentations 1-3

AUGUST 29

THE BLESSING OF BEING HIS

"I sometimes wonder whether all pleasures are not substitutes for joy." – C.S. Lewis

Have you ever noticed that most people are never satisfied regardless of their success? We work extremely hard at setting goals, fulfilling dreams, and pursuing careers; but once we have accomplished what we've set out to do, we quickly become restless. We want bigger homes, better cars, and broader horizons. There is nothing wrong with completing a task, but it seems as though we are never satisfied.

The apostle Paul experienced this same temptation, but he learned to be content apart from the external circumstances of life. When we base our joy upon all the "blessings of life" then our satisfaction comes and goes with every changing wind. Paul's joy and satisfaction was not rooted in this world, but rather came through his relationship with Christ. Our position in Christ is the greatest and final pursuit of the soul. Paul knew that his life was complete in Jesus.

That's what most of us are looking for, is it not? - to be complete, to be whole, to be satisfied. Your job, your money, your position, your friends, your possessions, your degrees will never fully satisfy you; they only accentuate a greater need in your life- the need to know God. Jesus fully satisfies. When you find yourself raptured in the simple bliss of knowing Him, you realize there is nothing greater than being His child.

DAILY SCRIPTURE READING: Lamentations 4-5

AUGUST 30

HUMILITY AND THE BIG PICTURE

---

*"Great leaders don't think less of themselves;
they just think of themselves less."* –Ken Blanchard

Large crowds always gathered to hear the famous Winston Churchill speak. His leadership, character, and influence were greatly admired during his tenure as prime minister of Great Britain. Just before delivering a speech to a large company, he was asked, "Doesn't it thrill you to know that every time you make a speech, the hall is packed to overflowing?"

Churchill replied, "It's quite flattering, but whenever I feel that way, I always remember that if instead of making a political speech I was being hanged, the crowd would be twice as big."

In his book, *Sometimes You Win, Sometimes You Learn*, John Maxell said, "Humility allows us to regain perspective and see the big picture. It makes us realize that while we may be *in* the picture, we are not the *entire* picture." Such humility was part of Churchill's greatness.

Pride boasts because of all that it has accomplished; humility bows because of all it is yet to learn. The difference between those who accomplish great things and those who think they are great is simply attitude. Self-consumed, self-serving people typically think the world revolves around them. Selfless people who live to serve others realize they are just part of a bigger picture.

DAILY SCRIPTURE READING: Ezekiel 1-4

AUGUST 31

WISE AS A FOX

"Wisdom is nine-tenths a matter of being wise in time; most of us are wise after the event." –Theodore Roosevelt

I love the old story of the fox, the wolf, and the bear who went hunting together. They each caught a deer and discussed how they would divide the spoils. The wolf said, "I think we should divide the spoils evenly." The bear suddenly ate the wolf. The bear then turned to the fox and asked, "How do you think we should divide the spoils?" The fox said, "I think you should have the wolf's deer, and I would like to offer you my deer as well." The bear asked the fox, "Where did you get such wisdom?" To which the fox replied, "From the wolf."

Learning from the mistakes of others is one of the best ways to gain wisdom; but such learning only comes with a spirit of humility. Wisdom is typically birthed out of our own experiences; but if we can gain wisdom from the adverse experiences of others, we actually save ourselves from unnecessary hurt and pain.

God oftentimes permits us to see the mistakes and failures of others so that we can better safeguard our own lives. Doug Larson said, "Wisdom is the reward you get from a lifetime of listening when you would have preferred to talk." Those who are wise learn the value in keeping their eyes open and their mouths shut. Lesson learned: be wise as a fox.

DAILY SCRIPTURE READING: Ezekiel 5-8

SEPTEMBER

SEPTEMBER 1

A LEAP OF FAITH

"Faith expects from God what is beyond all expectation." –Andrew Murray

The impala is an medium-sized antelope that roams the terrain of eastern and southern Africa. It is quick, agile, and swift on the run. It is primarily known as a fleet runner with an amazing ability to leap. It can jump up to ten feet high and thirty feet long. Quite literally, it can jump over any obstacle in the flatlands where it abides. But as nimble as the impala is, it has one limitation: the impala will not jump if it cannot see where it will land. Zookeepers can actually keep the impala enclosed with nothing more than a three feet wall.

I know a lot of Christians who live the same way. They have great abilities, God-given talents, and even passionate desires; but they have a hard time taking a leap. The reason being, they cannot see where God wants to take them.

Hudson Taylor said, "Many Christians estimate difficulty in light of their resources, and thus they attempt very little and they always fail." Those who refuse to take leaps of faith feel as though they are safer and more secure, when in reality, they actually position themselves as a prey. Faith is believing and trusting God even when we do not know where we will land. Take a leap of faith, and trust God to take care of the rest.

DAILY SCRIPTURE READING: Ezekiel 9-12

SEPTEMBER 2

ESCAPED BUT NOT DELIVERED

"All the great words of salvation have the same theme: the restoration of creation to the arena of the Father's glory." –Tom Marshall

There was a prisoner in Sydney, Australia who had planned his escape for quite some time. He noticed the delivery trucks that came in and out of the prison were supervised at all angles but from underneath. Cunningly, he positioned himself away from the other prisoners and secretly hid himself in the underpinnings of one of the trucks.

As the truck drove away, he held on for dear life. When the vehicle finally came to a stop, the prisoner released his grip, quietly dropped to the ground and secretly rolled out from beneath the truck. Unfortunately, he found himself just a few miles down the road, in the courtyard of another prison!

Freedom is God's gift to all humanity only in the saving grace of Jesus Christ. People go from prison to prison, bondage to bondage, addiction to addiction struggling with liberty because they have failed to accompany themselves with the only One who can save them.

Christ requires nothing at our hands for deliverance. He breaks through the iron gates of our confinement, releases us from the bondage of our sin, and freely pays the price for our freedom. By His grace, we go from glory to glory, not prison to prison.

DAILY SCRIPTURE READING: Ezekiel 13-15

SEPTEMBER 3
MAKING COFFEE FOR OTHERS

"God uses our adversity to loosen our grip on things that are not fruit." –Jerry Bridges

A young lady was facing an extremely difficult situation in her life when she went to her pastor for counsel. The pastor took her into the kitchen of the church and boiled a pot of water. He proceeded to take out a carrot, an egg, and some coffee beans, and tossed each into the boiling water. After a few minutes, he then asked the young woman to observe the items that were tossed into the pot.

He said, "Each ingredient was subjected to the same thing –the hot water, but each one responded differently. The carrot went in hard and came out soft. The egg went in fragile and came out hardened. However, the coffee beans actually changed the water." He then asked, "Will you allow your situation to change you, or will you change your situation?"

Robertson Davies said, "Extraordinary people survive under the most terrible circumstances and then become more extraordinary because of it." The truth is, from time to time, we all experience the hot waters of hardship. So the question is not, "Will trials come into my life?" They do and they will. The question is "How do I respond, and what will I do to make the situation better?" God uses adversity to grow and develop our faith. You never know, He may use your situation to prepare a pot of coffee for someone else.

DAILY SCRIPTURE READING: Ezekiel 16-17

SEPTEMBER 4

HOW WILL YOUR STORY END?

"One day I realized that my journal writing had been a memorial to God's sufficiency." –Gordon MacDonald

All of us have a story to tell. Our life unfolds as a book, on which every page articulates the essence of who we are. Allow me to ask you a question: up to this point, how is the narrative of your life unfolding? I like what author J.M Barrie said, "The life of every man is a diary in which he means to write one story and writes another; and his humblest hour is when he compares the volume as it is with what he vowed to make it."

Who are the characters in your story? What is the main plot? What about genre? Theme? Setting? What is the overall tone?

What we often fail to realize is that our story is being written every day; and the one disadvantage we have, is that we cannot go back and rewrite the narrative as it was. The previous chapters are exactly how they are and cannot be changed. What we can do, however, is begin today's chapter in a new direction. Today you can set a new tone, begin a new theme, and chart a new course. The way to do that is to spend time with the One Who is the Author and Finisher of our faith. Yes, God gives us the liberty to write the stories of our lives, but when we consult Him for continual direction, the ending will be much better.

DAILY SCRIPTURE READING: Ezekiel 18-20

SEPTEMBER 5

PEOPLE OF INFLUENCE

"The only inheritance that a man will leave that has eternal value is his influence." –Larry Dobbs

During his presidency, Woodrow Wilson was approached by his housekeeper concerning the position of the secretary of labor. She tried to convince President Wilson that her husband would be perfect for the job. She said her husband was a man of labor and understood how to interact with laboring people. President Wilson replied, "I appreciate the recommendation but you must remember, the secretary of labor is an important position. It requires a person of influence."

The housekeeper replied, "Well if you made my husband secretary of labor, he would be an influential person!"

There is a misconception about influence; having a title alone doesn't prove someone to be influential. Hanz Finzel said, "When all is said and done, the crowns of my achievements will not be the systems I managed, the things I wrote, or the buildings I built, but the people I personally and permanently influenced through direct contact."

Influence is guided by relationships, and relationships are formed only through trust. You may have a title but if others can't trust you I assure you, you have very little influence over them. Be the right kind of person and the position will find you.

DAILY SCRIPTURE READING: Ezekiel 21-22

SEPTEMBER 6

LEANING ON JESUS

*"Every evening I turn my troubles over to God;
He is going to be up all night anyway."* –Donald Morgan

The evening before Christ was betrayed, He spent several hours with His disciples sharing with them the details of His death. The Bible tells us that John, the disciple whom Jesus loved, was 'leaning upon the bosom" of Jesus, clinging to His every word. When Jesus told the disciples that one of them would betray the Lord, John went from "leaning on His bosom" to "lying on His breast." The more tense and dramatic the circumstance became, the closer John got to Jesus. He was leaning on the Everlasting Arms.

By definition alone, leaning implies placing all of your weight upon something or someone who is able to sustain the pressure. John so heavily leaned upon the Lord that if the Lord was to move John would have fallen. But Jesus didn't move, and John didn't fall.

As believers we are instructed to stand with Christ, walk with Christ, and even sit with Christ; but there are times when we have to lean. The confidence we have while leaning upon Christ is knowing that He can handle the weight. It is not coincidental that John was the only disciple who followed Jesus to the foot of the cross. Before he knelt at Calvary, he had been leaning on the Everlasting Arms. What have I to dread, what have I to fear when I am Leaning on the Everlasting Arms!

DAILY SCRIPTURE READING: Ezekiel 23-24

SEPTEMBER 7
ASSURANCE OF SALVATION

"He whose heart is in heaven need not fear to put his foot in the grave." –Matthew Henry

If salvation was merited by our feelings we would all be on a roller-coaster ride toward eternity. But salvation is not based on feeling, emotion, or intellect – it is based on faith. Therefore, as we put feelings aside we must consider the biblical approach to eternal life.

1. Salvation is Stated in the Bible. The foundation of salvation is the Word of God. With divine authority it tells us that whosoever calls upon the name of the Lord shall be saved. I am not trusting in the humble words of a prayer; no, I am trusting in the Holy Words of a Person.

2. Salvation is Secured by the Blood. The vicarious death of Jesus Christ allots the redemption for those who will place their faith in His finished work. His precious blood was shed so that we can have forgiveness of sins.

3. Salvation is Signed in the Book. When we place faith in Christ, our names are recorded in the Lamb's Book of Life, and nothing on our part can be done to erase what His blood has atoned.

4. Salvation is Sealed by a Birth. Salvation makes us His eternal children. We are adopted sons and daughters of the Heavenly Father, never to be cast aside. It is the new birth that seals us for all eternity.

DAILY SCRIPTURE READING: Ezekiel 25-27

SEPTEMBER 8

WHAT'S SO FUNNY?

"Contrary to popular belief, you can be saved and enjoy it." –Kenneth Kuykendall

Why did the monkey fall out of the tree? Punch line – because it was dead. I will confess: it is stupid, and doesn't make much sense, but whenever I hear that old joke, it makes me laugh; sometimes really hard. And laughter these days is a valued commodity.

I certainly agree that we have much to be concerned over during these turbulent, wavering times; but in spite of all the heralded doom and gloom, the church needs to reclaim its joy. Sometimes I wonder if people resist salvation simply because of their fear of becoming like the calloused and miserable Christians they encounter from week to week. Hypocrisy at its greatest height is to tell others of the sufficiency of Christ while wearing a frown on our face.

I wonder, do you laugh very often? If you are like me, you need a good prescription of it from time to time –"a merry heart doeth good like a medicine." When we live without the gleeful sounds of laughter, we actually diminish the joy God wants us to have. He has not only provided and prescribed joy in our life, I personally believe God, as our Father, delights in the joy of His children. Contrary to popular belief, you can be saved, and enjoy it! Laughing is scriptural.

DAILY SCRIPTURE READING: Ezekiel 28-30

SEPTEMBER 9
THE PRICE OF CHANGE

"Fasting helps confirm the resolution that we are ready to sacrifice anything for the kingdom of God." –Andrew Murray

Moses ascended Mount Sinai to experience the presence of God. For forty days and forty nights he deprived himself from the basic necessities of this world in order to find the nourishment and nutrition he so desperately needed from another. In short, that is the essence of fasting –starving our flesh, while God feeds our faith.

We hear very little of the subject these days; and that's not really a shock. We are so enamored with self-promotion, self-fulfillment, and self-advancement that we give very little thought to self-denial. We have traded the cross-centered life for the consumer-centered cross. The thought of giving up anything that feeds the flesh is an absurdity to this generation. We go to bed physically full but constantly rise spiritually hungry. The lacking dividends of our spiritual investment are a mere reflection of our failed sacrifice.

What are we willing to exchange in our lives for the power of God? Moses gave up food and water for an extended period of time but came down off the mountain a changed man. He was willing to give up so that he could go up. He descended with the worship of God in his heart, the Word of God in his hands, and the witness of God on his head.

DAILY SCRIPTURE READING: Ezekiel 31-33

SEPTEMBER 10
CELL PHONE INSANITY

"Man's mind, once stretched to a new idea, never regains its original dimensions." –Oliver Wendall Holmes

In 1876, an internal memo from Western Union read, "This 'telephone' has too many shortcomings to be seriously considered as a means of communication. The device is inherently of no value to us." Western Union, nor the world at large, could have ever imagined the revolutionary power they held in their hands. Like a small acorn that turned into a forest of oaks, that "worthless" device would become one of the biggest phenomenon of the next two centuries.

The full functionality of the phone is phenomenal. It has become an inseparable part of our lives. It is hard to go throughout the day without it in hand. It is borderline addiction. The compulsory usage is almost comical…maybe even a little sad.

Although I personally appreciate the benefits and convenience of the cell phone, I have come to realize that it can lead to an impersonal community and network. Instead of face-to-face interaction, we have reduced our relationships to words and imagines on a screen. Ironically, its time-saving functions have actually reduced the time we spend with those we love the most. From time to time, we should put it down, and reconnect with those in the next room.

DAILY SCRIPTURE READING: Ezekiel 34-36

SEPTEMBER 11
WATER-BOYS AND WARRIORS

*"Prayer puts God in full force
into God's work."* –E.M. Bounds

Of all the spiritual activities in which a believer is expected to embrace, prayer, at least in my own experience, is perhaps the most neglected and perplexing. I don't want it to be. I want, as I am sure you want, to be a prayer warrior. I want to be a champion of intercession and supplication, but to my chagrin, I fall short of such a title.

Instead of a warrior, I often feel like a water-boy: a weak, unlearned novice that half-heartedly mumbles a few sophomoric words of random religiosity. You know what I mean: vague, common, memorized statements that have little content or purpose (bless this food to the nourishment of our bodies; lead, guide, and direct us; Lord, bless my church). It's not that there is no value in such statements; it's just that they are substitutes for something else: intimacy.

And that's really the biggest problem in our prayer life: a lack of intimate fellowship with our Heavenly Father. For many people, prayer is difficult, not because they don't love the Lord, but because they simply don't know how to be intimate with God.

For the next few days, I want us to consider a few ways we can improve our prayer life, perhaps turning from water-boys to warriors.

DAILY SCRIPTURE READING: Ezekiel 37-39

SEPTEMBER 12

PRAYER IMPROVEMENTS

"Nothing has any power over the man who has fought out the battle before God and won there."–Oswald Chambers

Only in death will our prayer life come to perfect maturity. It is then we will accomplish the ultimate aim of prayer: to be in the perpetual and uninterrupted presence of God. But until then, we can make strides as the wanna-be-warrior, water-boys that we are. How can we improve?

1. Learn to Listen. We limit our prayer life when we do all the talking; half of prayer is listening. Be still, be quiet, and occasionally let Him speak without interruption on your part.

2. Move beyond Shallow, Meaningless Words. Empty statements and phrases are the curse of prayer. Whatever words we use, make sure those words are not ordered in vague generalities.

3. Be Gut-Wrenchingly Honest. C.S. Lewis said, "May it be the real I who speaks. May it be the real Thou that I speak to." Just be real with God, and move beyond the pretentious facades that fool everyone else.

4. Seek His Will in the Nuances. What really develops a strong relationship is seeking God's will in the minutiae of life. Such a pursuit will force you to your knees in the most inconspicuous moments. It is how we live consciously in the presence of God.

DAILY SCRIPTURE READING: Ezekiel 40-42

SEPTEMBER 13
MORE PRAYER IMPROVEMENTS

"Prayer is the first thing where a righteous life begins, and the last wherewith it ends." –Richard Hooker

As with any relationship, communication is vital for growth. I personally believe that prayer is an ongoing education; it develops, changes, and evolves over time. It intrinsically takes on the identity of our relationship with God in that particular season of life; it is an ongoing work in progress. Here are three more ways to improve your prayer life:

1. Pray for Others. When we adopt a selfless attitude toward prayer, and intercede continually for others, we not only strengthen the lives of other people, but God, in return, grows our faith and strengthens our communion with Himself.

2. Pray the Promises of God. Prayer and Scripture are mutually inclusive. Prayer is the venue in which we speak to God; Scripture is the venue in which God speaks to us. Read, study, and declare the promises of God through, in, and by your prayer life.

3. Pray Even When You Don't Feel Like It. Small, incremental prayers, on a daily basis transform our spiritual identity. I love how Henri Nouwen put it, "Sitting in the presence of God for one hour each morning- day after day, week after week, and month after month, in total confusion and with a myriad of distractions- radically changes my life."

DAILY SCRIPTURE READING: Ezekiel 43-45

SEPTEMBER 14

PRAY WITH EXPECTATION

"Prayer means keeping company with God Who is already present." –Philip Yancey

Expect God to hear and respond in prayer – because that is exactly what happens. Granted, His response may or may not be compliant with your desire; but it will be for your advantage. God either gives you what you ask for or something infinitely better.

Praying without expectation is like playing a piano without sound. What an absurdity to think that such an instrument would not sound forth once the keys are pressed. The secret, however, is getting it in tune with the Master's melody. Pray with expectation, and expect God to give the right song. Sing for God, and He will sing for you. The most beautiful prayers are those in which you and God sing together.

Expect God to save your children. Expect God to provide for your needs. Expect God to restore your family. Expect God to calm your fears. Expect God to mend your heart. This is not putting God in a box, this is simply claiming His promises for your life; promises substantiated by His Word. And if you fail to embrace those promises in and through prayer, your just might miss out on His very best.

Grab hold of the horns of the altar, and lay aside the garments of the water-boy. Dress as a warrior for battle, and expect great things from God.

DAILY SCRIPTURE READING: Ezekiel 46-48

SEPTEMBER 15

PRACTICES FOR PESSIMISTS

"The pessimists sees the difficulty in every opportunity; the optimist sees the opportunity in every difficulty" –Winston Churchill

I am not a naturally-optimistic person; as a matter of fact, I lean toward pessimism more times than I should. So for me to stay positive requires a lot of effort on my part. I have learned that being and staying positive really is a choice that we make about the everyday decisions in life. If you happen to see the glass half empty, give some thought to a few of these suggestions, and learn to appreciate what's in your cup!

1. Start Your Day with God. If you do not allow God to set the order of your day, someone else will do it for you. In solitude and quietness seek the Lord and ask Him to give you the right attitude for the day.

2. Stop Taking Yourself So Seriously. I am the most negative when I am the most selfish. I have learned that most of my pessimism is rooted in jealousy, bitterness, selfishness. Give yourself a break, and lighten up.

3. Learn a New Joke and Tell It to Someone Else. It is scientifically-proven that when we smile we produce more serotonin in the brain which is an antidepressant. A smile is only one step away from a laugh.

4. Celebrate Thanksgiving More than Once a Year. Self-explanatory.

5. Have a Spirit of Giving. Nothing takes the mind off of misery like giving. Giving what you have is *greater* than what you have! And when you exhibit a spirit of giving you'll be amazed at how quickly your outlook changes.

DAILY SCRIPTURE READING: Daniel 1-3

SEPTEMBER 16

AT REST IN CHRIST

"Peace is the continual rehearsal of standing in the right spot in the grand order of things —not lower or higher." –Mel Lawrenz

If you are like me, and just about everyone else I know, you find very little time for rest. The demands of life, career, schedule, ministry, and family keep you on the run. I rarely find a free moment to sit back, relax, and do…well, nothing. The reason being, things need to be done. Assignments need to be finalized. Appointments need to be filled. Homework needs to be completed. Projects need to be finished…there is always something. And once we complete the task, there is typically something else. Thus, we are restless creatures.

The only true rest I have found in this life is my rest in Christ. In Him, I have nothing left to do; as a matter of fact, I did nothing to begin with. Christ declared, "It is finished" on the cross. This life-altering, history-changing statement would constitute peace and rest for the restless, sinful souls of humanity.

In Him, I am secure. In Him, I am complete. In Him, I am at rest. This is not a pass of do nothing. Be sure, such rest constitutes a desire to work zealously and passionately for His cause and purpose. But I work not for merit or affirmation; I work because of the rest I have already found in Him. In this busy, chaotic, on-the-run world, take a few minutes today, and rediscover your rest in a Redeemer who can recharge your soul.

DAILY SCRIPTURE READING: Daniel 4-6

SEPTEMBER 17

SOMEBODY SAY SOMETHING

"What you are speaks so loudly that I cannot hear what you say." –Ralph Waldo Emerson

There was a disgruntled couple who decided to give one another the cold treatment. They both refused to say a word to each other and neither one wanted to be the first to speak. Realizing his alarm clock was broken he wrote a letter to his wife that evening and said, "Wake me when you get up at 5 o'clock in the morning, or I will be late for my appointment."

When the man woke up around 7 o'clock he realized he had missed his meeting. Next to his note was a note from his wife that read, "It's 5 o'clock dummy- wake up."

Communication is the key to any successful relationship. Without the proper communication no one will ever know where you stand or how you feel about anything in life. According to recent research from the Harvard Business Review, "The number one criterion for advancement and promotion among professionals is an ability to communicate effectively."

If you fail to communicate you have simply failed. If that is true in business, athletics, and education it is certainly true in your marriage. Choose your words wisely; articulate your words lovingly, and examine your words consistently. Failed communication is failed companionship.

DAILY SCRIPTURE READING: Daniel 7-9

SEPTEMBER 18

END OF CONSTRUCTION

"The greatest gift you can give anyone is your own personal development." –Jim Rohn

Recently while preaching near Charlotte, North Carolina, I went to the Billy Graham Library. As I walked through the larger-than-life facility, I watched videos, looked at countless pictures and artifacts, and read about the thousands of souls who came to know Christ through his ministry. The last stop of our tour was outside the facility in the memorial garden. And to be honest, it was my favorite part of the trip. In the garden, Ruth Graham is buried. Upon her gravestone are the simple words: "End of Construction –Thank you for your patience." A plaque near the grave gave detail to the unusual inscription:

While riding down the highway years ago, Ruth noticed a sign behind the road: "End of Construction –Thank you for your patience." With a smile, she said that these words the words she wanted on her gravestone.'

As I left the garden, I thought about the spiritual growth and development of my own life – it is a continual work in progress. God is constantly working, molding, shaping, and constructing my life. In that process, I fail and fall short of His glory; oftentimes at the expense of others. But there is coming a day when the construction will cease, I will take my last breath, and once and for all, I will be the masterpiece that God has fashioned me to be. Until then, thank you for your patience.

DAILY SCRIPTURE READING: Daniel 10-12

SEPTEMBER 19

SHOULD WE COEXIST?

"I am the way, the truth, and the life: no man cometh unto the Father but by me." –Jesus Christ

I am sure you have seen the bumper stickers. Engraved into the word COEXIST are the symbols of various religions, beliefs, and cults from around the world. The word may only be seven letters in length, but the effects of the message are far-reaching. The idea may seem innocent at first glance and thought. But the message behind the word is deceptive.

COEXIST packages itself as a free-love, free-choice, all-things-equal worldview. It promotes tolerance and acceptance of all beliefs. However, most of those particular religions inscribed into the word have less than tolerant views of each other. The concept is self-defeating.

COEXIST is nothing less than an attempt to promote universalism to a new generation. Its roots are planted in worldly and hellish soil. The message is simple: mankind can create a manmade Utopia. If we try hard enough, we can find various components of commonality. In our commonality we can discover world-peace and ultimately world-redemption. It is the devil's counterfeit to the millennial kingdom. Redemption of society is a future certainty, but such redemption is **only** obtained through the blood of Jesus Christ. Christ, and Christ alone, is the answer for global reconciliation. Only in Christ can we COEXIST.

DAILY SCRIPTURE READING: Hosea 1-7

SEPTEMBER 20

THE JOY OF AFFIRMATION

"There are high spots in all of our lives and most of them have come about through the encouragement of someone else." –George Adams

Not long ago, I attended the funeral service of a friend's mother who passed away. I drove a few hours to make the visit, and when I arrived I noticed that the family was surrounded by a host of guests and visitors. Inconspicuously, I sat down in the back of the church and waited for the service to begin. Not knowing I was there, my friend got up to say a few words and immediately recognized me sitting in the congregation. In front of the entire crowd he acknowledged my attendance and expressed his appreciation for my effort.

Though it was a small gesture, it made a big impact. Although I came to encourage and support my friend and his family, he, ironically encouraged me. In that brief moment, my friend did something that we all need to do from time to time: acknowledge the efforts of other people.

At the end of the day, all of us want to feel appreciated. We want to know that we are making a difference in the world. So when we acknowledge others, we are, in essence, bringing affirmation to their lives. Your children, your spouse, your friends, your pastor, your students –they all need encouragement. One of the greatest ways to encourage them is simply to acknowledge them in some small, simple way. Don't wait until they are in the casket – acknowledge them today.

DAILY SCRIPTURE READING: Hosea 8-14

SEPTEMBER 21
THE PRIVILEGE OF ACCESS

"Let us come boldly unto the throne of grace, that we may obtain mercy." –Hebrews 4:16

As a pastor, I have the unique privilege of access. There are certain situations and scenarios that allow me entrance simply because of my position. As a pastor, I am allowed into the ICU room when others are not permitted. As a pastor, I have the privilege of being with family during personal times of funeral visitation. By position alone I am given the right of entry. Those who grant me access have no way of knowing if I am a good pastor or a bad pastor. Again, I am admitted by position alone.

Believers have a similar privilege. Because of our position in Christ, we can gain access into the presence of God. We can boldly and righteously come before Holy God through our union in Christ. Our position in Him uniquely qualifies us for entry.

Access before God isn't determined by our goodness or worth. It is not allotted by intellect, ability, education, or assets. It is granted by position. As a believer, you can come before the Lord at any given time on any particular matter. The writer of Hebrews said, "Let us come boldly unto the throne of grace, that we may obtain mercy, and find grace to help in time of need" (Hebrews 4:16). Such boldness is only warranted by a relationship; and that relationship with Christ grants access.

DAILY SCRIPTURE READING: Joel 1-3

SEPTEMBER 22

WHO AM I?

"Sometimes our inability is the very reason why God appoints us to a particular assignment." –Kenneth Kuykendall

When God called Moses to deliver the children of Israel out of Egyptian bondage, Moses replied with the question, *"Who am I?"* He recognized his weakness and inability, and felt incapable of such a monumental task. But God didn't respond to the insecurity of Moses; instead, He answered the question *"Who am I?"* with a revealing statement about Himself. The Lord said, "I AM WHO I AM."

Sometimes our inability is the very reason why God appoints us to a particular assignment. God works through our infirmities, our handicaps, and our weaknesses. Who, but God, could take a stuttering, backslidden, nomad-on-the-run and use him to deliver millions of Jewish slaves out of the world empire of Egypt? Who, but God, could take a little shepherd boy and use him to slay the gargantuan Philistine? Who, but God, could take a thorn in the flesh of an apostle and use it to advance the gospel throughout the province of Rome?

Our ability for ministry is not substantiated through self-sufficiency or self-revelation. You may ask, "Who am I?" and never receive an answer. But when you know the GREAT I AM, you are equipped to accomplish any assignment – not by your strength, but His.

DAILY SCRIPTURE READING: Amos 1-5

SEPTEMBER 23

MOTIVES AND METHODS

"There is no point in praying for God's help if we have not made a commitment to obedience without exception." –Jerry Bridges

King David had a great desire. He wanted to move the ark of God, which had been captured by the Philistines, back to Jerusalem. He took counsel from his leaders, and an opinion poll from the people. All agreed; they too wanted the ark back home. With a procession of music, laughter, and jubilation, David and his large company began making the journey with the ark of God. The ark rested upon a new cart and was being carried by a team of oxen, led by Uzza and Ahio.

During the transportation, the oxen stumbled and Uzza put his hand upon the ark to secure it. The Bible says that God was angered at the occurrence and smote Uzza for touching the ark. The death of Uzza may seem harsh and unfair, but God had strict orders on handling the ark of God; and David failed to comply. Only the priests were to bear the ark, and they were to carry it with staves, not on a cart. The death of Uzza was an indictment upon the camp of Israel and their handling of things divine.

There is a great lesson in this story for believers as well. Our methods should coincide with our motives. David had a good motive, but followed through with ungodly methods. Remember: how we do something is just as important as why we do something.

DAILY SCRIPTURE READING: Amos 6-9

SEPTEMBER 24

PATIENCE PAYS OFF

"People can generally make time for what they choose to do; it is not really the time but the will that is lacking." –John Lubbock

There was an inch-worm that began its long arduous climb up an apple tree when it was spotted by a bird. The observant bird asked the worm what it doing to which the worm replied, "I am going after an apple." The bird just laughed and said, "You are in the wrong season, there's not an apple up there." The worm nonchalantly replied, "There will be by the time I get there."

Timing is everything. Oftentimes we miss great opportunities because we arrive too early or too late. We become too aggressive or too lazy. Timing involves a spirit of discernment and understanding about a particular circumstance.

In order to have the right timing in life we must make preparation, have patience, and ultimately trust in God. One of the hardest things to do is wait on the right season to arrive. Most of us want the "apple" here and now without doing the hard work of climbing the tree.

Don't miss the blessing of God because you were either impatient or apathetic. Remember, the early-bird may get the worm, but the patient, consistent, and trusting worm gets the apple. Timing is everything.

DAILY SCRIPTURE READING: Obadiah 1-Jonah 4

SEPTEMBER 25
ONE PROBLEM, THREE TIMES

"Anything big enough to occupy our minds is big enough to hang on a prayer." –George MacDonald

It is possible to face the same problem three different times: before it occurs, when it occurs, and after it occurs. Many people face their problems before they actually happen- this is called fear. Then they face their problems when they actually occur –this is called reality. Then they face their problems after they are over –this is called regret.

If you will notice, much of our anxiety is based upon something that has not happened, or has already occurred, to which we can do nothing about. I believe much of our worry is unsubstantiated. The enemy causes us to see things that are not real. He manipulates circumstances, relationships, emotions, and decisions causing us to consider the worst possible scenario. Many people experience restless and sleepless nights due to unwarranted worry and fear.

If the enemy cannot plague you with worry, he will torment you with regret. He pushes the rewind button over and over again in your mind. He causes you to relive bad decisions, knowing you can do nothing to change the outcome. He is a master manipulator and works fervently to discourage your life. Face only those problems that are a reality of today. Refuse the worry and regret of problems that are nonexistent.

DAILY SCRIPTURE READING: Micah 1-7

SEPTEMBER 26

SIGNS IN THE SKY

"I'm not looking for the second coming of Jesus, I am looking for Jesus at the second coming." –Clarence Sexton

The technology we now have to determine weather patterns is truly amazing. Through satellite and radar systems, meteorologists are able to verify the path of a storm, the size of a storm, and the severity of the storm. This has been greatly beneficial to society in that we now receive warnings much earlier than we did years ago. But in all of the advancements we have made to determine the weather, a majority of our society is still clueless about the signs of the times.

Jesus said this was somewhat problematic. Listen to His scathing words in Matthew 12:56, "Ye hypocrites, ye can discern the face of the sky and of the earth; but how is it that ye do not discern this time? Yea, and why even of yourselves judge ye not what is right?" Isn't it ironic that we can determine the path of a storm down to the very street that will be affected, yet much of the world cannot see or discern the soon return of the Lord Jesus Christ?

We can determine the schedule of seasons by the signs that are associated with them; even so, we should be aware of the signs that accompany the return of the Lord Jesus Christ. He is soon to appear in the clouds –you don't have to be a meteorologist to see how close we are to His arrival.

DAILY SCRIPTURE READING: Nahum 1-3

SEPTEMBER 27

IN GOD WE TRUST

"The liberties of a nation will be insecure if we remove the conviction that these liberties are the gift of God." –Thomas Jefferson

Since 1864 the motto, "In God We Trust" has appeared sporadically on our coins and currency. The phrase originated from the song, *The Star Spangled Banner,* during the War of 1812. The fourth stanza reads, "And this be our motto, In God is our Trust." It was an unofficial slogan for many years, but in 1956 it became the official motto. The law requires the motto to appear on all currency and coinage. This came at a time during the Cold War when America wanted to make refute the cold, atheistic tendencies of Communism and Marxism.

Although "In God we Trust" hasn't always been our official motto, it has been the anthem of our nation since its inception. Our founding fathers believed and trusted in the sovereign God of all creation. It was John Quincy Adams who said, "The highest glory of the American Revolution was that it connected, in one indissoluble bond, the principles of civil government with the principles of Christianity."

The providential care of God has historically been our anthem. Sadly, these days, we trust our money and markets more than our Maker. May God stir our hearts back to Himself, and may we realize our lives are guided by the One Who is worthy of our trust.

DAILY SCRIPTURE READING: Habakkuk 1-Zephaniah 3

SEPTEMBER 28

BROKEN ON THE INSIDE

"In the presence of the Great Physician, my most appropriate contribution may be my wounds." –Philip Yancey

Pastoral care often requires being there for people during times of personal and intimate healthcare. I have sat with family members on multiple occasions as they waited for the results of CT scans, X-rays, and MRI's. One thing I have learned about such tests is that they never detect emotional or spiritual pain. An X-ray can confirm a broken bone, but it will never reveal a broken heart.

Physical pain is typically evident and normally treatable; emotional pain…now that's another story. Most people you encounter today will have smiles on their faces and courteous words on their lips; but I assure you, underneath, they are probably dealing with some pain. And even the most scientifically, technologically-advanced equipment in the world cannot identify their hurt and discomfort.

There is One, however, Who sees where others cannot see. The Great Physician is able to detect the problem-areas of our lives. His power is not limited by the latest inventions or medical devices. He knows where the pain is, and is able to bring healing and grace to that particular area. God sees the depths of our soul and knows how to heal the brokenness on the inside.

DAILY SCRIPTURE READING: Haggai 1-2

SEPTEMBER 29

HOLY HONKING

"Those who are observing your testimony are not only watching what you do, but why you do what you do." –Paul Chappell

Recently, I was out of state for a revival meeting. Leaving my hotel a little late, I realized I would need to hurry if I was going to arrive at the church on time. As I quickly made my way through traffic, I got behind a "Sunday driver" and it wasn't even Sunday. Their slow and leisurely pace competed with the steady and consistent tick of the car clock. Needless to say, when I found my opening, I quickly swerved around them. Anxious and frustrated, I lightly tapped on the horn so they would know I was passing them.

You could imagine my embarrassment when I saw their blinker in the rearview mirror. We both made "rights" into the church parking lot. Yes, unbeknownst to me, I had just honked at the pastor of the church. My only consolation was that he was late too.

Of course, we laughed and joked once we got out of our cars; he even said he would honk if my preaching went on too long. Although the lesson was somewhat embarrassing, it was very valuable: my testimony is evident in everything I do. From driving a car, to buying groceries, to walking in the neighborhood – somebody somewhere is watching my life. Therefore, whatever I do, I should do it for the honor and glory of God.

DAILY SCRIPTURE READING: Zechariah 1-7

SEPTEMBER 30

THE KEY CONNECTION

"Better is the poor that walketh in integrity, than he that is perverse in his lips, and is a fool." –Proverbs 19:1

Not long ago, I stood on my front porch trying to get into my home. As I fumbled through my big, bulky key chain, I noticed that I was having difficulty finding the right key. After a few moments of frustration, I paused to consider how large my "key collection" had become. Some keys have been on there for years without ever being used. Some are old, some are duplicates, and some are just mysterious. I have no idea how they got on there, or what they unlock. These excess keys are cumbersome to say the least, and serve no purpose. So I did the unthinkable...

I purged my key chain.

Yes, I began to eliminate those mysterious keys that are never used. It was quite liberating. Am I the only one, or is your key ring becoming a little obnoxious as well?

Sometimes it is hard to unlock the right doors in life because we simply have too many distractions. These distractions may seem necessary and essential, but in reality, they are useless. From time to time we need to simplify our lives and rid our chain of unnecessary keys.

DAILY SCRIPTURE READING: Zechariah 8-14

OCTOBER

OCTOBER 1

CANDLE CHRISTIANITY

"If there is anything in you that doesn't worship God, then there isn't anything in you that does worship God very well." –A.W. Tozer

The candle-making business is a multi-billion dollar industry. I am amazed at the various smells that are now manufactured and produced through wax. From the fresh smell of a home-made apple pie to the natural scent of an open-camp fire, you can now capture just about any fragrance you like in a can.

Suppose your life was a candle. What would it smell like to God? How would the label describe your odor? Cold and indifferent? Backslidden? Joyful? Thankful? Jealous? Sour? Gracious? What does "cheerful" smell like? How about "anger?"

When Noah came off the ark, he built an altar and made sacrifices unto the Lord. The Bible says that God smelled the fragrance and was well-pleased with his worship. When Mary knelt at the feet of Jesus, she opened her alabaster box of spikenard and the house was filled with the odor of the ointment. When the sacrifices were made in the temple, the smell of the offerings pleased the Lord.

The truth is, your life does give off an odor to the Lord. Is that odor pleasant or repulsive? Sweet or bitter? Holy or worldly? What kind of fragrance describes your life?

DAILY SCRIPTURE READING: Malachi 1-4

OCTOBER 2

SHARING YOUR FAITH

"It is the truth of the Gospel, reaffirmed in our hearts daily, that puts desire in our duty." –Jerry Bridges

Stop just for a moment and ask yourself a personal question: when was the last time I shared my faith with someone who is lost? I meet people all the time who have a sincere desire to see others saved, but they find being a witness for Christ difficult and cumbersome. For whatever reason, they feel inadequate, unprepared, or simply uncomfortable in sharing the gospel.

If this describes you, let me give you a simple thought: just tell them what Jesus did for you. The greatest tool in our soul-winning endeavors is simply the witness of a transformed life. Sharing the faith with others means sharing *your* faith, and how God changed *you*. Soul-winning is not just a science, it is an art. We can become so mechanical, robotic, and step-by-step in our methods that we fail to express how Christ personally and dramatically changed *us*.

Unsaved people may argue with your logic, your tract, your methods, and even your style, but they cannot refute your transformation. Share the gospel today with someone just by telling them how Christ changed your life. The power of the Gospel does not just exist on paper; it exists and is confirmed through the people it radically transforms.

DAILY SCRIPTURE READING: Matthew 1-4

OCTOBER 3

5 "BE'S" FOR SOUL-WINNING

"Tell someone today about God's grace in your own life to see their life changed." –Kenneth Kuykendall

Soul-winning visitation, campaigns, tracts, door-knocking, and crusades are only effective when authentic, genuine, radically-transformed grace is exposed through those who labor. Remember, if God has saved you, He has given you the power, the witness, and the ability to lead others to Himself. This is grace at work. This is our greatest strategy in the harvest fields. Too often we depend upon a method or tactic more than our actual experience of grace. Remember these five simple truths when sharing your faith with others:

1. Search your heart for any indifference and **be clean.**

2. Ask God to open the door with someone who is lost and **be ready.**

3. Look for those openings that God may send and **be sensitive.**

4. Understand that you are equipped by the Spirit and **be reliant.**

5. As you speak to the individual, simply tell him what God has done for you and **be real.**

Soul-winning can be summarized in this simple thought: it is ordinary people telling ordinary people about an extraordinary God. Tell someone today about God's grace in your own life to see their life changed.

DAILY SCRIPTURE READING: Matthew 5-6

OCTOBER 4

SAY NO TO THE NOBEL

"Sign your work at the end of each day. If you can't do that, find a new profession." –Jeff O'Leary

In his book, *Sometimes You Win, Sometime You Learn*, John Maxwell tells about his visit to the Nobel Museum in Stockholm, Sweden. After several hours of touring the museum and hearing about all the various people who have won the prestigious award, he was surprised to hear about a little-known fact. The tour guide revealed that very few people, after receiving the award, go on to do anything else significant in life.

In the book, Maxwell quoted T.S. Eliot, who actually won the award in literature, "The Nobel Prize is a ticket to one's own funeral. No one has ever done anything after he got it."

If we are not careful, we can allow yesterday's success to become tomorrow's failure. Many people get so caught up in the accolades, awards, and applause of their previous accomplishments that they never do anything worthwhile again.

We should constantly push ourselves to grow and become better. Don't allow your life to be defined as a trophy on a mantle, or a badge on an old jacket. Keep pushing, keep pressing, keep progressing. So "no" to the Nobel mentality and say "yes" to something new today.

DAILY SCRIPTURE READING: Matthew 7-8

OCTOBER 5

OUR GOD IS ALIVE!

"Long-lasting victory can never be separated from a long-lasting stand on the foundation of the cross."–Watchman Nee

There was a period in Martin Luther's life when he experienced a great depression. Day in a day out, Luther was discouraged and despondent. One morning he awoke to find his wife Katherine dressed in black from head to toe. Luther asked why she was dressed like she was going to a funeral. Katherine said, "Oh, you haven't heard? God is dead." Martin Luther was appalled by her statement and said, "Woman, that's blasphemy!" to the which she replied, "Oh, I'm sorry, by the way you've been acting lately I just presumed that God had died."

I do not know a believer who would contend that God is dead; however, oftentimes we live that way. To look upon the faces of some believers you would think their God is dead, their joy is gone, and their mansion in glory has foreclosed.

There is good news today! Heaven has not faded. The blood has not lost its power. The grave has not won. The Bible is still true. The Spirit is still our Comforter. And the cross is still worth the crown. In a world full of turmoil and tears there is one victorious truth to live by: God is not dead, He is very much alive!

DAILY SCRIPTURE READING: Matthew 9-10

OCTOBER 6

A TREASURE OF TRUTH

"My conscience is held captive by the Word of God." –Martin Luther

In 1640, Puritan settlers printed the "Bay Psalm Book," a translation of the biblical psalms. Known as the first book printed in the United States of America, it recently sold at a Sotheby's auction as the most expensive book in the world. The bidding opened at $6 million and within a few moments closed at the astronomical price of $14.16 million. Some contend the winning bidder got a bargain; the book has an estimated value of $15-30 million.

The truth is the most valuable book in the world is the Holy Bible. Though I have seen it on sale for a low as a $1 dollar, the contents therein cannot be defined by monetary measurement. Solomon said the word of God is more precious than gold or silver.

The Bible is the only book in the world that offers hope to the hopeless, life to the dying, bread to the hungry, water to the thirsty, peace to the weary, and salvation to the sinner. The Bible is God's revelation of Himself to fallen humanity. It is the key that unlocks the door to God's glory and grace.

Rejoice today in the Word of God. Be thankful that you found eternal life in its pages. That, my friend, is more worth more than $14.16 million.

DAILY SCRIPTURE READING: Matthew 11-12

OCTOBER 7

THE OTHER END OF THE TABLE

"Why value humility in our approach to God? Because it accurately reflects the truth." –Philip Yancey

A rich man once invited many honored guests for a feast of celebration. His chair was highly decorated and placed at the end of the table. While he was out of the room, many noblemen came and took their seats according to the position of the rich man's chair so as to get close to the master of the house. When time came, the rich man returned to the feast and moved his chair to the other end of the table, thus sitting with the peasants and servants.

The moral of the story is simple: to get close to the Master we must assume the position of humility and service. Jesus, during His public ministry, never jockeyed His way to notoriety. His fame and popularity was built upon the virtues of compassion, humility, and service.

If we are going to sit in the greatness of Christ we must be willing to sit on the other end of the table. We must be willing to wash the brow of the leper, feed the homeless, love the orphan, bow in service, and reach the outcast. God is not concerned with our successes as much as He is concerned with our likeness to Christ. And one can never be like Christ until he bows before his brother and offers the better chair.

Take a seat at the other end of the table, Christ will meet you there.

DAILY SCRIPTURE READING: Matthew 13-14

OCTOBER 8

HOW DO YOU SIGN YOUR NAME?

"If you have integrity, nothing else matters. If you don't have integrity, nothing else matters." –Alan K. Simpson

Most people use the word "sincerely" just above their signature to close out their correspondence. The origin of this practice stemmed from the phrase "sin cerely" which meant "without wax."

Ancient sculptors and artisans would use wax to conceal defects in their work. If a sculpture had an exposed fracture, then wax was used to cover up the imperfection. Therefore, when someone signed "sin cerely" they, in essence, were signing off on their documentation, having closely examined their correspondence. They were satisfied in what they said. There were no flaws, defects, or errors – they were sincere (no need to use wax).

Can you honestly write "sincerely" in the letters of your life? At the close of this day will you be able to say that you were honest, thorough, and genuine? Does your family, ministry, career, finances, or relationships suffer from your insincerity? Jeff O'Leary said, "Sign your work at the end of each day. If you can't do that, find a new profession."

In order to sign "sincerely" above your name, you will have to constantly and continually evaluate your motives and intentions. You will have to strive for excellence as you depend upon the Spirit of Christ. Proofread your life, edit if necessary, and close this day "sincerely."

DAILY SCRIPTURE READING: Matthew 15-17

OCTOBER 9

DON'T GET USED TO IT

"You can spend your life any way you want, but you can only spend it once." –John Maxwell

There was a man who walked into a fortune teller's tent at a carnival to enquire of his future. As he sat down with the mysterious woman, he looked into her crystal ball. The teller quickly said, "I see many things in your future." Intrigued, the man asked what she saw. She replied, "You will be poor, miserable, and unhappy until you are forty-five." Unsettled by her prediction, he asked, "What will happen when I turn forty-five?" She said, "You will get used to it."

Sadly, this is an all-too-common prediction for many people. Instead of changing their circumstances, they simply allow their circumstances to change them. They embrace the status quo of life, and plod through their journey without ever reaching their potential or dreams.

This is not the way God wants us to live. Christ came so that we may have life and life more abundantly. He didn't burst forth from the grave, defeat death, and impart eternal life so that we could have a sad, sub-par existence. John Maxwell said, "You can spend your life any way you want, but you can only spend it once." This is the only shot you get. Don't get used to the mediocrity and misery of hum-drum living. Shut the mouths of the naysayers, and do something today to change your course.

DAILY SCRIPTURE READING: Matthew 18-19

OCTOBER 10

DO YOU HAVE TWO CANVASES?

"My interest is in the future because I am going to spend the rest of my life there."–Charles F. Kettering

I read of a painter who had two canvases for every picture he painted. He always hung a blank, white canvas just above every painted canvas. His reasoning for the unusual habit was simple. The blank canvas contained all that he envisioned the picture to be, this was where the real work took place. The other was simply the reality of all he considered in his thoughts and dreams.

The most laborious part of making something a reality is the forethought. This is where vision is vital. You can paint your life in one of two ways. You can live by the paint-by-number design, where all you have to do is stay between the lines with the prescribed colors. Or you can live by vision, and allow the blank canvas to become the palette where your dreams come true.

Do you have two canvases? Oswald Sanders said, "Eyes that look are common, eyes that see are rare." The only way to "look" at the God-given reality of your painted canvas is to "see" with the eyes of faith what the blank canvas could become. Have a vision for the canvas of your life; the result will always lead to a beautiful picture.

DAILY SCRIPTURE READING: Matthew 20-21

OCTOBER 11

TIME IN A BOTTLE

"The clock and the light – they gifted us with time, and then stole it away."–Richard Swenson

Jim Croce was a popular singer/songwriter in the 1970's. One of his most famous songs was *Time in a Bottle*. The lyrics of the song suggest that Croce wanted to capture time in a bottle so that he could spend it later with someone he loved. Unfortunately, and ironically, Jim Croce died in a plane crash before the song hit the airwaves.

Capturing time is like capturing a vapor – it can't be done. We only have one life set before us. There are no do-over's, this is it. When Croce penned down those haunting words, he didn't realize how close he was to the end of his life.

The truth is neither do we. None of us know with great certainty when and how we will die; we only know that we will. Most of us have no trouble with the *fact of death*; I think the real issue is the *act of death*.

I think all of us would like a few extra bottles of time stored up somewhere for later use. But life is less like a bottle, and more like an hourglass. With each passing moment we draw closer to our eternal destiny. Time is not stored in a bottle –it is stored in a body, and once that body is gone, so it your time.

DAILY SCRIPTURE READING: Matthew 22-23

OCTOBER 12

CHRIST IS ENOUGH

"What Christ was in His life is the object of our desire; and how He lived is the copy of our imitation." –F.E. Marsh

I see it more and more these days: division among brethren. I hear, and thanks to social media, see the contention that is taking place among the body of Christ. And it doesn't matter what group, denomination or "movement" you may be associated with- bickering in this generation is rampant.

Do not get me wrong, there are some things to which we must contend. The precious doctrines of the church are worth separating over. I cannot stand in fellowship with someone who refuses to believe in the virgin birth, the deity of Christ, the imminent return of the Lord, or the inspiration of Scripture, etc. Some things not only warrant our division, but our death if necessary.

Many, who are adamantly fighting for whatever reason has in reality, hindered the body of Christ through their criticism and contention. Our **focus** should be in the same direction as our **faith**- looking unto Jesus. Christ did not die for me to argue about carpet, songbooks, or screens. He died to redeem sinners from their sin; furthermore, He called us to be co-laborers. Instead of striving together, many want to be in strife with one another. For me Christ is enough, my liberty is in Him!

DAILY SCRIPTURE READING: Matthew 24-25

OCTOBER 13

5 GOOD USES OF SOCIAL MEDIA

"Character is the only sure foundation of the state."–Calvin Coolidge

Like any other form of media, social outlets can be used for good or evil. We can try to discredit its influence, or we can embrace it with the intent to use it for good. I choose to do the latter. Consider these five fruitful functions of Facebook:

1. Use it to Testify of God's Goodness. Post the blessings of God. Tell of His goodness. Recall and retell answered prayers. Brag on Jesus, uplift His name, and make much of Him.

2. Encourage Someone Randomly, Privately, and Publicly. I cannot tell you how many times I have been encouraged in my spirit by the kindness of a simple post from a friend.

3. Post Scriptural or inspirational quotes. Just a line of Scripture or a good quote from a book may be exactly what someone on another screen needs to read.

4. Advertise your Church and its Ministries. Link your church's website to a post and invite others to attend. Specify a particular ministry and tell others what God is doing through children's church, bus ministry, choir practice, etc.

5. Stay Connected with Your Children. Monitor their status, review their pictures, check out their friends. Stay connected with them, and keep them accountable.

DAILY SCRIPTURE READING: Matthew 26

OCTOBER 14

CHRISTIANS WHO COMPARE

"If you do not follow the nature of Jesus, the name of Jesus will not mean anything to you." –A.W. Tozer

It's human nature. We compare, contrast, and weigh our lives by the successes, failures, and expectations of others. The overachiever in us all wants to excel and advance. We want to win souls, build buildings, book meetings, grow ministries, speak frequently, minister often, and increase our network. However, some men, in the name of ministry, are simply trying to make a name for themselves. In this process, we can compare and contrast our lives with others thus affecting our motivation for what we do.

Have you ever felt inadequate or superior as a result of comparison? Let's be honest, all of us at one time or another have grappled with this temptation. I certainly have; but one of the greatest days in my ministry was when the Lord showed me I had been measuring by the wrong standards. My success or failure is not determined by another's experience; it is measured by my obedience to God's word, and my acceptance to God's will.

So how do we overcome such a disparaging subject? How can you get victory over comparison? Tomorrow we will at five things we can do to overcome this prideful temptation.

DAILY SCRIPTURE READING: Matthew 27-28

OCTOBER 15

OVERCOMING INSECURITY

"Conscience is God's spy, and man's overseer." –John Trapp

If you stand in constant need of approval or validation from others, you may very well have a heart problem. Here are five ways to overcome the dangerous temptation of comparison:

1. Realize the Consequences. When we compare our ministries with others one of two things will happen: we will be full of pride, or full of pity. We may become full of pride if we are doing "better" than the next guy; full pity if we fall short of his success.

2. Don't Believe Everything You Read. One of the dangers of social media is all the hype that goes on in particular ministries. Rule of thumb: don't believe everything you read; I assure you, on the other end, they are having some hard days as well.

3. Measure Your Success by Your Obedience to Christ. God doesn't give everyone the same ministry. Most of the time we get in trouble when we covet what God allocates to others.

4. Keep Your Motives in Check. From time to time, we should take inventory of our motives and ask ourselves this one prevailing question: is this for the glory of God? If it is, keep it there! If it is not, get it there.

5. Repent. Yes, this word should be part of our modern vernacular. If this insidious habit of comparison has captured your heart and attention, ask the Lord to forgive you, and keep a wall around your intentions.

DAILY SCRIPTURE READING: Mark 1-3

OCTOBER 16

HOW FAITH IS LIKE A G.P.S.

"Extreme faith is built upon the greater curiosities, those themes that are deep – taking a lifetime to explore." –Gordon MacDonald

As a child, I remember having a very large, plastic map in the glove-department of our family car. It was rarely used, but from time to time, it would make an appearance whenever we traveled somewhere new. Usually my dad would pull off the side of the road, trace his finger along the miniscule highways, and try his best to determine the location of the next turn. This antiquated method of traveling was time-consuming and often times inaccurate. Once the map came out of the dash, it usually stayed out until we reached our desired location.

Technologically speaking, we have traveled a long way since those days, and primarily without a cheap, annoying, plastic map. Like most of you, I use my GPS extensively in my travels. To say the least, it has put the plastic map out of business. Consider how faith is like a GPS:

1. You Have to Listen to Others
2. You Have to Start Where You Are
3. You will have to Re-route from Time to Time
4. You will be Responsible for the Drive

God not only knows the way – He knows the best way, and He knows the way you should take today. By faith, trust Him, listen to Him, and enjoy the ride.

DAILY SCRIPTURE READING: Mark 4-5

OCTOBER 17

THE SEVEN-DAY FORECAST

---

*"If God sends us on stony paths,
He provides strong shoes."* –Corrie Ten Boom

My wife is a weather fanatic. Every evening she faithfully watches the weather channel to see what the conditions will be for the upcoming days. Her favorite part of the program is the seven-day forecast. Though not always correct in their predictions, they are surprisingly accurate a majority of the time. Imagine such a thing – the ability to know what lies ahead for the next seven days.

There are many things that we cannot predict. There are many unforeseen events that take place in our lives each and every week. However, there are three things that we can bank on for the next seven days. Here is the seven-day forecast for the child of God:

1. God's Promises are Reliable. The next seven days will be filled with the promises of God. They are all around us. They sustain us. They give us life, joy, sustenance, and hope.

2. God's Providence is Real. The world was created by Him. He holds it in His hands. He is holding your life in His hands. All things are made and kept by Him. Live with great resolve knowing He is in control.

3. God's Pardon is Reachable. Each and every morning He makes His mercy new. In our daily failures, God offers daily forgiveness.

DAILY SCRIPTURE READING: Mark 6-7

OCTOBER 18

THE LAW OF HARVEST – PART 1

"For he that soweth to his flesh, shall of the flesh reap corruption." –The Apostle Paul

The law of harvest is pretty simple. You reap what you sow. Never has a farmer planted corn hoping to harvest beans. You wouldn't knowingly plant apple trees in the anticipation of growing oranges. No one plants tomato bushes hoping they will sprout pecans. Such a notion is absurd in farming – so it is in living.

If we all understand this basic and fundamental concept of harvest, then the question is apparent – what are you reaping from your life? That question can be answered with another question –what have you been sowing?

The apostle Paul said, "For he that soweth to his flesh shall of the flesh reap corruption; but he that soweth to the Spirit shall of the Spirit reap life everlasting. And let us not grow wearing in well doing: for in due season we shall reap, if we faint not" (Galatians 6:7-8).

If you are dissatisfied with the harvest of your life, it may very well be time to change what you are sowing. When we sow to the flesh and the world, we will reap things that bring death (corruption); but when we invest in spiritual things, we reap life and spiritual reward. Change seed, and you will change harvest.

DAILY SCRIPTURE READING: Mark 8-9

OCTOBER 19

THE LAW OF HARVEST – PART 2

"And let us not be weary in well doing: for in due season we shall reap, if we faint not." –The Apostle Paul

The Apostle Paul, writing to the churches of Galatia, gave them some specific instructions about harvest. One of the key elements of understanding sowing and reaping is the time frame in which it is accomplished. Sowing is done in one season. Reaping in another.

This concept, though basic and elementary, is foreign to our modern culture. We live in an instant society. Instant food, instant information, instant gratification…if we want it, we can easily obtain it. The law of harvest doesn't work that way.

The law of harvest invests in the "here and now" for the benefit of the "then and later." Yes, the law of harvest says the unthinkable…wait! I know, I know, that is a "curse word" in our culture. No one likes to stop at red lights, or sit in waiting rooms, or pause for silence. Waiting is old-fashioned; yet it is one principle that cannot be altered when it comes to harvesting.

Paul said, "…for in due season we shall reap, if we faint not." (Galatians 6:9). You may not see instant results, but if you keep working at it, a harvest is in the making. If you want a season of harvest, you will have to invest in a season of sowing. And then simply wait.

DAILY SCRIPTURE READING: Mark 10-11

OCTOBER 20

THE LAW OF HARVEST – PART 3

"God will give you to give, more than He will give you to keep." –Unknown

I remember when me and Heather were first married. Trying out our green thumb, we planted tomato bushes in the back yard of our home. Over the next few weeks we planted, cultivated, watered, and nourished those seeds until the bushes sprang forth. The process truly amazed me. From a few handfuls of seed came forth an abundance of fruit.

Those green and red tomatoes taught me a valuable lesson of harvest: not only do we *reap* what we sow, and reap *later* than we sow; we also reap *more* than we sow.

Someone has rightly said, "God will give you to give, more than He will give you to keep." When we sow into the work of God, He abundantly provides above and beyond our initial seed. This is true in all areas of life. The divine dividends of God far outweigh our initial investments.

Unfortunately, this universal truth can also work to the detriment of mankind. Split homes, divided churches, rocky marriages, and destroyed lives are all the result of reaping more than initially sown.

Therefore, sow good seed, and you'll be able to enjoy the tomatoes!

DAILY SCRIPTURE READING: Mark 12-13

OCTOBER 21

ARE YOU FLIRTY OR FAITHFUL?

"Commitment only bothers us if we don't have it." –Kenneth Kuykendall

When I first met Heather I knew I wanted to marry her. I had always heard about such sappy love stories, and thought such a notion was only written in the pages of a Hollywood manuscript. But I can honestly say, I knew immediately that I wanted to spend the rest of my life with her. In those initial days, I did what many other guys were doing – I flirted with her. You know what I mean, the subtle innuendos of romance…the sentimental gestures of infatuation: the winks, the calls, the goofy names.

More than likely, some form of flirting initiated your relationship with your spouse as well. Flirting – it means to "behave amorously, to show superficial or casual interest." Flirting is a simple way of showing someone that you like them.

There came a point in time however, that flirtatious gestures could not sustain our sophomoric relationship. I needed to make a commitment. I needed to show her that I was willing and able to enter into a faithful bond.

Some folks need to make the same decision about their relationship with the church. Ask yourself this question: am I flirting with my church or am I faithful to my church. It may be time for you to get hitched!

DAILY SCRIPTURE READING: Mark 14

OCTOBER 22

STOP WINKING, START WORKING

"A commitment to something you believe in is a commitment that is easier to keep." –John Maxwell

Church membership seems to be a deemphasized subject of commitment these days. For whatever reason, people are expected to fulfill requirements in every area of life (home, job, sports, relationships, investments, etc), but when it comes to church membership, there seems to be a lot of wiggle room. In an effort to grow the masses, we have failed to call believers to faithfulness. We may be growing our congregation, our buildings, and our programs, but the church itself is suffering. Flirty Christians make goo-goo eyes at the steeple, blow meaningless kisses at the altar, and seem to be interested only when it is fun and exciting. Come Monday, they are flirting with something else.

Flirting requires no commitment. It requires no real love. It requires little time, devotion, or energy. Anybody can flirt.

Faithfulness on the other hand puts the ring on the proverbial finger. It is the manifestation of love and honor. It requires much time, attention, investment, devotion, prayer, and affection. It is not always fun or exciting, but it indeed has its advantages! Anybody can flirt, but only the committed are faithful.

DAILY SCRIPTURE READING: Mark 15-16

OCTOBER 23

IN THE GARDEN WITH GOD

"Solitude is the furnace of transformation." –Henri Nouwen

In one of his earliest recordings, Jonathon Edwards made mention of his wife's intimate relationship with God. He said of her, "She (Sarah) hardly cares for anything, except to meditate on Him. She loves to be alone, walking in the fields and groves, and seems to have someone invisible always conversing with her."

It was said of Sarah Edwards that she spent much of her time walking in the garden alone with God.

Such solitude is rare in our generation. We wake up to a screeching alarm clock and go to bed with a blaring television. We are enamored with noise. We are surrounded by sounds. We are enclosed with clamor and clatter. Such constant commotion is the enemy of meditation, reflection, prayer, and solitude.

Jesus understood the value of quietness. He often would slip away from the busy schedule of ministry to spend time alone with His heavenly Father. Suffice it to say, if the Lord Jesus needed a break from the bustling busyness of life, we too need to spend some time in the garden walking with God. Find a quite place today, drown out the noisy distractions, and let the only sound you hear be the sound of His voice.

DAILY SCRIPTURE READING: Luke 1

OCTOBER 24

SETTLING OUT OF COURT

"Your worst days are never so bad that you are beyond the reach of God's grace." –Jerry Bridges

In the first chapter of Isaiah, the Lord Himself gave an invitation to wayward Israel. He said, "Come now, let us reason together, saith the LORD: though your sins be as scarlet, they shall be as white as snow; though they be red like crimson, they shall be as wool" (Isaiah 1:18).

Although Israel had been faithful to the religious requirements of the day, they were spiritually distant from God. They had "gone away backward" from His presence. They were being sentenced to court by the Lord because of their spiritual condition. The indictments against them were severe, but God made a plea to "Come now, let us reason together."

This was a judicial phrase. The Lord was literally asking them to "settle out of court." He wanted their case to be resolved before the judgment was final. In His longsuffering and grace, Israel's divine Judge was giving them an opportunity to be forgiven.

If God gives you the chance to "settle out of court," it would be wise to "reason together" with Him. The Lord pleads with us all today to approach the stand, settle the matter, and get things right before the final verdict is declared. It is better to accept His plea-bargain than to be sentenced by His justice.

DAILY SCRIPTURE READING: Luke 2-3

OCTOBER 25

SANCTIFICATION IN THE SNOW

"No man has the right to ask God for peace of mind unless it's founded on righteousness." –J. Sidney Harris

Years ago, famed scholar and theologian F.B. Meyer, went on a visit to a home in Scotland. The lady of the house was doing laundry that day and had all of her clothes hanging on a line in the backyard. During the visit, it began to snow extremely hard. The whites on the line suddenly looked more dingy than before. Meyer commented how different the clothes looked against the fresh snow. The lady of the house replied, "What can stand against God's almighty white?"

Too often we measure our holiness by the wrong standards. When we compare our lives to wicked men, popular culture, or the entertainers of our day, we may become prideful in our thinking. Andrew Murray said, "There is no pride so dangerous, none so subtle and insidious as the pride of holiness."

The truth is, when we compare our lives to the righteousness of "God's almighty white" we realize that we are not as clean as we previously thought. Again, we need to put our standards in the right perspective. God doesn't challenge us to simply be "a little better" than the ungodly world. No, their trends, values, and lifestyles are constantly fluctuating. God orders us to live by the eternal Word of God. It is then we see ourselves in light of His glory.

DAILY SCRIPTURE READING: Luke 4-5

OCTOBER 26

FOUNDATIONAL TRUTH

"In matters of style swim with the current; in matters of principle stand like a rock." –Thomas Jefferson

In His closing remarks during the Sermon on the Mount Jesus gave the parable of the foundation. He likened the man who was a doer of the Word of God to a person who built his house upon a rock. The fellow in the parable invested his time, money, and energy to secure the stability of his home by digging deep and building upon the strength of a boulder. When the floods came the house was not exempt from the storm, but it was able to survive because of its foundation.

You see, the house was not holding up the foundation, the foundation was holding up the house. What gave the home the ability to stand during the raging storm was the part of the home that was unseen to the world.

The same principle is true in our own lives. Just because we work hard at being faithful and dedicated to the Lord does not mean we will avoid the storms of life. We will certainly endure hardships and adversities; but the difference between those who survive and those who fall is the unseen foundation.

Show me someone who has a secure and sturdy foundation and I will show you someone who will survive the most tempestuous moments of life. It's not what you see that makes us strong; it's what you cannot see.

DAILY SCRIPTURE READING: Luke 6-7

OCTOBER 27

THE DIFFERENCE GRACE MAKES

"Some people's religion is like a guitar strapped around an unskilled musician...beautifully worthless." –Kenneth Kuykendall

There is no such thing as under-cover Christianity. Those who are *saved* by grace will *exude* grace from their lives. Hudson Taylor said, "If your father and mother, your sister and brother, if the very cat and dog in the house, are not happier for your being a Christian, it is a question whether you really are."

Some people's religion is like a guitar strapped around an unskilled musician...beautifully worthless. How can our faith be beneficial to others if they never see it working in our own lives? God's work of grace is not cold, stagnant, or unnoticed. On the contrary, it revolutionizes who we are, how we act, and what we do. Its transformational power is a testimony of regeneration. How does it work in your life?

Do people see God's marvelous grace through your attitude, behavior, actions, and words? Does your family notice a change in you? What about your co-workers, neighbors, or associates? As Taylor contends, even our dogs and cats should notice a difference that grace makes.

Come out of the secret-service mindset. Let your faith be known; not just by the words in your mouth, but by the witness in your life. Show the world what kind of difference grace makes.

DAILY SCRIPTURE READING: Luke 8-9

OCTOBER 28

THE FAITH OF YOUR CHILDREN

"If you want to make a lasting difference, you had better make a commitment to endure." –Albert Mohler

Under the leadership of Moses, the children of Israel wandered in the wilderness for forty years. When Moses died, Joshua took over the reins. Joshua's generation would experience the mighty works of God as they crossed the Jordan River and captured the land of Canaan. God gave them clear instruction to make no league with the inhabitants of Canaan, but to rather throw down their altars and drive them out of the land.

Joshua's generation partially obeyed the Lord and failed to purge the Promise Land from the false gods of the Canaanites. As a result, the next generation would suffer greatly. The Bible says in Judges 2: 9-10 that Joshua died, and so did his generation; however, "there arose another generation after them, which knew not the LORD, nor yet the works which he had done for Israel."

The disobedience of Joshua's generation had a long-lasting, far-reaching effect on their children and grandchildren. When we fail to comply with God's instruction, we not only hinder our growth and development as a believer, but we set the groundwork for future disobedience in the next generation. Obey the Lord with ALL your heart, your children's relationship with God may very well depend on it.

DAILY SCRIPTURE READING: Luke 10-11

OCTOBER 29

TAKING STEPS, MAKING STOPS

"It's the quiet life of obedience that will earn a hearing." –Steve Farrar

A young child in Sunday School class was writing out Psalm 37:23 for his teacher, *"The steps of a good man are ordered by the Lord; and he delighteth in his way."* As the teacher reviewed the verse she noticed a misspelled word in the passage. The student wrote, "The STOPS of a good man are ordered by the Lord…" The teacher said, "Bobby, do you know that you misspelled STEPS?" Bobby replied, "No ma'am, I am ready for this class to STOP so that I can STEP somewhere else."

Walking with God means knowing when and where to step, but it also means knowing when and where to stop. Too often we are traveling so quickly down the road of life that we run through spiritual red-lights and stop signs. We have no time to pause, reflect, relax, and renew our strength.

The Lord understood the benefits of stopping. Oftentimes He would dismiss Himself from the multitude, ascend into a mountain, and spend some time with His Heavenly Father. If Jesus needed those down times, we do as well. As you walk with the Lord today, get a sense of His presence. If He instructs you to take a step, take it; if He instructs you to make a stop, make it.

DAILY SCRIPTURE READING: Luke 12-13

OCTOBER 30

CONTENT IN CHRIST

"I sometimes wonder whether all pleasures are not substitutes for joy." –C.S. Lewis

Have you ever noticed that most people are never satisfied regardless of their success? We work extremely hard at setting goals, fulfilling dreams, and pursuing careers; but once we have accomplished what we've set out to do, we quickly become restless. We want bigger homes, better cars, and broader horizons. There is nothing wrong with completing a task, but it seems as though we are never satisfied.

The apostle Paul experienced this same temptation, but he learned to be content apart from the external circumstances of life. When we base our joy upon all the "blessings of life" then our satisfaction comes and goes with every changing wind. Paul's joy and satisfaction was not rooted in this world, but rather came through his relationship with Christ. Our position in Christ is the greatest and final pursuit of the soul. Paul knew that his life was complete in Jesus.

That's what most of us are looking for, is it not? We want to be complete, whole, and satisfied. Your job, your money, your position, your friends, your possessions, your degrees will never fully satisfy you; they only accentuate a greater need in your life- the need to know God. Jesus fully satisfies – there is nothing greater than being His child.

DAILY SCRIPTURE READING: Luke 14-16

OCTOBER 31

WHO IS SPEAKING FOR YOU?

"We apprehend that the finished work of Christ is the hub in which all the spokes of our blessings meet." –F.E. Marsh

Years ago, a man by the name of Marshall Cummings was accused of stealing a purse in Tulsa, Oklahoma. Cummings opted to be his own lawyer in the trial, but was not very successful. As he cross-examined the victim he asked, "Did you get a good look at my face when I took your purse?" After realizing what he said, he tried to retract his question, but to no avail. The state jury convicted Cummings and sentenced him to a ten-year prison sentence.

In the divine courtroom of justice, we are all guilty before the Holy Judge. If we try to defend ourselves by our own merit, works, goodness, or knowledge we will stand condemned. As Cummings would attest, it is not wise to try and defend yourself; especially before God.

We desperately need an advocate to speak on our behalf. John wrote, "And if any man sin, we have an advocate with the Father, Jesus Christ the righteous: And he is the propitiation for our sins: and not for ours only, but also for the sins of the whole world" (1 John 2:1-2). As believers we do not have to defend ourselves, we cannot defend ourselves: we are guilty. Christ however approaches the bench and declares us righteous before the throne of God. His atonement declares our freedom.

DAILY SCRIPTURE READING: Luke 17-18

NOVEMBER

NOVEMBER 1
INVESTING IN YOUR HOME

"A happy family is but an earlier heaven." –John Bowring

Time with family is like investing for retirement: small and consistent contributions compounded over an extended period of time leads to a valuable return. Ronald Reagan said it like this, "Great change in America begins at the dinner table." Reagan understood that the betterment of our civilization was not through the channels of legislation or political platform. It was, and is, through the teaching and training arm of the home.

The kind of family you have tomorrow is determined by the kind of investments you make in your family today. What kind of contributions have you been making lately? An investment doesn't just happen. You have to be intentional and deliberate when putting money into a particular account. The same is true with our families.

Sporadic investments are good, but they will never build a healthy portfolio. In large, your legacy will be defined, not by the buildings you erect, the degrees you earn, or the positions you acquire; but by the lives you touch. The building blocks of your home are laid day after day in the efforts of continual and consistent labor. Build a family, and you'll have a place to live for a long time.

DAILY SCRIPTURE READING: Luke 19-20

NOVEMBER 2

GO AND GET YOUR SCAR

"An aura of authenticity, created by the scars on our souls, connects us with the deepest hurts of others." –Jeff Iorg

When the knights of King Arthur's court returned from battle, they were examined for bruises, cuts, and wounds. If they did not bear any ailments in their bodies they were thrust out of the king's presence and back into the battle with a direct command, "Go and get your scar!"

Without a scar, King Arthur believed, you didn't really engage in the warfare. Sometimes the greatest badge of courage is the scar we received from the conflict.

Scars are to be expected. In his book, *The Painful Side of Leadership*, Jeff Iorg writes, "Sometimes God allows us to experience pain so we can help others with similar problems. An aura of authenticity, created by the scars on our souls, connects us with the deepest hurts of others. There is no shortcut to being equipped to offer genuine comfort to hurting people. Wounded people give the best comfort."

It is a misnomer to think that as soldiers of the cross we will have no scars. On the contrary, we will bear wounds, endure battles, engage the enemy, and have some pain along the way. Though scars can be painful and excruciating, they prove one glorious truth: you have made it through the battle! Now, go and get your scar.

DAILY SCRIPTURE READING: Luke 21-22

NOVEMBER 3

THE END OF THE ROPE

"When you reach the end of your rope, you may very well be at the beginning of your hope." –Kenneth Kuykendall

I recently heard a story about a man who descended into a well by sliding down a rope. He supposed the rope to be ample in length, but as he reached the end of the rope his feet had not yet touched the bottom of the well. He had exhausted his strength and therefore could not climb back up; and he feared to let go lest he be dashed into pieces. He held on as long as he could until sheer exhaustion set it. When he let the rope slip from his grasp he fell to the bottom of the well – just three inches.

Sometimes it can feel like we are at the end of our rope. Inch by inch we descend into the darkness until our grip becomes loose and weak. Fear, fatigue, and exhaustion sets in, and then we let go. It is then we realize something: the ground was closer than we thought; soon we are back on our feet.

When you reach the end of your rope, you may very well be at the beginning of your hope. It's true, there are times we need to strengthen our grip and pull ourselves back up. But then there are those moments when we have to let go, and simply trust God. Hold on as long as you can, and then trust God to be your solid ground.

DAILY SCRIPTURE READING: Luke 23-24

NOVEMBER 4

THE BLUE-PRINTS FOR LIFE

"All things desirable for man is contained in the Bible." –Abraham Lincoln

It doesn't matter how much money you spend on material, or how many contractors you schedule, or how many hours you invest into a building, if you do not have the right blue-prints for the construction, you will waste your time.

No one would flippantly start a building project without securing the appropriate plans. Such a strategy would bring chaos and confusion. Intentions are wonderful, but intention without preparation is futile. Let's face it, buildings need blue-prints…the same is true with our lives.

God has given us the blue-prints for spiritual success. He doesn't expect us to live for Him without proper instruction. He has a set of signed and sealed plans known as the Word of God. These plans provide the foundation and framework for faithful living.

How ludicrous would it be to go to the local hardware store and spend thousands of dollars on material without knowing the design? The same holds true in the spiritual realm. Don't expect to build a life of honor and glory without referring to God's specific plans. Measure your life by His Word, and God will provide a good place to live.

DAILY SCRIPTURE READING: John 1-2

NOVEMBER 5
SERVANT LEADERSHIP- PART 1

"In the kingdom of God, service is not a stepping stone to nobility; it is nobility." –T.W. Manson

Christ is the embodiment of servant leadership. His incarnation not only authenticated His deity, it also accentuated the manner in which He would lead His disciples. Christ was not a go-with-the-flow pushover who excused all and any activity from those around Him; but neither was He an in-your-face-tyrant who coerced His followers to make decisions for egotistical purposes. Christ did not seek self-fulfillment or self-validation; more times than not He actually refused recognition and pointed men to the Father.

As spiritual leaders, we have a similar responsibility–we should cause men to bypass the titles, positions, and futile accolades of our prideful accomplishments, and simply direct them to the great God of glory.

We must be careful however when we categorize the leadership style of Jesus. Yes, we can study His actions, decisions, words, accomplishments and try to implement them in the corporate or ministerial world. We can use His lessons and put them into practice on the ball field, the business meeting, or the political stage. But Jesus did more than just model a particular method of leadership. He demonstrated the essence of a selfless life. Jesus taught that glory, power, and honor are the fruit of humility.

DAILY SCRIPTURE READING: John 3-4

NOVEMBER 6

SERVANT LEADERSHIP- PART 2

"Honor is a guaranteed triumph for the humble life, but I assure you, it is not the aim." –Kenneth Kuykendall

The essence of servant leadership is the act whereby you *lead* others by *serving* others through humility. Most leaders like the recognition, enjoy the applause, and gladly receive the awards. But for the servant leader, the true reward is not fame, it is actually service. T.W. Manson said, "In the kingdom of God, service is not a stepping stone to nobility; *it is* nobility, at least the only kind that is recognized."

And be sure, God recognizes service and humility. Jesus was given a name by the Heavenly Father…a name that will be applauded, recognized, and worshiped by all men. Indeed, every knee will bow to the Potentate King of Glory. However, the seat of Christ's greatness was stitched with the fabric of selfless humility. Therefore, the bigger question is not "who are you leading?" but rather "who are you following?"

Honor is a guaranteed triumph for the humble life, but I assure you, it is not the aim. Servant leaders spend little time trying to hit the bull's eye for their own glory; instead, they invest time, energy, and effort in helping others hit the mark. Helping others find their way…this is the essence of servant leadership; this is the glory of Christ.

DAILY SCRIPTURE READING: John 5-6

NOVEMBER 7

DON'T BE A BALL HOG

*"A deaf ear is evidence
of a closed mind."* –John Maxwell

The term "ball hog" was a name we used growing up to describe someone who would never share the limelight with his teammates. Once the ball got in his hands, you could count on him keeping it for awhile. The "ball hog" made it his personal goal to score every time he touched the ball. Rarely passing or seldom giving, the "ball hog" monopolized the game.

I have not only played with "ball hogs" throughout the years, I have also talked with them. Have you ever talked with someone who controls and monopolizes the entire conversation? (I am sure you are thinking of someone right now). Some people give very little opportunity to reply or respond while engaged in conversation with others. Although this may come off as a habit or personality trait, it is nonetheless uncomfortable and oftentimes frustrating. If not careful, the "ball hog" can seem self-absorbed and uninterested in what other people have to say.

The Bible challenges the "ball hog" with these convicting words, "Wherefore, my beloved brethren, let every man be swift to hear, slow to speak, slow to wrath" (James 1:19). There is a reason why God gave us two ears and one mouth. Let's pass the ball around from time to time and give someone else the opportunity to score.

DAILY SCRIPTURE READING: John 7-8

NOVEMBER 8

APPLYING GOD'S WORD

"Your knowledge of God's Word only brings Him honor when it is applied." –Kenneth Kuykendall

Our biggest problem when it comes to the Word of God is not reading it, memorizing it, learning it, or even embracing it; it is implementing it. The true test of our spiritual character is not how we receive the Bible; it is how we appropriate it in our lives. How do we do it? How do we take what we have read from Scripture and carefully give application? Consider a few suggestions:

1. Read and meditate daily. Reading and meditating alone will not bring application, but you have to start somewhere. If you are not reading His Word, you cannot apply it. Get the Word in your heart and mind.

2. Pray for wisdom. As you meditate on the Word, ask the Lord to give you remembrance and discernment. Pray over the text and ask God for spiritual enlightenment.

3. Ask Questions. As you read through a passage, ask yourself plenty of questions. Who is the author? To whom is he speaking? What is he saying? What is God saying to me? How do I make application?

4. Look for situations. Expect opportunities to occur in which you can apply what you have learned. Filter each situation through the Word of God, and make decisions in accordance to Scripture.

DAILY SCRIPTURE READING: John 9-10

NOVEMBER 9

SPIRITUAL FLOSSING

"Sanctification is a work of God, conducted through life and completed in death." –William Plumer

My wife is a dental hygienist. She constantly stresses to my family the importance of flossing. Most people have no problem brushing their teeth multiple times a day, but flossing is another story. The American Dental Association recommends flossing at least once a day, but a majority of Americans disregard the recommendation. Brushing alone will not give a person the total dental health that they need.

From time to time we should do some spiritual flossing. Oh sure, we have a daily regimen of brushing, but what about those hard to reach areas that are underneath the surface? This is not about having a bright, religious smile; no, this goes beyond vain cosmetics. This involves your overall health. This is about reaching places that are typically unseen.

Over time we accumulate worldly plaque. This not only gives off a foul smell, it actually causes other health problems. According to WebMD, studies indicate that a build-up of plaque can lead to heart disease and dementia. If this is true in the natural sense, it is certainly true in the spiritual.

Add spiritual flossing to your daily routine. Get below the surface by wrapping God's Word around every area of your life.

DAILY SCRIPTURE READING: John 11-12

NOVEMBER 10

THE TRUTH ABOUT TWIST-TIES

"It's easy to dodge our responsibilities; but we cannot dodge the consequences of our responsibilities." –Sir Josiah Stamp

I never knew the proper name of this grand invention. I believe the term is twist-tie. To be honest, I never gave much attention to the little metal-wire contraption attached to the end of a loaf of bread; but recently I wanted to make a sandwich and realized the twist-tie was nowhere to be found. As I reached into the plastic bag, I suddenly discovered the importance of this seemingly insignificant device. Sliced ham doesn't taste as good on stale bread.

Little things make a big difference. When we fail to take care of the little things in our life, larger problems seem to follow. It's a little thing to put gas in the tank; it's a big problem when we are on the side of the road. It's a little thing to tie your shoes; it's a big problem when trip and fall. It's a little thing to lock up the fence; it's a big problem when the dog runs the neighborhood.

A successful life is comprised of doing a lot of little things right. At the end of the day, little things aren't that little at all. They are the things in which make life what it is. Don't be misled. God honors people who honor Him in the little things. Make sure the twist-tie is in its proper place today…and you'll not have to worry about growing stale.

DAILY SCRIPTURE READING: John 13-15

NOVEMBER 11

THE HEART OF THE GOSPEL

"My only rest is in Christ; all other areas remain unfinished." –Kenneth Kuykendall

Christendom is becoming increasingly man-centered these days. Books, religious shows, conferences, and particular movements are birthed from self-centered perspectives trying to achieve self-centered goals. Like the church at Laodicea, we leave Christ out of the equation, and then wonder why our lives lack purpose and meaning.

The message of the Gospel however, is not man-centered. Oh sure, it is for man, and because of man that Christ came to die for our sins. But at the heart of the Gospel we discover more than ourselves.

The Gospel is God-Centered. The plan of salvation derived from the heart of God. It is His plan, the original plan, the only plan. Such a plan could have only been birthed from the wisdom of Almighty God.

The Gospel is Golgotha-Centered. God's plan takes His Son to a rugged cross. It transfers the weight and penalty of man's sin on the spotless Lamb of God. Without Calvary, the gospel would never be a reality.

The Gospel is Grace-Centered. All of the gospel is grace. Grace is from God, faith is from God, salvation is from God. The unmerited favor of God is exactly that: unmerited. Man is the recipient of this marvelous message, but at the heart of this plan is a gracious God who forgives.

DAILY SCRIPTURE READING: John 16-18

NOVEMBER 12

GOD DOES THE RIGHT THING

"God invites us to take a holiday, to stop being God for awhile, and let Him be God." –Simon Tugwell

As a leader, I oftentimes have to make tough decisions. Many of those decisions are based off of information that is not known by the masses. Sometimes a decision has to be made that seems unpopular to others; but if they knew all the information, they would better understand the thought-process. I learned years ago that my job as a leader isn't to make popular choices; it is to make the right choices with the information I have. God does the same thing, the only difference: He has all the info.

Sometimes we question why particular things transpire in our lives. We suffer loss, experience difficulties, and endure problematic circumstances. In our limited knowledge, we question why God allows such things to occur. We have thousands of questions…what we do not have is all the information. But God does.

God sees farther than us. As a matter of fact, He sees it all, the end from the beginning. He is not concerned about what is popular, He is concerned about what is right. God can't help but be anything but right. He is righteously right. If you are having a hard time understanding the Lord in this particular season of life, just remember this: God has all the information; He is doing the right thing at the right time for the right reason.

DAILY SCRIPTURE READING: John 19-21

NOVEMBER 13
KEEP THE NAME ON THE SIGN

"It is certainly true that hardly anything is missing from our churches these days – except the most important thing." –A.W. Tozer

Can you imagine how frustrating it would be if restaurants took their names off the buildings and marquees? You would have to wonder what kind of store it was and what services it offered. Suppose hospitals took down their ER directional signs. Many sick and injured people would wander aimlessly as they sought medical attention. Such a scenario would be annoying because, as a culture, we like signs, symbols, and names. They point us in specific directions about specific places.

Restaurants, businesses, professional offices, and the like have particular identities that describe a particular service…and for the most part, we insist on such things. However, when it comes to God's House there is a growing trend of shallow, vague, superficiality concerning identity.

Why do people insist that the church to be something it is not? Furthermore, why do spiritual leaders try to revamp the image, identity, and purpose of the church? God didn't permit His Son to die on the cross so that we can have a coffee shop, nightclub, or strip mall. The church at large has converged with the popular trends of the world thus losing its identity in the process. We are salt and light. To be anything different is to promote a nameless Savior and a Christless eternity.

DAILY SCRIPTURE READING: Acts 1-3

NOVEMBER 14

BEFORE YOU QUIT

"By prevailing over all distractions, one may unfailingly arrive at his chosen goal or destination." –Christopher Columbus

Have you ever felt like quitting? Be honest. Have you told yourself you couldn't continue under the current pressures of life? The job is too demanding; the schedule is too hectic; the ministry is too discouraging; the traffic is too congested; the family is too dysfunctional; the church is too indifferent; the relationship is too taxing. Sure, we have all been faced with the temptation of walking away from circumstances. But before you throw in the proverbial towel, remember a few things:

The Past Generation Reminds Us. Look at the patriarchs of old. They faced giants, lions, barbarians, and great battles of the faith. They too had moments when they wanted to quit, but they endured and remained steadfast in the heat of the conflict. They remind us that we can make it.

The Next Generation Resolves Us. Where will your children and grandchildren be in 5, 10, 20 years from now if you decide to lay down your faith today? What kind of heritage will your family, church, or ministry have? The answer depends on you.

This Generation Requires Us. Look around; I am sure someone in close proximity is facing a greater, more pressing situation. They need you to be faithful. Pick up the towel, take a few more steps and keep going for God.

DAILY SCRIPTURE READING: Acts 4-6

NOVEMBER 15
SITTING IN HOT WATER

"Many blush to confess their faults, who never blush to commit them." –William Secker

It has been said of Dr. Paul Brand, medical physician and leprosy missionary, that he would regularly take scalding hot baths after long arduous days on the field. His reason for the baths was simple: he wanted to see if any parts of his body had lost feeling, an initial symptom of leprosy. It was his way of self-examination in relation to working so closely with those who had the skin-eating disease.

The psalmist invites us all to do the same. Psalm 139 records, "Search me, O God, and know my heart: try me, and know my thoughts: And see if *there be any* wicked way in me, and lead me in the way everlasting." The scalding hot waters of judgment may initially be uncomfortable and painful, but they reveal life-threatening diseases that need spiritual remedy.

Living in this world can affect our faith. We are surrounded by those who have a spiritual disease. And though it is our responsibility to love them and lead them to Christ, we must be cautious that we are not infected with the very plague we seek to cure.

Climb into the tub. Let the waters pour over your soul, and ask God to search your heart for anything that may hinder your service in the Lord.

DAILY SCRIPTURE READING: Acts 7-8

NOVEMBER 16

POP QUIZ

"A mark of Christian maturity is to continually trust the Lord in the everyday minutiae of life." –Jerry Bridges

Do you remember taking pop quizzes in school? You were supposed to read carefully the given text that previous night with the anticipation that an official test would be given in a few days. A pop quiz came intentionally unannounced. There was a reason for its name: it popped the joy out of the rest of your day. Its design was simple: it was to reveal if you had done the assignment or not; and to see how well you knew the subject.

The intention of the pop quiz was actually beneficial. It was a wakeup call to your understanding of that subject's content. Suppose the Lord did a pop quiz on your spirituality today? Yes, one day we will all appear before the Judgment Seat of Christ. We will give an account for our lives; but suppose we had a few pop quizzes along the way? How well would you do?

Have you read your Bible lately? Have you spent time with God in prayer? Who was the last person you spoke with about Christ? Have you been faithfully going to church? Have you spoken poorly about someone recently? How is your worship? Your service? Your devotion? How well would you do if the Lord gave you an impromptu test today? The only way to pass such an exam is to make sure you do your homework.

DAILY SCRIPTURE READING: Acts 9-10

NOVEMBER 17

INTERIOR CULTIVATION

"I must secure more time for private devotions. I have been living far too public for me." –William Wilberforce

The great devotion writer Oswald Chambers said, "If God allows you to be stripped of the exterior portions of your life, He means for you to cultivate the interior." Cultivating the interior is the essence of devotion. True devotion is knowing that you will never be able to repay Christ for Calvary, but giving it a daily attempt. So what are the essential elements of interior cultivation?

1. Devotion requires a quiet place. We are addicted to noise. We wake up to a screeching alarm only to go to bed with a roaring television. Escape from the clamor of life and find a place alone with God. Jesus did.

2. Devotion requires a quiet hour. Jerry Bridges said, "Just as a house must have a foundation and framework to hold it together, so our all-day communion with God must have a foundation and a framework to hold it together. The foundation of our communion with God is the morning quiet time." Seek God early, and He will be found throughout the day.

3. Devotion requires a quiet heart. Steve Farrar contends, "It is entirely possible for a man to appear perfectly fine, to live an outward life of doing all the right things, and yet to be completely isolated from God in his heart." Above all, devotion is about getting your heart in tune with God. To do such a thing, we must hear the melody of the master in solitude.

DAILY SCRIPTURE READING: Acts 11-13

NOVEMBER 18

MUSIC WITH THE MASTER

"The love of God, and only the love of God, secures the vision of God, and keeps God constantly before our mind." –Dallas Willard

Devotion may include certain disciplines of writing, journaling, Bible-reading, and meditating, but it requires much more than ink, paper, and thoughts – it demands that we empty ourselves before a Holy God and drink from His fountain. It is turning from our ornately-designed tables of the flesh, denying ourselves of temporal desires, and taking a seat at His table where the meal is prepared and provided from ovens beyond this world. In short, it is taking wings toward heaven where our landing will be in the very presence of the Holy Lamb of God.

A.W. Tozer, the eccentric prophet from yesteryear said, "Retire from the world each day to some private spot. Stay in the secret place till the surrounding noises begin to fade out of your heart and a sense of God's presence envelopes you. Deliberately tune out the unpleasant sounds and come out of your closet determined not to hear them. Listen for the inward Voice till you learn to recognize it."

Devotion is about getting your heart in tune with God, again and again. To do such a thing, we must hear the soft melody of the Master as He plays to our soul in quiet solitude. Too often we barge into the holy place with loud, obnoxious, out-of-tune sounds from the world. Be still, know that He is God, and hear His sympathy of grace.

DAILY SCRIPTURE READING: Acts 14-15

NOVEMBER 19

WALKING WITH GOD

---

*"We never grow closer to God when we just live life;
it takes deliberate pursuit and attentiveness."* –Francis Chan

I recently invited my children to go on a jog with me through the neighborhood. Strong-willed, growing, and full of energy, they turned the jog into a competition. As we began the route, one of my sons took off full speed trying to outdo his brother. We watched as he sped hundreds of feet ahead. Occasionally he would turn back and give us a smile as though he was winning. It did not take him long to realize that he could not keep that pace up for 2.5 miles.

Once we caught up to him, he was so winded that he fell behind. This now stirred my other son to speed far pass his brother. Now I have one son hundreds of feet behind, the other, hundreds of feet ahead. Suddenly, I am jogging all by myself, thus defeating the purpose of my invitation. I just wanted to be with them.

The noise of six marching feet soon softened to the sound of my own steps; it was then I thought about my own walk with God. Like my two sons who turned the expedition into a competition, I suppose sometimes I do the same thing – I forget why I am on the journey. Sometimes I get so far ahead of God that I get winded; other times I lag so far behind that I get discouraged. Either way, I am missing out on the whole point of the walk –spending time with Him.

DAILY SCRIPTURE READING: Acts 16-17

NOVEMBER 20

RESOLVED IN THE FAITH

"Holy resolution, built on fast principles, lifts up its head like a rock in the midst of the waves." –William Gurnall

Missionary E. Stanley Jones spent much of his life in India preaching the gospel and making a cultural impact. He spoke to millions of souls, traveled extensively, met with presidents and peasants, and led many to the Lord Jesus Christ. At the age of 83, Jones suffered a stroke that left him without speech or mobility. In the last few months before his death, he was able to dictate, through his paralyzed lips the manuscript of a small book. In one of his last statements about life and faith he said:

"There are scars on my faith, but underneath those scars there are no doubts. Christ has me with the consent of all my being and with the cooperation of all my life. The song I sing is a lit song. Not the temporary exuberance of youth that fades when middle and old age sets in their disillusionment and cynicism...No, I'm 83, and I'm more excited today about being a Christian than I was at 18 when in first put my feet on the way."

Can you say with a resolved heart that you are more excited today about Christ than you were yesterday? Perhaps you have been saved for some time and your faith has grown mundane and monotonous. Ask the Lord to give you more zeal and passion today than ever before.

DAILY SCRIPTURE READING: Acts 18-20

NOVEMBER 21

GOD FUNDS HIS WORK

---

*"The God that answereth by orphanages,
let Him be God."* –Charles Spurgeon

William Quarrier was heavily involved in the Orphan Homes of Scotland during the late 1800's. He, along with Annie MacPherson, desired to take homeless children off the streets of London and place them in cottage-style orphanages where they could develop a sense of community, family, and faith.

Quarrier was responsible for balancing the finances for the institution. When the accounts fell into the red, he would call on his associates to join themselves together in prayer. Whenever the group came together in prayer, invariably, the funds would always show up in some manner, sometimes that very day. At the close of his life, William Quarrier testified about God's provision, "We have never been in debt one hour."

God always funds His work. It may be a ram in the thicket, a handful of meal, a cruise of oil, or a few little fish and some bread – but mark it down, God always funds His work. Whatever He calls us to do, He adequately and sometimes overwhelmingly provides for the venture.

Embrace His call, accept His plans, and experience His provision. If God has supernaturally sent you, He will supernaturally support you.

DAILY SCRIPTURE READING: Acts 21-23

NOVEMBER 22

THE AFTER-EFFECT OF THE SPIRIT

"The world needs to see God doing things only God can do instead of man doing things others can do." –Kenneth Kuykendall

Jesus gave His disciples some last-minute instructions before His ascension to Glory. He told them to wait in Jerusalem until the arrival of the Holy Spirit. He said, "But ye shall receive power, after that the Holy Ghost is come upon you..." (Acts 1:8). There is one very important word the church needs to familiarize itself with once again: **after**. The power, ability, and authority of the first-century disciples depended solely upon the effect of the Holy Spirit; without Him they could do nothing.

The world needs to see God doing things only God can do instead of man doing things others can do. A.W. Tozer said, "No one dare be so rash as to seek to do impossible things unless he has first been empowered by the God of the impossible." We are trying to accomplish divine acts without the support of the Divine Spirit.

Jesus was clear: preaching, teaching, witnessing, evangelization, church-planting, missionary endeavors, and the like were to be done AFTER the Holy Spirit came. When we work in the energy of the flesh, we not only become frustrated, tired, and weary, but we accomplish nothing of eternal significance. They were found praying before His arrival, the modern-day church should follow their practice.

DAILY SCRIPTURE READING: Acts 24-26

NOVEMBER 23

PAINTING THE WORLD

"Church is not a place where people go, it is something that people are." –D. Stuart Briscoe

For several years, I worked as a paint-contractor for residential home-builders in metro-Atlanta. Almost every day I would place an order with the local paint store for various colors and shades of paint. I was always interested in the method of their formulation. The computer they used would shoot various colors into the bucket. The "shaker" would fiercely mix the colors together until it became the color of my choosing. When the lid was opened, it always matched the color on the chart. Even though there were multiple tints in the mix, they all worked together to produce one color.

The body of Christ works in a very similar fashion. The Holy Spirit gives different gifts with different functions to different people to blend together for one common goal: to glorify God. The apostle Paul said, "Now there are diversities in gifts, but the same Spirit. And there are differences in administrations, but the same Lord. And there are diversities in operations, but it is the same God which worketh all in all" (1 Corinthians 12:4-6).

The church, though comprised with various gifts and colors, is used to paint a picture of His grace and mercy to the world. The only color the world needs to see in the church is the precious red blood of His Son.

DAILY SCRIPTURE READING: Acts 27-28

NOVEMBER 24

IMPRESSIONS OF LIFE

"I was set up from everlasting, from the beginning, or ever the earth was." –Proverbs 8:23

If you are familiar with the Impressionistic paintings of Claude Monet, you already know that his portraits look better the further away you get from them. This was his intention, this was his genius. If you view his works at a close perspective, they look like chaotic, disordered, messy strokes of paint. Ironically, as you step away, the painting actually begins to come into focus. The impression of the work is better experienced at a distance.

This is a method that works in life as well.

Sometimes in order to see the big picture, it is necessary to step back, get the entire scene in view, and order accordingly. Monet was not concerned with all the particulars as much as he was the grand scheme of things. Yes, we should take care of details; we should plan, organize, and make certain preparations for life. However, if we get so caught up in the minutiae, we may very well miss out on the masterpiece.

When was the last time you took a few steps back? When was the last time you saw your life from a big-picture perspective? If it has been awhile, you may want to put the brush down, walk away from the picture, and take a look at what you are painting on your canvas.

DAILY SCRIPTURE READING: Romans 1-3

NOVEMBER 25

GOING BACK WITH GRATITUDE

"Keep your face to the sunshine, and you cannot see the shadow." –Helen Keller

Jesus healed ten lepers one day on the outskirts of Samaria. These men were physically diseased, spiritually despondent, and socially dejected. When they saw Christ, they begged for mercy. Jesus, in His grace and compassion, commanded that they present themselves to the priest. This was an act of faith on their part. They were to head in the direction of the temple, believing and trusting they would be whole.

As they went their way, they were all cleansed. Out of the ten, only one returned to give thanks and honor to the Lord. The Bible says, "And one of them, when he saw that he was healed, turned back, and with a loud voice glorified God" (Luke 17:15). One of them "turned back." This is the essence of gratitude: returning to the place where the blessing was given. Thankfulness is rooted in our acknowledgement of grace. It is turning our hearts, minds, and sometimes our physical body back to the place where God imparted blessing and favor.

Have you gone back recently? The other nine were so engrossed with having a religious experience at the temple that they failed to turn their appreciation to the one who gave the healing. Take a few minutes today and return to the place where God healed your soul. Give Him the glory that is due His name.

DAILY SCRIPTURE READING: Romans 4-7

NOVEMBER 26

GIVING THANKS

"Careful for nothing, prayerful for everything, thankful for anything." –D.L Moody

Giving thanks is more than an expression of gratitude. It is that, but truthfully we can say "thank you" to someone and not really mean it. Gratitude is more than words communicated; it is ultimately a mindset, a mentality. It is a keen awareness of our dependence upon a particular thing or person, and then demonstrating that appreciation through a charitable relationship.

Thanksgiving is not really a holiday of indulgence and stuffing, it is a lifestyle that actually sacrifices and succumbs to the reality of grace – God's grace imparted and enjoyed. So what does it really mean to give thanks?

Most of the time we reduce our blessings to those tangible items found around the home. But what things unseen? Joy, peace, grace, contentment, assurance, hope, rest, and security: all of these deserve our gratitude and appreciation.

Giving thanks means assessing your life and recognizing all that you have. As the word suggests, thanksgiving is not just about "thanks," it is equally about "giving." Thanksgiving is about returning our appreciation to the One who abundantly gives daily to our needs, and even our desires.

DAILY SCRIPTURE READING: Romans 8-10

NOVEMBER 27

A PSALM 100 KIND OF DAY

"Thou who has given so much to me, give me one more thing – a thankful heart." –George Hebert

The very first passage of Scripture that I memorized by heart was Psalm 100. My motivation for learning the passage was prompted by my Sunday School teacher. She promised a gift to every student who could quote the passage verbatim.

That was over thirty years ago, and I have no idea what she rewarded me for memorizing the verse. The reward was short-lived and quickly discarded. As a child, I didn't realize that the true gift would be the passage itself. Through the years, this verse has challenged me to live a life of praise and worship. On this Thanksgiving Day, I challenge you to have a Psalm 100 kind of day.

1. Be Heard! – (v1) Make a joyful noise unto the Lord

2. Be Happy! – (v2) Serve the Lord with gladness

3. Be Humble – (v3) Know the Lord has made us, and not we ourselves

4. Be Holy! – (v4) Enter His gates with thanksgiving

5. Behold! – (v5) The Lord is good; his mercy is everlasting; and his truth endureth to all generation

Will you do all of these today? Don't let Thanksgiving pass without spending some time in praise and worship to your Heavenly Father.

DAILY SCRIPTURE READING: Romans 11-13

NOVEMBER 28

FORGIVEN AND FORGIVING

"None of us has a claim to superiority over any other in God's presence." –Gordon MacDonald

Living with an unforgiving heart produces emotional misery and spiritual indifference. Is there anyone in your life that needs to be forgiven? That is a very easy question to ask, but a very difficult question to answer. But such a question is required to be in good standing with God.

In his book, *A Resilient Life,* Gordon MacDonald speaks about his difficulty with forgiveness. He writes, "In the maturing years of my life, I learned much about forgiveness. Forgiveness, I came to see, is about cleaning up the memory by renouncing and flushing vengeful feelings about other people. Forgiveness is about surrendering the right for vengeance and retribution. It is about acknowledging that we are all failures in one way or another and that we stand on level ground with any offender before the cross, where God, in Christ forgave us. None of us has a claim to superiority over any other in God's presence."

Calvary is the solution for the unforgiving soul. God's mercy and grace displayed on the cross is the divine remedy for my own unforgiving heart. When I consider how God forgave me of my wicked and foul trespasses, how can I hold a grudge against another? The most obvious validation of a forgiven heart is a heart that forgives. Being forgiven gives way to forgiveness.

DAILY SCRIPTURE READING: Romans 14-16

NOVEMBER 29
CONVENIENT CHRISTIANITY

"The world is put back by the death of everyone who has to sacrifice his peculiar gifts to conventionality." –Florence Nightingale

David Livingstone, the missionary hero to Africa, was asked by a missionary society if he knew of any easily-accessible roads to which some of their interns could travel. They wanted to get a taste for mission life and desired to spend some time with Livingstone. David Livingstone replied, "If you have men who will only come if there are good roads, I don't want them. I want men who will come even if there are no roads."

One may contend that Livingstone replied harshly to the missionary society, but I contend that Livingstone knew what it meant to count the cost.

We are living in a convenience-minded society. Oftentimes when something is too difficult or inconvenient we hesitate to move into action. Too often we allow obstacles to hinder us from an opportunity. The Lord teaches us to sit down and count the cost before we attempt anything for him. Being his disciple involves problems, persecutions, and paths that are not cut down.

We must be willing to go for God regardless of the convenience factor. Christ did not die a convenient death; we cannot assume a convenient life.

DAILY SCRIPTURE READING: 1 Corinthians 1-4

NOVEMBER 30

HOLINESS WITH THE HAMMER

"Whoever is careless with the truth in small matters cannot be trusted with the truth in important matters." –Albert Einstein

A pastor told his congregation one Sunday that he would be taking a few weeks off to repair a fence in his backyard that needed mending. A little boy heard the announcement and showed up the next day at the pastor's home. As the pastor began working on the fence the little boy just stood there silently and watched the man of God as he worked.

The next day the little boy showed up again at the same time and just stared intensely as the preacher hammered away at his work. This went on for several days until the preacher asked the boy if he would like to help. The boy responded, "No sir, I just want to see what a preacher does when he hits his hand with a hammer."

Be certain- someone one is watching your life. Odds are it is someone who is younger. The children in your home, the students in your class, the kids down the street are looking for someone to admire and esteem. It is easy to stand behind a pulpit and pronounce to others how to live, but those words will only have validity when they see character while working on the fence. You are someone's favorite Christian. What kind of testimony will they see in you today?

DAILY SCRIPTURE READING: 1 Corinthians 5-8

DECEMBER

DECEMBER 1

IT'S A WONDERFUL LIFE

"Life's value is not in its duration but in its donation. It's not how long you live, it's how fully you live." –Unknown

In the classic movie, *It's a Wonderful Life*, George Bailey failed to realize how he affected others until he saw what the world would have been like had he never been born. His community at large was drastically different as a result of his absence. Though he faced many disappointments throughout the movie, he finally came to realize that life was indeed wonderfully good.

Imagine just for a moment what the world would be like had Christ never been born. Such a notion is hopelessly sobering. Suppose there had never been a cross or an empty tomb. The world today would be radically, and awfully different. Consider the dismal thought of a Christless world…or even worse, a Christless eternity.

But the glad reality is that Christ was born. He really came, He really died, and He really rose from the grave. He changed the scope and landscape of humanity. More importantly, today He changes hearts.

Therefore, with resolute spirit we offer praise and honor to the Lamb of God Who takes away the sin of the world. We lift His name above all others. Because of His presence in the world we can gladly and confidently say "it's a wonderful life!"

DAILY SCRIPTURE READING: 1 Corinthians 9-11

DECEMBER 2

THE VALUE OF A SECOND

---

*"Time is what we want the most,
but what we use the worst."* –William Penn

World-class runners understand the importance of living with grueling discipline. They train day after day, week after week stretching and pushing their bodies to the limits. They endure harsh elements, early mornings, and late evenings in preparation for the next race. Their discipline is rooted in the perspective of time. To the passionate runner, half a second could very well mean the difference between first or last place.

The older you get the more you value every second in the race of life. In his book, *Margin*, Dr. Richard Swenson said, "This present moment is, literally, so narrow that it is impossible to conceive. We live our entire lives in an inconceivably thin slice of reality. Reflecting on this for many years now, I have arrived at a corollary understanding –that this present moment is not only infinitely narrow, but also infinitely deep."

What a thought…each moment is infinitely narrow, infinitely deep. No wonder athletes discipline themselves with such resolve: they are trying to get the most out of every second. Do you? Do you value the depth of each moment? As William Penn said, "Time is what we want the most, but what we use the worst."

DAILY SCRIPTURE READING: 1 Corinthians 12-14

DECEMBER 3
CRYING ON THE WRONG ROAD

"You cannot repent too soon, because you do not know how soon it may be too late." –Thomas Fuller

The word repentance derives from the ancient world of travel. Before the invention of modern-highways, maps, GPS, or road signs, travelers would easily and frequently get lost in their journey. Once a traveler acknowledged their lost state, they had to retrace their steps, often turning around from the direction in which they were headed. It was at this point they began to pursue the right path.

Therefore, repentance is not just about *turning away from*, it is equally about *turning toward*. Kevin DeYoung says, "There is an eternal difference between regret and repentance. Regret feels bad about past sins. Repentance turns away from past sins. Regret looks to our own circumstances. Repentance looks to God. Most of us are content with regret. We just want to feel bad for awhile, have a good cry, enjoy the cathartic experience, bewail our sin, and talk about how sorry we are. But we don't want to change."

Change…this is the essence of repentance, a change of direction. Too often we have ourselves a good cry and feel sorry about a particular thing, and may even confess our faults to God. But if we do not turn from such a practice, we have not truly repented – we are just crying about the fact we are on the wrong road.

DAILY SCRIPTURE READING: 1 Corinthians 15-16

DECEMBER 4

THE VALUE OF 50 SOULS

"I consider the success of my day based on the seeds I sow, not the harvest I reap." –Robert Louis Stevenson

A few years before his death, Charles Spurgeon was approached by an American lecture bureau team about coming to the United States. They wanted the 'prince of preachers' to give fifty lectures in all the major cities of America. The compensation would be one thousand dollars per lecture, thus totaling $50,000 in 50 days. Spurgeon replied to the offer, "I can do better. I will stay in London and try to save 50 souls."

What is the worth of a soul? How can you measure the value of eternity in monetary increments? You simply cannot. Money dissipates, decreases, and departs; but the soul lives on. This was Spurgeon's motivation for ministry, and it should be ours.

Peter instructed the spiritual leaders of his day, "Feed the flock of God which is among you…**not for filthy lucre**, but of a ready mind" (1 Peter 5:2). Peter referred to money as a dirty, vile, and corrupt motivation for service. When finances become the determining factor of ministry, we have in essence prostituted ourselves to the devil's commerce.

We must see the souls of men in light of eternity. As Spurgeon said, "If they perish, let them perish with our arms around their knees, let no one go to hell unwarned or unprayed for."

DAILY SCRIPTURE READING: 2 Corinthians 1-4

DECEMBER 5
NOT SO SUPER MAN

"God's one goal for us is Himself." –Francis Chan

You may have never heard of Jerry Seigel or Joe Shuster, but you probably know their creation: Superman. In the early 1930's, they developed the man-of-steel character and forever changed the landscape of comics and superheroes. Not realizing how wildly successful the series would eventually become, they sold their rights to Action Comics for a measly $130 dollars. Not a super idea.

Superman would become a multi-billion dollar brand. The cultural icon would be seen in comics, movies, toys, advertisement, television, and even broadway. In 1966, Shuster said that he stood on the sidewalk in the opening night of Superman's broadway musical début. Unfortunately for Shuster, he had no money to pay for a ticket. He said, "I just huddled out there, while the celebrities arrived. I couldn't get in to see my own creation."

"I couldn't get in to see my own creation." Those words are ironically haunting. In the third chapter of Revelation, we read of Christ standing on the outside of the church, knocking, seeking, asking to come in. Christ is no poor beggar without a place to stay, but He does long to be with His estranged creation. What a poor commentary of the last days: while we play the part of Supermen, the Creator gets little glory.

DAILY SCRIPTURE READING: 2 Corinthians 5-9

DECEMBER 6

ONE LIFE TO LIVE

---

*"Life is too short not to be happy,
and too long not to do well."* – Bryan Dodge

In the book of James we are asked a very important question, "What is your life?" The writer was not trying to wax eloquent or engage in some philosophical debate; no, he quickly answered his own question with these words, "It is even a vapor, that appeareth for a little time, and then vanisheth away." James was trying to give us a measurement. He was not speaking of the substance of life; he was speaking of the shortness of life.

The singular is in mind. We do not have "vapors" of life; we have only one to live. Fred Smith said, "You only live once, but if you work it right, once it enough." I would contend the only way to "work it right" is to receive forgiveness of your sins through faith in Christ. The earlier in life you find the Lord, the fuller your life becomes.

No one fully comprehends the brevity of life until one comes to the end. We look back and realize that James was right, a vapor is fleeting. Its benediction is as short-lived as its appearance. Therefore, to really live life, we must live life today. James also said, "Whereas ye know not what shall be on the morrow." Yesterday cannot be redone, tomorrow is not promised, so today is the only opportunity to bring meaning and purpose to this fleeting life. James gave us the measurement; it's our responsibility to define the meaning.

DAILY SCRIPTURE READING: 2 Corinthians 10-13

DECEMBER 7

ARE YOU A SAVED CHRISTIAN?

"You can name the name of Jesus, but if you won't follow the nature of Jesus, the name means nothing to you." –A.W. Tozer

That seems to be a strange question doesn't it: are you a saved Christian? In our culture, religious terms constantly need to be defined. The word "Christian" can mean a lot of things these days. Someone may contend they are Christian because of the following reasons:

- Someone told them they were Christian
- They grew up in a home where Christians lived
- They were born in a Christian country
- They are members of a church
- They have participated in Christian ordinances

The list could go on and on, but the point is simply this: someone who identifies themselves with Christianity may not necessary be saved.

I like what Bill Hull says, "You can follow your heart, your dreams, your gifts, and your personality profiles, and you can seek the right fit, but all of that is inferior to following Christ." Being saved is simply that: following Christ. Christianity identifies itself with religion; salvation identifies itself with relationship. Christianity can be broad, general, and corporate in its nature whereas being saved is about a specific, personal, intimate bond with Christ. Are you a Christian or are you saved?

DAILY SCRIPTURE READING: Galatians 1-3

DECEMBER 8

DO YOU HAVE AN ACCENT?

"Sanctification is the work of the Holy Spirit in us whereby our inner being is progressively changed." –Jerry Bridges

Do you have an accent? Think about it for just a moment. If you are saved, you are not a citizen of this world; you are a citizen of heaven. And those in the world should notice the difference. When someone is from another country, they carry with them the dialect, language, and vernacular of that country.

The apostle Paul said, "For our conversation (citizenship) is in heaven; from whence also we look for the Savior, the Lord Jesus Christ" (Philippians 3:20). The writer of Hebrews, speaking about those who have died in the faith said, "…they were pilgrims and strangers upon the earth" (Hebrews 11:13). Jesus told the disciples that they were "not of this world" (John 15:19). Suffice it to say, believers should have a heavenly inflection in their voice. Our language, our mannerisms, our speech should be different from the dialect of the world.

There was a time when I was a citizen of the world and a foreigner to heaven, but when Christ saved my soul, He changed my citizenship. Now, I am a citizen of heaven and a foreigner in this world. Through Christ, I am no longer a stranger to heaven, but a "fellowcitizen with the saints, and of the household of God." The world needs to hear the accent of heaven in my voice.

DAILY SCRIPTURE READING: Galatians 4-6

DECEMBER 9
THAT ONE SPECIAL GIFT

"Anything less than Jesus is a letdown; anything more than Jesus is an impossibility." –Kenneth Kuykendall

As a parent, I typically try to buy my children that one special gift at Christmas time. You know, the one they have been asking for all year long. The one you leave wrapped until the very end. It is the one gift they really, really want. It could be a new bike, a dollhouse, an iPod, a new computer, or those really expensive shoes. Whatever it may be, it is typically the gift they remember for years and years to come.

Did you know that God did the same thing for us? At Christmas, He gave humanity that one special gift – the unspeakable gift of Jesus Christ. Just as you prepared that special gift for your child, God too, prepared for us the gift of Christ. Oh sure, there were plenty of gifts prior to the coming of Christ. God gave the law, the prophets, signs, wonders, and covenants. But He saved the best for last.

This gift was the most precious, the most expensive of all gifts. It was concealed and hidden, wrapped in swaddling clothes. The world at large didn't know where this gift was until the stone was rolled away, thus revealing the glorious package of divine resurrection.

As I watch my children open that one special gift, I can't help but think that God, too, feels elation and joy when the world receives His Son.

DAILY SCRIPTURE READING: Ephesians 1-3

DECEMBER 10

DIVINE, MUNDANE MOMENTS

"The soul which turns to God may clothe itself in quietness, even in the crowded concourse or hurrying streets." –David MacIntyre

Nicolas Herman, or Brother Lawrence as he was commonly known, was a dishwasher in the institution where he lived. He often spoke about washing those dishes for the glory of God. When finished with his menial work in the kitchen, he would fall down on his knees and thank God for the opportunity to serve. He said, "I wouldn't as much as pick up a straw from the floor, but I did it for the glory of God."

You may think this sounds silly or extreme, but hear the words of the apostle Paul, "Whether therefore ye eat, or drink, or whatsoever ye do, do all for the glory of God" (1 Corinthians 10:31). The same sentiment is applied in Colossians 3:17, "Whatsoever ye do in word or deed, do all in the name of the Lord Jesus, giving thanks to God and the Father by him."

Glorifying God is typically an act achieved in the mundane. We tend to think that God is only honored when we lift our hands or voices in some corporate experience of worship. But the truth is, we have the opportunity to glorify God in every moment of life, even in the most boring and seemingly unproductive. Today you have a great opportunity set before you: to glorify God in all that you do. Transform each mundane moment into a cathedral of praise by honoring and glorifying God in all things.

DAILY SCRIPTURE READING: Ephesians 4-6

DECEMBER 11
HAPPY BIRTHDAY TO YOU

"For unto you is born this day in the city of David a Savior, which is Christ the Lord." –Luke 2:11

My youngest son's birthday is today. I will never forget how I felt when I saw him for the first time. Little did I know that he would steal my heart, and forever change the dynamic of our family. His birthday is *his* day, and we try to make it as special as we can. Cakes, parties, balloons, gifts…yes, we make much of this day because it is day that God gave us Carson.

Now imagine how silly it would be to have a party for Carson, and not invite him to the activities. What a ludicrous notion. Such a thought sounds ridiculous when it comes to our children, but that is exactly what the world does when it comes to the birth of Christ.

The world loves Christmas. They embrace all the activities, the trees, the gift exchange, the lights, the bows, the parties, the songs, and the actual date. They just refuse to invite Jesus to the party. They want to celebrate the day without knowing the divine.

As *His* day approaches in the next few weeks, let's make much of Jesus. Sing to Him, worship Him, and acknowledge Him in all that we do. Don't have a party and fail to invite the honored Guest. (By the way, Happy Birthday, Carson! I love you.)

DAILY SCRIPTURE READING: Philippians 1-4

DECEMBER 12

THE PRAYER OF THE MINDFUL

"Woe to the generation of sons who find their sensors empty of the rich incense of prayer." –E.M. Bounds

In 1550, a number of religious and influential people met in Essex to discuss the position of one's posture in prayer. Some contended that prayer should be observed while standing, others said prayer is at its best when kneeling. They also discussed whether or not a covering should be placed upon one's head while entering into the prayer closet.

After much discussion and debate, the council agreed by in large that attitude, not position, was the greatest condition of prayer. Bodily posture, though important in prayer, should never supersede the posture of the mind. The question therefore stands to be asked: where is your mind when you pray?

If you are like most people, your mind drifts, wonders, and gets off track. What good is it to bow before the throne of God, if your mind is standing in the courts of man? No matter what position you choose in prayer, one thing is certain: wherever your mind is, your prayer will follow. I wonder how often our prayers really reach the throne.

Today when you pray, evaluate the posture of your mind. Have you bowed your thoughts to God? Have you directed your mediation toward heaven? What is really on your mind when you speak your mind to God?

DAILY SCRIPTURE READING: Colossians 1-4

DECEMBER 13
5 WAYS TO GET FOCUSED

"Is it not a wonder that our words, which almost die in the coming out of our lips should climb as far into heaven."–Robert Blair

If the posture of the mind is critical when you pray, it is imperative to discipline your mind when you come into the prayer closet. Here are a few suggestions to help direct your mind and thoughts toward God during the hour of prayer.

1. Remove Distractions. When I say remove distractions, I mean primarily from your mind. How often do you go into the prayer chamber only to think of other things?

2. Keep a Good Mental Prayer List. This list doesn't have to be on paper, but if you compile certain things to pray about BEFORE you enter prayer, you will be more prone to stay focused.

3. Pray the Scriptures. This will help your mind absorb spiritual truth while at the same time rid your mind of carnal thoughts.

4. Think about Christ, Glorify Christ. See Christ on the cross dying for your sins. Embrace an empty tomb and see the Resurrected Christ in His glory. How can we think of anything else when we really understand Who it is we are conversing with?

5. Rely on the Holy Spirit. There are times when we do not know what to say. This is when the Holy Spirit gives utterance to our prayers.

DAILY SCRIPTURE READING: 1 Thessalonians 1-5

DECEMBER 14
DOING CHURCH TOGETHER

"For we are labourers together with God." –The Apostle Paul

The power of the early church was experienced in group dynamics. God Himself calls the church a Body, a Building, a Bride. Each of these descriptive terms alludes to unity, harmony, and togetherness. This is not a suggestion…this is what we are. Therefore, to function properly the church must work together in order to fulfill its God-given assignments. Consider the following passages:

Romans 1- We are comforted together
Romans 6- We are planted together
Romans 8- we will be glorified together because we groan together
Romans 15- We are to strive together
1 Corinthians 1- We are perfectly joined together
2 Corinthians 6- We are workers together
Ephesians 2- We are quickened together, raised together, called to sit together, fitly-framed together, and built together
Philippians 3- We are followers together
Colossians 2- We are knit together
1 Thessalonians 4- We shall be caught up together and live together forever

Our togetherness is not just a Sunday adventure. God designed the church to experience all of life together. Therefore, the strength of a church is not found in its size, programs, or gifts, but rather in its unity.

DAILY SCRIPTURE READING: 2 Thessalonians 1-3

DECEMBER 15

THE TABLE OF FELLOWSHIP

"We are, at this moment, as close to God as we chose to be." –Oswald Chambers

I have fond memories of my grandparents, many of which occurred around their kitchen table. It was just a brown maple table, nothing fancy, nothing large, nothing expensive. When I visited them that is where we would spend a majority of our time. There we talked about life and its problems. We prayed at that table, discussed the Bible at that table, and even worshipped at that table. We cried at that table, we laughed at that table, we ate at that table. We shared holidays at that table; I even drank my first cup of coffee at that table.

I now realize what made the table so special was not really the table at all but the people that gathered around the table. A table speaks of fellowship and intimacy with those you love. In the Word of God there are many different tables, and all of them point us to communion with God.

There is nothing like pulling up a chair at His table. He daily prepares a meal for His people. He lavishes goodness and grace before us and prepares a table in the presence of our enemies. The more you eat at His table however the more you realize the greatest part is simply being with Him. Go ahead and pull up a seat, He's been waiting on you to arrive!

DAILY SCRIPTURE READING: 1 Timothy 1-6

DECEMBER 16

SHEPHERDS AND STAR-GAZERS

"The Son of God became man to enable men to become the sons of God." –C.S. Lewis

I always stand amazed at the striking differences between the Wise Men and the shepherds. They literally were worlds apart. These two groups were different socially, financially, religiously, and even intellectually.

The Wise Men were more than likely from oriental descent. They studied the cosmos and gave much attention to the mysteries of the universe. They were affluent, educated, and respected men of degree. The shepherds on the other hand were considered unlearned and unclean men. In many ways, they were much lower on the social ladder. They were poor, common, and men of low estate.

As different as these men were they had one thing in common: they both came to Christ. Interestingly enough, Christ came into their world to unite those who were worlds apart. In Christ there is neither Jew nor Greek, male or female, bond or free. Faith in Christ guarantees our position in His body, thus uniting the most diverse and varied men. In the book of Revelation, John testified that people from all nations, all tribes and all tongues were singing praise unto the One that united them together. Christ gives all men, regardless of ethnicity, economics, or environment, the opportunity to become part of one family- the family of God.

DAILY SCRIPTURE READING: 2 Timothy 1-4

DECEMBER 17
5 SIGNS OF NEGATIVITY

"I am looking for some men with an infinite capacity for not knowing what cannot be done."–Henry Ford

Winston Churchill said, "The pessimist sees the difficulty in every opportunity; the optimist sees the opportunity in every difficulty." The major difference between a negative and positive person is attitude. The way you view something ultimately determines how you feel about that particular thing. Here are a few ways to determine if you are negative.

1. Lack of Appreciation. Those who are negative very seldom express gratitude or give thanks. They rarely acknowledge the goodness of God.

2. Constant Drama. Negative people typically feel like they have been wronged in some capacity. Their lives are filled with endless issues and constant frustration.

3. Critical Spirit. The negative person finds fault in everything and in every situation. To them, no one is ever right, and nothing is ever good enough.

4. Selfishness. Negativity is the breeding ground for selfishness. The negative person rarely thinks of others or makes decisions with the interests of others in mind

5. Unforgiving Heart. Negativity and bitterness go hand in hand. The pessimist usually holds grudges and keeps records.

DAILY SCRIPTURE READING: Titus 1- Philemon 1

DECEMBER 18

DON'T MISS THE BIG NEWS

"God sends His Son – herein lies the only remedy. The image of God has entered our midst." –Dietrich Bonhoeffer

The year was 1903, the Wright brothers had been working tirelessly to get their plane off the ground. In December, after many failed attempts, they finally took flight. Excited about their historic accomplishment they telegraphed their sister this message, "We have actually flown 120 feet. We will be home for Christmas!"

Thrilled about the news, their sister immediately went to the local newspaper and showed the message to the editor. Briefly glancing at the message he said, "How nice, the boys will be home for Christmas!"

I would say that he missed it.

Imagine...such an historical and monumental event taking place, but completely disregarding its reality. I would say that many people "miss it" this time of year as well. In the hustle and bustle of celebration, we tend to overlook the big news of Christmas. The big news in December is not that man has taken flight toward heaven, but rather that God has condescended to earth for man. This is the big news! Christ has come.

He cared, He came, He conquered, and He is coming again. No other news in history can surpass the glorious truth that the Savior of the world has made a way for us to reach heaven...and that, without a plane.

DAILY SCRIPTURE READING: Hebrews 1-6

DECEMBER 19
A BOX FULL OF INTENTIONS

"Action is less vague than intention; it begins with intention but it is unknown to others without the act." –Bill Hull

I recently found an old stack of Christmas cards in our basement. There they were: signed, sealed, and ready to be delivered. The names of our friends and family were on the envelopes, but in the hustle and bustle of the holiday season we forgot to mail them out. They had been in the basement for over two years and never reached their intended destination. One of the cards was addressed to a lady who recently passed away. She passed without ever receiving that card. Obviously her life was not drastically changed because we failed to mail out a cheap Christmas card, but seeing her name on that red envelope caused me to think about missed opportunities.

Oftentimes our intentions are good, but our follow-through needs work. The truth is no one ever sees our intention. No one sees an old dusty box in a basement full of Christmas cards. Intention has no value unless action is involved. Bill Hull said it like this, "Action is less vague than intention; it begins with intention but it is unknown to others without the act."

Regret is the consequence of failed intentions. Don't stock-pile your intentions down in a dusty basement with the hopes that others know you care. If need be, hand-deliver your intention to its final destination and see to it that your card is opened before another season passes.

DAILY SCRIPTURE READING: Hebrews 7-10

DECEMBER 20

THE ECHO OF GOD'S VOICE

"He that hath ears to hear, let him hear." –Jesus Christ

In his book, *The Crucified Life*, A.W. Tozer points out a sobering trend in modern Christianity. Tozer, who had the voice of a prophet, proclaimed, "Modern Christians are so busy doing this and that, going here and there, that they know God only in hearsay. We hear of this and that, but we never hear it for ourselves. We too easily settle for substitutes rather than the real thing. Under these circumstances, the most we can expect to hear is the indistinguishable echo of God's voice."

Imagine such a thing: Going through life and only hearing the echo of God's voice. Some believers only faintly hear an undetermined sound from the corridors of glory. They have forgotten the bliss of hearing the Father speak their name as only He can. They have allowed horns, cell phones, worldly music, and a hundred other noises to fade the voice of God to a mere reverberation. They only hear what has been spoken in days gone by, and try to substantiate yesteryear as a valid place to maintain their relationship with the divine. All the while, God is speaking. He is speaking today, but they do not hear.

It is time that we hear "what the Spirit sayeth to the churches." Jesus invites us to put on our spiritual hears so we can clearly discern His Father's voice, not just the echo.

DAILY SCRIPTURE READING: Hebrews 11-13

DECEMBER 21
CHRISTIAN CHARACTER

"Integrity is doing the right thing, even if there is no chance you would be caught doing the wrong thing." –Dave Cottrell

In ancient times artisans of all sorts were known primarily for the mark or "character" they engraved upon their vessels. They left their mark to identify themselves with whatever product they produced. This secured integrity in their work. They could not produce a substandard product without others knowing who it was that made it. In essence their "character" represented the quality of not only their work, but their lives.

Whether we know it or not we also leave a mark on the things we do. Our mark is only as good as the product we create. I like what D.L. Moody said years ago, "If I take care of my character, my reputation will take care of itself." Those who worry about their reputation without being concerned with their character have failed in their labor.

What kind of mark are you leaving? What does your character say about your vessel? Nathanial Hawthorne said, "No man for any considerable amount of time can wear one face to himself and another to the multitude without finally getting bewildered as to which is the true one." You may fool people for a little while, but at some point they will identify the quality of your life with the character upon your vessel. As Dave Cottrell says, "Integrity is doing the right thing, even if there is no chance you would be caught doing the wrong thing."

DAILY SCRIPTURE READING: James 1-5

DECEMBER 22
THE INCARNATION OF CHRIST

"The greatest man in history was the poorest." –Ralph Waldo Emerson

The incarnation of Jesus Christ is one of the dearest doctrines of the church. Perhaps no other Scripture more clearly validates this cardinal truth more than Philippians 2:5; it says of Jesus- "who being in the form of God thought it not robbery to be equal with God, but gave Himself of no reputation and took upon Him the form of a servant and was made in the likeness of men."

God became man. The Creator of heaven and earth subjected Himself unto the elements of earthly experience. He condescended to man's low estate and donned Himself with the wardrobe of flesh. "God with us" is His name- Emmanuel, the great God of glory dwelling among men.

This is the very essence of Christmas. He who was rich became poor, so that we who were poor might become rich. The Light came into the darkness. Life entered into a world plagued with death. The Hope of Heaven appeared in humility with the face of humanity. Oh, the mystery and the majesty of that first Christmas morning!

Our anthem should ever be "Christ the Savior is born!" Intentionally celebrate the true meaning of Christmas by acknowledging the historical truth that God became one of us.

DAILY SCRIPTURE READING: 1 Peter 1-5

DECEMBER 23

A CHANGE OF PLANS

"God estimates us not by the position we are in, but by the way in which we fulfill it." –Tryon Edwards

Joseph was a man of character, conviction, and compassion. He had great plans for his life and eagerly awaited his wedding with Mary. Like any young man making preparation for the future, Joseph had big dreams and aspirations. But God changed his course. God changed his plans. In a moment's time, an unexpected, unpredictable situation arose in Joseph's life forever changing the landscape of his home and heart.

God's plan for Joseph was far greater than Joseph could imagine. Consider the awesome responsibility of being the step-father of Israel's Messiah, God's own Son. Consider the pressure of raising the Redeemer of the world. Can you imagine the daunting task of being a parent to the Prince of Peace?

When God changes our plans, it is ultimately an invitation to be part of a much greater plan – His plan. When we trust and follow the Lord we can expect the unexpected. Faith is an adventure; an adventure that follows the divine steps of God.

The job loss, the broken car, the bad report, the failed dream…the unexpected trials of life may very well be the door that God opens to reveal His plans…plans infinitely better than your own.

DAILY SCRIPTURE READING: 2 Peter 1-3

DECEMBER 24

GOD IN US

"The incarnation is the ultimate reason why the service of God cannot be divorced from the service of man." –Dietrich Bonhoeffer

All throughout the Old Testament we find men and women who demonstrated faith in God. From Genesis to Revelation this is the essence of salvation. By grace we are saved through faith. Faith *in* God is the bedrock of our redemption. But when the Holy Spirit conceived Jesus Christ into the womb of Mary, we have, for the first time in Scripture, a picture of salvation *in* the life of a believer.

Faith in the Old Testament had been defined as *"faith in God"* but when we see Mary with child we discover *"God in faith."*

Christ was living *inside* Mary. Christ, the Savior of humanity, the promised Messiah was residing *in* the body of a young Jewish girl. This is the true picture of salvation. Paul said that "Christ *in* you" was the hope of glory. John said, "Greater is he that is *in* you" than he that is in the world. Even Christ said that He would be *in* us and we would be *in* Him, and He would be *in* God.

Like Mary, believers have Christ on the inside. We have the indwelling presence of Almighty God. Therefore, salvation is not just faith in God; it is ultimately God in us!

DAILY SCRIPTURE READING: 1 John 1-5

DECEMBER 25

GOD WITH US

---

*"Let Him into the mire and muck of our world.
For only if we let Him in can He pull us out."* –Max Lucado

The long-awaited pronouncement finally came. Messiah had come. The promised seed of woman, the incomparable Prince of Glory, the Savior of souls had arrived. Emmanuel, as Isaiah prophesied, was His name: God with us. The most unthinkable, unbelievable, yet undeniable event in history occurred at the birth of Christ: God became man.

This is not only a foundational doctrine of our faith; it is the one of the most comforting truths in history. God came to us. God became one of us. He placed Himself in the human experience. The Creator condescended to the elements of creation. He did this so that He could sympathize with our grief and sorrow. He knew what it was like to cry, to sweat, to grow weary, to become hungry, to laugh, to sing, to suffer. He experienced life "with" us.

Today, He is still with us. This is the reality of Christmas. He is with us in our pain. He is with us in victories. He is with us in our loneliness. He is with us at all times. Christmas not only reminds us that Christ came, but that Christ abides. No, Christmas is not a once-a-year holiday from work and school; it is an ever-present truth about the ever-presence of Christ. Because God is for us, He is in us, and forever with us! Emmanuel: a name like none other.

DAILY SCRIPTURE READING: 2 John, 3 John, Jude

DECEMBER 26

GOD FOR US

"What shall then we say to these things? If God be for us, who can be against us." –The Apostle Paul

In our culture, Christmas time is associated with family, presents, giving, hospitality, and seasonal warmth. However, during that first Christmas season there was a threatening charge laid against Christ and His family. Herod had issued a murderous decree to have all children, two years and under, executed in the surrounding areas of Jerusalem.

In the midst of such horrific violence, the message of Christmas sounded forth: fear not. God warned Joseph in a dream to depart from Nazareth and into Egypt for the safety and protection of the newly-born Messiah.

God was for them…guiding them, guarding them, keeping them, and fulfilling His promise of protection. He does the same today for those who carry the hope of Jesus Christ.

God is not only in us, He is not only with us, but He is for us defending His cause in the world. He never said we would be exempt from the violent, antagonistic culture, but He did promise to lead, guide, and direct us for His name's sake. As the apostle Paul said, "If God is for us who can be against us?" (Romans 8:31).

DAILY SCRIPTURE READING: Revelation 1-3

DECEMBER 27

TELESCOPIC VISION

"The best work we can do is so important, so big, so visionary, that it cannot be completed in a lifetime." –Mel Lawrenz

As you approach the New Year, how do you see things? Do you have telescopic vision? What I mean to ask is, can you see the entire year? Look at your calendar and start making plans for the ending as well as the beginning. Vision requires seeing things far off. Mel Lawrenz said, "Sometimes, instead of asking if our vision is big enough, we should be asking, is it far enough? The best work we can do is so big, so important, so visionary, that it cannot be completed in a lifetime."

As another year begins, look at the end, not just the beginning. Anyone can look ahead far enough to see the starting line, but only those with the right kind of patience, strength, vision, and fortitude will see the finish line. See the big picture and plan accordingly.

Look through the telescope at each month, each week, and each day. What do you want to accomplish? Where do you want to be in a year's time? What about five years from now, or ten, or twenty? Pray and plan something so big that it is bound to fail unless God intervenes.

E. Paul Hovey said, "A blind man's world is bound by the limitations of his touch; an ignorant man's world by the limit of his knowledge; but a great man's world is bound by the limitation of his vision."

DAILY SCRIPTURE READING: Revelation 4-8

DECEMBER 28

MICROSCOPIC VISION

---

*"Eyes that look are common,
eyes that see are rare."* –J.Oswald Sanders

Having telescopic vision is only the start. Once you see the big picture you must find ways to facilitate the vision. It is imperative to see your goals in totality (losing weight, reading the Bible, developing relationships, etc.), but that is only the beginning. Once you have a good idea of the vision, it is vital to start focusing in on the details.

If a telescope gives the ability to see things far off, a microscope affords the opportunity to see things up close. Both are equally important in having and maintaining a vision.

In his book, *Understanding Leadership*, Tom Marshall said, "Leaders not only have a vision for the future, but they must also conceptualize their vision into goals. Leaders must not only conceptualize their vision into goals, but they must also articulate them and communicate them to other people." In short, we must work from the outside in.

Through the lens of a telescope we see vision, the goal, the aspiration, the dream. From there, we put that vision under the microscope and start focusing on how that vision can be a reality. With these two perspectives, we keep a balanced approach to life, family, and our goals at large. Constantin Brancusi said, "To see far is one thing; going there is another."

DAILY SCRIPTURE READING: Revelation 9-12

DECEMBER 29

HINDSIGHT VISION

"Hindsight vision is a gift from God to enable and encourage us for change." –Kenneth Kuykendall

When we think of vision, we generally think in futuristic terms about futuristic plans. We look ahead, plan, strategize, and make efforts to facilitate the goals. However, in order to properly move ahead, we have to, from time to time, look back. We look back to evaluate, estimate, and change accordingly.

A.W. Tozer said it like this, "If we do not know where we have been, how in the world are we going to determine where we are going? That is the only reason for looking back. We do not look back in order to go back. Rather, we look back so that we can make sure we are going in the right direction."

As you look ahead to the New Year, have you looked back? Have you traced your steps making notes of failures and mistakes? If not, I encourage you to assess the past twelve months. Examine your attitude, relationships, habits, and spiritual disciplines. Have you failed in some areas? If so, don't hide your mistakes and shortcomings. Rather, present them to God, ask forgiveness, seek counsel, and make changes.

Hindsight vision is a gift from God to enable and encourage us for change. In the coming days, don't forget to look back before you look ahead.

DAILY SCRIPTURE READING: Revelation 13-16

DECEMBER 30

CLEAR VISION

"By prevailing over distractions, one may unfailingly arrive at his chosen goal or destiny." –Christopher Columbus

Life is full of distractions. If we are not careful, we can become so enamored with disruptions that we lose sight of what's important. Henry Ford said, "Obstacles are those frightful things you see when you take your eyes off the goal."

Whatever clouds your vision will control your direction. Whatever controls your direction will ultimately characterize your life. I like what T.E. Lawrence said, "All men dream; but not equally. Those who dream by night in the dusty recesses of their minds awake to find that it was vanity; but the dreamers of the day are dangerous men, for they may act their dreams with open eyes, to make it possible."

Without a clear vision you will have difficulty going where God directs your life. Press toward the prize for the high calling of God in Christ Jesus. The only reason we should look behind us, beside us, or below us is to keep our bearings of where we are and where we are going. Therefore, keep looking ahead. Keep pressing on. Keep your sights on the finish line. Keep your vision undisturbed. Perhaps Christopher Columbus said it best, "By prevailing over distractions, one may unfailingly arrive at his chosen goal or destination."

DAILY SCRIPTURE READING: Revelation 17-19

DECEMBER 31

GODLY VISION

"If our vision is not of and from God, it is not worth a second glance." –Kenneth Kuykendall

When all is said and done, the only vision that really matters is our vision of God. The prophet Isaiah saw the Lord high and lifted up. When he saw the Lord in His exalted position, the prophet ultimately, and dreadfully, saw himself. Life only makes sense in relation to our view and vision of God.

George Barna said, "Vision for ministry is a clear mental image of a preferable future imparted by God to his chosen servants and is based upon an accurate understanding of God, self, and circumstances." Such a vision is not only necessary for ministry, but for life itself.

Goals, dreams, aspirations, and resolutions only seem valid in light of the honor and glory of God. The further along I get in the journey of faith, the more I realize the significance of God's glory. No wonder the apostle Paul said, "...whatsoever ye do, do all to the glory of God" (1 Corinthians 10:31).

We should not be asking whether or not our vision includes God. We should be asking, is our vision of God? If our vision is of God and from God, He will give us the means, resources, and abilities to see that vision fulfilled. If it is not from Him or of Him, it is not worth a second glance.

DAILY SCRIPTURE READING: Revelation 20-22

www.crossroadspublications.org

- Commentaries
- Devotionals
- Lesson/Sermon Outlines Books
- Christian Living
- Audio Resources
- E-Books
- Discipleship Resources

Other Titles by the Author

A Collection of Seasons

The Private Life of the Preacher

The Joy of Devotion

The Six Senses of the Spiritual Leader

Principles from the Parables

The Evidence of Faith

Find the Blessing in the Testing

He Restoreth My Soul

All Things Are New

Meditations for Ministry

Somewhere in the Shadows

5 Reasons Why a Believer Faces Trial

6 Cures for the Common Cold

200 Sermon Outlines from the Gospels

100 Sermon Outlines from the Old Testament

150 Sermon Outlines from the Pauline Epistles

Preaching through the Psalms Volume 1,2,3

A Fresh Encounter with God

Visit Us Online at

www.crossroadspublications.org

www.crossroadsbap.org

www.kennethkuykendall.com

www.seeds4thesoul.com